Evidence-based practice
in social work

Evidence-based practice in social work

Edited by Andy Bilson

Whiting & Birch Ltd

MMV

Whiting & Birch Ltd are registered with
the Publishers Licensing Society, London, England and the Copyright
Clearance Centre, Salem Mass. USA.

Published by Whiting & Birch Ltd,
PO Box 872, London SE23 3HL, England.

USA: IPG, 614 N Franklin Street, Chicago, IL 60610.

British Library Cataloguing in Publication Data.
A CIP catalogue record is available from
the British Library

ISBN 1 86177 047 2

Chapters 2 to 8 first appeared in *Social Work and Social Sciences Review*
10(1) and 10(2). Chapter 1 is a revised and expanded version of a
paper which first appeared in *Social Work and Social Sciences Review*
10(1).

Contents

Introduction

Andy Bilson

Evidence-based practice in social work is subject of considerable debate relating to a range of issues from the nature of evidence through to the possibility and appropriateness of transferring this idea from health to the 'messier' world of social work practice. This debate is increasingly important as government initiatives in a number of countries attempt to promote a more 'scientific' approach to social work policy and practice. This book contains a range of views which look at this subject from different perspectives. Before discussing these chapters and their place in this debate it is worth examining some of the background.

Evidence-based practice (EBP) as a movement in social work is drawing strength from the developments of evidence-based medicine (EBM) most notably promoted by David Sackett and his colleagues. When putting the articles together for the special edition of the journal *Social Science and Social Work Review* on which most of this book is based I approached David Sackett for a contribution. His reply to this request was relevant to some of the central issues in this book. He gave me advice on others to contact and said 'I am not the person to provide an EBP perspective, since I don't write or lecture about EBM any more' (see Sackett, 2000, for an explanation). Intrigued by this response I looked up the article he cited to find in it a description of why he had 'retired' from the field of EBP. This was not because of any change of heart about the subject but rather that he had taken a position that 'new ideas and new investigators are thwarted by experts, and progress toward the truth is slowed.' He concluded that to avoid this negative effect experts should retire from the field and turn their attention to new problems where, without prestige and commitment to prior pronouncements, they would be able to consider new ideas and evidence and judge these on their merit. In fact this tacit acknowledgement that science is a human endeavour subject to our peculiar human frailties and strengths is central to the debate about the nature and possibility for evidence based practice in the messy world of social problem solving. So at the centre of the debate is the nature of evidence-based practice itself. Sackett *et al.* define evidence-based medicine as

the conscientious, explicit and judicious use of current best evidence in making decisions about the care of individual patients, based on skills which allow the doctor to evaluate both personal experience and external evidence in a systematic and objective manner. (Sackett et al., 1997, p.71)

This definition gives a flavour of the issues in developing EBP in practice. The contributors to this book put different stress onto the need to combine evidence and experience and whether personal experience is seen as necessary. There is also the question of whether the approach is as relevant in social work as in medicine and this particularly leads to the issue of how evidence based practice can be promoted within the 'messy' environment of social work. The following chapters deal with these key issues relating to the nature of evidence and how it can be or is being put into practice.

With regard to the issue of evidence, EBM has developed views about the most appropriate research methodologies which can provide the 'external evidence' on which to act. A hierarchy of methods for evaluating treatment effects is proposed (Guyatt et al. 1995) with research not directly relating to clinical practice excluded altogether. This hierarchy is topped by systematic reviews and meta-analyses, randomised control trials, through cohort studies down to case reports. It will be evident to anyone with knowledge of research in social work that the forms of research at the top of this hierarchy are almost totally absent (see, for example Maluccio's 1998 review of the research evidence in the USA). Trinder (2000) has argued that this lack of the type of 'evidence' favoured by evidence-based medicine is not simply caused by the lower levels of funding available for social work research but by real methodological and practical problems in the application of RCT's and similar approaches in the messy world of social work. She states that

2

... social work encounters are not straightforward or linear relationships, but multiple, multilayered, relational and complex, and located in a social and political context. Within this framework of the inherently messy and complex nature of social work and probation, classic formulations of evidence are impoverished and potentially constraining. (Trinder, 2000, p. 149)

The book is organised in three parts. The first part deals with establishing the case for evidence based practice in social work. Part 2 looks at critical reflections on the application of evidence based practice. The final part considers the directions for application. Each part has three chapters dealing with these linked themes.

Part 1 starts with Brian Sheldon, Rupatharshini Chilvers, Annemarie Ellis, Alice Moseley and Stephanie Tierney's chapter, which puts forward a robust argument for evidence-based practice, and considers the use that social workers make of research. He reports on a major survey of over a thousand social work staff in England. Whilst he finds social work staff have enthusiasm for the idea of evidence-based practice there is also a worrying lack of knowledge of evaluative research. This is not dissimilar to the findings of a smaller survey in the United States (Mullen & Bacon, 1999) and demonstrates the work that needs to be done to increase knowledge of research.

Chapter 2 is by Frank Ainsworth and Patricia Hansen from Australia. They develop an argument for evidence-based practice as a basis for the social work profession's ethics. They stress how research from both the quantitative and qualitative arenas have different and complementary roles in the creation of an evidence base for social work. They see the current education system for social workers as being the key area for reform to promote evidence-based practice and argue for major reforms in areas including the selection and recruitment of both staff and students as well as in the content and focus of the training.

Stephanie Tierney continues this theme in chapter 3 and argues that EBP can have democratising, empowering and protective elements for practitioners and service users.

Part 2 of the book provides critical reflections on the application of EBP in social work.

As a counterpoint to part 1, in chapter 4 Carolyn Taylor and Sue White warn of the danger that evidence-based practice is becoming an orthodoxy without proper critical appraisal of its core ideas. In particular they focus on the hierarchy of evidence and the process by which practice becomes evidence-based. They suggest that, in its current form in social work, EBP is too strongly associated with deductive reasoning and suggest that practice needs both induction and deduction. They argue that EBP forces too much of the attention onto intervention and outcome underestimating the problems of diagnosis, assessment and case formulation. Their call is for a more inclusive version of EBP that is more able to respond to the uncertainties of social work practice in the real world.

In Chapter 5 David Smith takes a critical look at the limits of a positivist approach to EBP. He points out the importance of context and process in making any real sense out of measures of outcomes. Thus the same intervention will have different outcomes if the context or process of its delivery is changed. He considers implications from philosophy and uses examples from his evaluation of social work with offenders to highlight problems in providing evidence. This leads him to suggest that there is a less ambitious but more helpful role for science than providing 'hard' evidence. In social work science needs to provide middle range theories which give indications of helpful approaches and that allow practitioners to develop an integrated approach able to draw flexibly on a range of theories and be responsive in their practice to changes in the social, political and policy environment.

Finally in chapter 6 Nick Frost provides a critique of EBP arguing that it does not take adequate account of the value conflicts that permeate research and practice. He argues for the need to consider research utilisation within a wider framework that recognises the political and economic contexts of social work as well as the values that social workers use to steer their practice.

In Part 3 we start to consider the directions that implementation of EBP can take. This starts with Mike Fisher in chapter 7 who provides a detailed description of the UK Government's initiative to promote evidence-based practice, the Social Care Institute for Excellence (SCIE). SCIE was established in October 2001 with the aim of improving standards in social work and social care in England and Wales by promoting the better use of research and knowledge. Mike Fisher is SCIE's Director of Research and Reviews. He provides an overview of the current state of research in England and Wales highlighting that service users and social care practitioners are often marginalised in the production of research. In looking at how to categorise research he concludes that 'a system for assessing the quality of social care knowledge will need a more subtle and inclusive approach than a simple hierarchy in which findings from experimental studies take precedence.' He also stresses the need for inclusive approaches to knowledge generation rather than those which favour the academic as the producer of knowledge.

In Chapter 8 Tony Newman and Di McNeish write about their experience of promoting evidence based practice in a major child care charity. They discuss the creation of the 'What Works?' series on child care and some early but encouraging signs of change in practice in their organisation.

In chapter 9 John Lawler and I reflect on the earlier chapters and provide some ideas about dealing with the implementation of a more reflective and research aware social work practice in organisations and teams. We provide a 5 part model for interventions to implement better use of research. We argue that there has been a substantial focus on the responsibility of the individual professional for using best evidence to guide their practice and that there is a need balance this by an increased focus on the organisational and team context in which social work takes place. We draw on the literature on organisational change and social work research to develop principles for encouraging greater reflexivity and developing a more open participative approach to the use of evidence to shape new practices in social work at the local level.

The way forward?

In considering what the authors in this book say about the future of evidence-based practice there are two issues which still need to be considered if it is to fulfil its potential to guide and improve practice and policy. The first concerns the nature of EBP and the form it will take and the second is the process of its implementation.

Evidence-based practice is currently in its early stages in social work and there are many avenues still open for its development. In a number of countries its introduction is within a political climate in which social work is coming under increasing attack and where government wants to centralise its control. EBP has the potential to become part of this political process or be the profession's defence against it. A crucial element in determining the part EBP plays is its ability to reflect the complexity of the problems social workers face in their day-to-day work and to challenge overly simplistic and populist policies (for evidence of this look no further than the punitive policies for offenders and the scapegoating of asylum seekers common in many parts of the world). For EBP to take on this role will require it to not only overcome the divide between quantitative and qualitative research and find a synthesis able to use the strengths of all research approaches, but it will also have to include many other forms of knowledge including professional experience, theory, knowledge and experience of service users and so on (see for example le May, 1999). One way to achieve this is for the profession to embrace the concept of EBP and at the same time redefine it as a framework for social work which values the contribution of practitioners and service users; supports professional discretion; and celebrates the complexity of social work practice.

The second issue concerns the process by which EBP is implemented. It is ironic that, in looking at practice, those promoting EBP call on practitioners to have regard to research whilst in their consideration of how EBP is implemented in organisations little regard is given to the substantial literature on such issues as change in organisational culture and professional practice. The naive view that all that is needed is better dissemination and access to research has long been discredited and more complex multifaceted approaches are needed (for an overview of the effectiveness of different dissemination and implementation interventions in health see NHS Centre for Reviews and Dissemination Bulletin 5 no.1 1999). Some of the drive for evidence-based practice comes from the frustration of researchers who feel their findings have little effect on practice. A danger of this is that as EBP takes hold researchers will become more influential at policy level, forgetting that the strength of their insight into practice is that they have an alternative perspective rather than the whole truth, and they may try to use their new found influence to control practice and force it to improve. This can take the form of developing lengthy and compulsory assessment or recording forms to force social worker's attention onto what researchers see as key issues, or by encouraging government to set targets for practice based on their research interests. Much of the literature on organisational and professional change calls for an inclusive process that engages staff at all levels in a process of ownership of change and in an environment that tolerates and learns from mistakes rather than top down instructions, procedures and target setting. For effective implementation of evidence based approaches this complex process of change needs to be properly planned and resourced if it is to be effective.

Finally the need to base social work practice and policy on sound evidence is rarely denied, but there is a danger in concentrating too much on practice and its limited use of evaluative research. We need to heed Trinder's warning of the need to respond to the social and political context of our actions. For example, the probation service in England and Wales represents the agency which, in its policies, procedures and directives, has been amongst the strongest in promoting evidence-based practice. It is worth noting that this has taken place against a background of national policy that has seen continual condemnations of community based work with offenders and the biggest increase in the prison population, an intervention whose spectacular failure is well documented.

Thus it is clear that there is still a long way to go to help to develop a more reflexive, research aware social work practice. This book provides a comprehensive overview of developments in evidence-based practice in social work and highlights many important debates and dilemmas. I hope it has shown that these debates are not, as some have suggested, a sterile fight between entrenched camps fighting for empiricism or a postmodern perspective. Rather it addresses fundamental issues about ethics, the nature of social work, research and its applicability and gives clear pointers to the need for a new direction for the partnership between research, policy and practice able to promote better more effective services.

References

Guyatt, G., Sackett, D., Sinclair, J., Haywood, R., Cook, D. and Cook, R. (1995) User guides to the medical literature 9. A method for grading health-care recommendations. *Journal of the American Medical Association*, 274, 1800-1804

Le May, A. (1999) Evidence-based practice *NT Monologs no.1*. London: NT Books. http://www.nursingtimes.net/

Maluccio, A. (1998) Assessing child welfare outcomes: The American perspective. *Children and Society*, 12, 161-168

Mullen, E.J., and Bacon, W.F. (1999) 'A survey of practitioner adoption and implementation of practice guidelines and evidence-based treatments.' Paper presented at the 2nd International Inter-Centre Network for Evaluation of Social Work Practice Conference, Stockholm, Sweden.

NHS Centre for Reviews and Dissemination (1999) Effective health care: Getting evidence into practice. *Bulletin* 5:1

Sackett D.L. (2000) The sins of expertness and a proposal for redemption. *British Medical Journal*, 320, 1283

Sackett, D.L., Richardson, S., Rosenberg, W. and Haynes, R.B. (1997) *Evidence-Based Medicine: How to practise and teach EBM*. Edinburgh: Churchill Livingstone

Trinder L. (2000) Evidence-Based Social Work/Probation. in L. Trinder and S. Reynolds (Eds) *Evidence Based Practice: A critical appraisal*. Oxford: Blackwell Science

Part One

Establishing the case

1

A pre-post empirical study of obstacles to, and opportunities for, evidence-based practice in social care[1]

Brian Sheldon, Rupatharshini Chilvers, Annemarie Ellis,
Alice Moseley and Stephanie Tierney

Messages from history: The case for evidence-based practice

The concern that measurably effective help should be available to poor, troubled and otherwise needy people is as old as Social Work itself. Joseph Rowntree was much concerned with the issue, and the American pioneer researcher Mary Richmond was writing about the impediments to its realisation on the eve of the Russian revolution, particularly in respect of the need for a common language (which we still do not quite have) in which to discuss questions of evidence:

> With other practitioners – with physicians and lawyers, for example
> – there was also a basis of knowledge held in common. If a neurologist
> had occasion to confer with a surgeon, each could assume in the
> other a master of the elements of a whole group of basis sciences and
> of the formulated and transmitted experience of his own guild
> besides. But what common knowledge could social workers assume
> in like case?' (Richmond, 1917, p.5)

Or, consider this politically savvy statement from the President of the American National Association of Social Workers, but then note its date:

I appeal to you, measure, evaluate, estimate, appraise your results in some form, in any terms that rest on anything beyond faith, assertion, and the 'illustrative case'. Let us do this for ourselves before some less knowledgeable and less gentle body takes us by the shoulders and pushes us into the street. (Cabot, 1931, p.6)

Then there is this little poem to the principles of evidence-based service-development contained in the 1968 Seebohm Report:

The personal social services are large-scale experiments in helping those in need. It is both wasteful and irresponsible to set experiments in motion and to omit to record and analyse what happens. It makes no sense in terms of administrative efficiency, and however little intended, indicates a careless attitude towards human welfare. (Seebohm Report 1968, p.142)

Not just another new fad then, and not just another 'initiative' deserving of a 'Good Soldier Schweik' response: enough collaboration not to get into trouble, too little to make it work (see Haslev, 1921).

Yet the Social Work field, particularly in the United States, tried hard to put the question of its usefulness beyond the reach of shifting political ideologies as early as did any of the other helping professions. The first large-scale controlled trials were begun in the 1930s and were reported in the 1940s and 1950s (Lehrman, 1949; Powers & Witmer, 1951: see Sheldon, 1986, for a review of this and later British work). The first medical trials (of streptomycin for pulmonary tuberculosis: see Daniels and Hill, 1952) brought an experimental approach into clinical medicine at about the same time. The agriculturalists beat us all to this, but then, conveniently, their subjects stay put while being observed[2].

The problem was that the results from the first Social Work experiments were almost wholly nil-nil draws, or worse, (see Mullen & Dumpson, 1972; Fischer, 1976). Indeed these brave, early studies should have taught us long ago something that all the helping professions (including medicine) have only recently begun seriously to acknowledge, namely, that it is perfectly possible for good-hearted, well-meaning, reasonably clever, appropriately qualified, hard-working staff, employing the most promising contemporary approaches available to them, to make no difference at all to, or even on occasion to worsen, the condition of those whom they seek to assist. It still happens today (see Marshall *et al.*, 2000; Byford *et al.*, 1999; Wessely *et al.*, 2000, Tolley & Rowland, 1995; for a general treatment of these issues, see Hunt, 1997).

Clear negative findings do not, in a strict scientific sense, matter. Lost hopes aside, methodologically kosher but disappointing findings are very precious (see Macdonald, 2004). They tell us, particularly in combination, what *not* to do and, potentially at least, provide arguments for the release of resources for more promising ventures. These large (and for the most part) well-conducted studies did eventually lead to a series of changes in practice favouring more focused and better-organised approaches which later stood up well under test, (see Reid & Hanrahan, 1981; Sheldon, 1986, 1995, 2000; Macdonald & Sheldon, 1992; Thyer, 1995; Macdonald, 2000). However, there are some more detailed points to be made.

1. The early negative findings came as a great surprise to everyone, both to those closely involved in the research, and later readers of it. When consulted at intermediate stages in the conduct of studies staff were always sanguine about the undoubted gains being made (see Jones & Borgatta, 1972). However, these alleged improvements disappeared when the control data were added to the equation – as is common today (see Macdonald, 2004).

2. The publication of scattered single studies with clear negative findings did little to alter professional attitudes, and where they were known about at all, they were seen as flukes. It was *reviews*, that is, collections of experimental material, that urged the conclusion upon us that just because particular approaches or patterns of service-provision were routine, congenial and familiar, this nevertheless told us little at a scientific level about their effectiveness.

3. Standards regarding acceptable levels of evidence vary greatly across disciplines and circumstances. At a multi-disciplinary mental health conference two years ago, the

following quotation from a systematic review of approaches to relapse prevention in cases of schizophrenia was read out, but amended, so that wherever the phrase 'case-management' occurred, the name of a mythical neuroleptic medication, *Lususproxine* was substituted (lusus is Latin for playfulness):

> *Case management increased the numbers remaining in contact with services. Case management approximately doubled the numbers admitted to psychiatric hospital. Except for a positive finding on compliance from one study, case management showed no significant advantages over standard care on any psychiatric or social variable. Cost data did not favour case management but insufficient information was available to permit definitive conclusions. (Marshall et al., 2000, p.34)*

The audience was then asked what they thought should happen regarding this treatment, and overwhelmingly suggested that it should no longer be used. However, when they were let in on the little thought experiment, a substantial number, though sympathetic to the *principle*, thought that little could be done about social care interventions since they were embedded in national and local policies, and that different rules applied. A 'Mexican Wave' shrug rippled through the audience to accompany these comments. *Should* different rules apply though, is the question, since both constitute *interventions*? Our tendency to fall in love with favourite theories, methods or concepts, and to question the motives of any critics; our tendency to follow, rather slavishly, the routine but often uninformed prescriptions of government are not always cost-free to our clients.

The position in the early 1990s was that both reviews and single studies were showing clearly positive results (e.g. in 78% of the 94 screened outcome studies reviewed by Macdonald and Sheldon, 1992) but that staff, inhabiting a workplace culture favouring action over reflection, and much pre-occupied with the new commercial principles which accompanied community care reforms (see Griffiths, 1988) appeared rarely to have heard of these more promising findings (see Sheldon, 1987a). However, as a result of the work of a few irritatingly persistent Social Work academics, and under the influence of developments in the Health field, particularly those brought about by the Cochrane Collaboration (see Cochrane, 1973; Maynard & Chalmers, 1997) new impetus was given to research programmes which had service development objectives as their *raison d'être*. Most notably in our own field was the funding (£5 million to date) of the Centre for Evidence-Based Social Services (CEBSS) at the University of Exeter[3] - a partnership project originally involving the Department of Health and (to date) 20 social services departments, and charged since 1997 with the following aims:

1. to translate the results of existing research into service and practice development;
2. to ensure research findings are available to social services departments when reviewing and changing service delivery, and are fed into the review process;
3. to collaborate with providers of DipSW and post-qualification courses to ensure that education and training in Social Work incorporates the knowledge available from research;
4. to improve the general dissemination of research findings to local policy makers, managers, practitioners, carers and service users;
5. to commission new research where significant gaps in knowledge are identified.

With such promising contemporary developments in hand, why dwell on historical matters at all? Well, there are three good reasons:

1. One of the more sensible views of Karl Marx (paraphrasing Hegel) was that 'those who know no history are often condemned to relive it'. If there is any field in which this is true it is Social Work, wherein old ideas (whether plausible or whacky) frequently just acquire new names and are recycled.
2. Our common experience in the social services is that new initiatives which ignore their historical roots wither quickly when the limited supplies of political fertilizer dry up (just

think back five to 10 years).

3. Large enterprises, when they seek to change behaviour within organisations rather than merely the terms of discourse, depend upon a widespread discussion of aims, purposes, and desired results if they are to secure 'informed consent' from staff regarding the extra work to be done.

In other words, regarding this promising idea of evidence-based practice, current enthusiasm should be tempered by remembering that the sieve of history has large holes.

The concept of evidence-based social care and its implications.

Having had a look at the origins of the idea, we must now consider what it implies. Here is a short definition containing the principal features (freely adapted from the work of Sackett *et al.*, 1996 in evidence-based medicine):

> *Evidence-based social care is the conscientious, explicit and judicious use of current best evidence in making decisions regarding the welfare of those in need.*

Conscientiousness

How do the key words in this quotation translate to the Social Work field? *Conscientious* surely reminds us of our ethical obligations to clients, not least among which is to try to keep up to date on research which (a) helps us understand the nature and development of personal and social problems, and (b) requires that we keep abreast of studies on the effectiveness of particular interventions which might ameliorate these. This is, after all, what we as, generally speaking, rather less up-against-it consumers expect of the services that *we* use - from medical and nursing staff to gas fitters (plumbers are, of course, a different matter entirely). Surely social workers, concerned with the well-being of the most vulnerable in society cannot be exempt from a similar obligation?

Hippocrates (400BC) counselled his student physicians on the moral imperatives of intervention thus: 'First, do your patient no harm'. Can it be said that the social services do no harm? Just to mention the events on the Orkney Islands (see Dalrymple, 1994; Sheldon, 1995[4]) or at Cleveland (Butler Sloss, 1988) sadly puts this matter beyond doubt. Then there are sins of omission rather than of commission to consider, as in the many reports of the deaths of children in our care (see Howitt, 1992; Sheldon, 1987b; Laming, 2003). The problem is that 'hard cases make bad laws'. Child death from abuse is statistically rare, but below this visible iceberg tip is a much larger mass of children suffering non-fatal, but serious physical (and sometimes more cruel) emotional injuries. True conscientiousness would imply much greater attention to these, whose cases do not make the Daily Mail leader page (see Macdonald & Macdonald, 2000). All of the above points apply equally well to the fields of mental health, and the care of frail, elderly people (see Sheldon, 1994; Trappes-Lomax *et al.*, 2002).

Explicitness

Explicitness, that is, the recommendation that we work in as open and contractual way as possible with clients, has emerged as a key ingredient in effective helping over the last three decades (see Reid & Shyne, 1968; Stein & Gambrill, 1977; Sheldon, 1980, 1986; Macdonald & Sheldon, 1992). It causes some problems though, and has done for some time, as this quotation (from two pioneer experimentalists addressing the issue of what exactly is the distinctive contribution of Social Work) shows – and frustratingly, continues to show:

> *These qualities cannot reside in the mind of someone in the agency who knows what they think is important but cannot express it because it is too subtle to be communicated or because it is a relationship so fragile that any attempt to measure it would destroy it. (Jones & Borgatta, 1972, p. p.112)*

The idea that basic scientific procedure is much too blunt an instrument with which to poke about in the inevitably mysterious dynamics of what passes between would-be helper and might-be helped was once the major obstacle to the goal of explicitness in our dealings with clients. Indeed, the idea is still in circulation (see Webb, 2001; Sheldon 2001). However, a new version of this problem has now arisen. Its origins lie in the community care reforms of the 1990s (a great, but politically compromised cause which nevertheless quietly achieved most of what was intended) wherein initially heart-warming phrases about 'needs led' services were later nullified by decisions that 'needs' for which there were no budgets, no facilities, or no conveniently available expertise, did not (in true Orwellian fashion) really count as needs. Transparency of decision-making and honesty about what existing funding can and cannot provide should surely be our aim in these matters. All the rest must be passed on fearlessly to democratically elected politicians – whether they like it or not.

Then there is the curse of Carl Rogers to contend with (some good ideas, but nothing to justify his Guru status on Social Work courses). Why is it that 'I can feel your anger' is seen as a much cleverer statement than, 'have you ever thought of ...?' Imagine meeting Carl Rogers on campus and asking the way to the library and getting back, 'I sense you feel lost'. Respondents in client-opinion studies have been telling us for forty years that they value explicit advice (which of course they are entitled either to take or ignore) but that this approach was/is seen as low trade by social workers. In any case, in-depth relationships instead of help with utility arrears has gone out of fashion as a problem and has been replaced by a 'B & Q' approach to welfare: 'if we have it, it will be on the shelf', and 'no, we only do the one size'. A rather injudicious development this, since research favours tailor-made solutions.

Judiciousness

This next word in our definition concerns the exercise of sound, prudent, sensible, judgement. Our stock is not high in this regard, and considered pragmatism has been out of fashion for two decades at least. We seem instead, lacking a healthy professional immune system, to be prone to infection by fads and fashions: some, on the face of it plausible, some less so (see Sheldon, 1978; Sheldon & Macdonald, 1999). Incidentally, Tallyrand, Napoleon's foreign minister, gave the following advice to passing-out graduates of the elite *corps diplomatique...* 'but above all, gentlemen, please, no zeal'. Neglected advice, perhaps.

The case here is that not all that could be done should be done; and that not all things that staff like the idea of are reasonable; but that equally, some things that appear demanding or expensive in the short run turn out to be a bargain in the longer run. Potential risks arising from some, or no intervention, either in cases or in policies, should of course be thoroughly assessed and evaluated, but in the sure and certain knowledge that not all eventualities can be predicted (see Macdonald & Macdonald, 2000). All else is dangerous pretence and comes back to haunt us. So much so that social services staff now spend only 13-16% of their working week in face-to-face contact with clients, the rest of the time is spent on 'virtual reality Social Work', i.e., preparing a case for a possible Inquiry – statistically unlikely, but then (to invert the National Lottery slogan) 'someone has to loose' and it could be you.

Organisational obstacles to evidence-based service provision

If evidence-based social service provision were to become a reality, as opposed to just a laudable aspiration, then we would expect to see the following changes in the way the Social Work profession organises itself.

- There would be in place a well-qualified workforce within which knowledge and experience are regularly up-dated by training courses which make regular reference to research firstly on the nature and development of social problems and secondly on what is known at an empirical level about the effectiveness of different approaches designed to address them.
- There would be qualifying courses, which, as a matter of

priority, would address and review the literature on the effectiveness of services and equip students critically to appraise the results reported therein rather that relying upon comfortable notions of 'eclecticism' (see Sheldon, 1978).

- The profession would nurture a system of staff supervision which regularly draws upon research to inform decisions made about cases and projects, and wherein questions such as 'why are we proceeding in this way?' and, 'on what evidence?' would be seen as routine professional enquiries, not as personally threatening questions (see Macdonald & Sheldon, 1998).

- Departmental meetings would regularly include references to research on what has been tried elsewhere, regionally, nationally and internationally, when services are being monitored or reviewed, or where departmental restructuring is in the offing, which ubiquitously it is, but often without benefit of supportive evidence for the changes envisaged and the value versus the costs involved. Those who doubt whether scientific principles can properly be applied to human behaviour should consider Sheldon's three laws of reorganization, which have proved to have Newtonian, solar eclipse- prediction precision: i) If your director of social services leaves and is replaced you *will* be reorganized; ii) This will happen however recently you have been reorganized; iii) This will happen no matter what the size of the budget deficit regarding front-line care services (Q.E.D.). A single contravening example would of course refute these laws (see Popper, 1963), however none is evident to date. The American biologist Paul Ehrlich offered some good advice when he wrote that 'the first rule of intelligent tinkering is to save all the parts until you understand what they do'.

- There would be a range of support facilities available to assist staff in their efforts to keep abreast of research relevant to their field, e.g., departmental library and information services capable of efficiently delivering books and journal articles to enquirers and able to distribute summaries of available evidence, with those in charge of them able to show that such services are regularly used. There would be subscriptions to research databases[5] so that staff can search the literature in their field; and subscription to key journals containing empirical research.

- There would be better and more Internet access (see Moseley, 2004) so that systematic reviews and studies of good quality, both on problems and plausible solutions could be readily accessed (for example, www.cochrane.org; www.campbellcollaboration.org; www.ex.ac.uk/cebss; www.be-evidence-based.com; www.york.ac.uk/inst/crd/). There are some remaining chaff/wheat ratio problems with some of the research reported on websites, but with a little trained-in discrimination (see the CEBSS critical appraisal skill courses documentation on www.ex.ac.uk/cebss/casptraining.html) these should recede. All this *will* happen, but is presently happening much too slowly in the Cinderella services and we should probably jump up and down about the fact more. The remnants of commercially-minded service managers, who made their names with 'spreadsheet accountability' and top-down 'workforce compliance strategies' in the 1980s should have thought more about the fate of British Leyland perhaps.

- At an attitudinal level, there would be a workforce which takes some personal responsibility for acquainting itself with the empirical evidence on service-effectiveness (this is beginning to happen, see below), with a reasonably well-founded expectation of practical support from management for this necessary task.

- There would exist a range of collaborative arrangements between social services departments and local and regional universities and research institutes, so that each tangibly influences the work of the other, and within which each group of staff might unexceptionally be encountered on the corridors of the other pursuing common purposes. In other words, Social Work academics and social services managers should get out more.

Wishful thinking? We think not given the new resources now available, but whether or not this wish list is ever granted will depend upon those at the sharp end backing the *idea* with more than concerned, Rogerian nods and sighs. 'Cognitive-behavioural therapy', rather then insight-giving is, at an organisational level, closer to what we need.

There was great pressure at the inception of the CEBSS project to 'hit the ground running', just as there are pressures in day to day practice to do 'something' - whatever it is - quickly. Our approach in CEBSS was to argue that we could not live up to our name, if we did not have an evidence-base of our own. Therefore, (military analogies still in place note) we agreed to take some 'aerial photographs' of 'the ground' first. This exercise took the form of a large-scale questionnaire exercise, the results of which are summarized below. The purpose of the questionnaire was to establish the level of support amongst staff for the idea of evidence-based social care and to gauge the prospects and problems for the development of an evidence-based culture within departments. As will be evident in the graphs and tables which follow, this questionnaire exercise was then repeated, to see whether, or to what extent, attitudes and knowledge had changed over four years.

Design and content of the questionnaire[6]

The sample was drawn from information supplied by (though, 'midwifed out of' might be a more accurate phrase) social services departments participating in the CEBSS project. At the time of data collection, all of these departments but one were in the South West of England. It consisted of social workers, team leaders, care or case managers, heads and deputies of residential facilities, occupational therapists, and a small number of nurses and teachers (all employed in social services departments). A proportionate stratified random sample of 2285 professional grade, frontline social services staff were contacted in 1998 (time 1) to participate in the study, from a population of 6994. In 2002 (time 2), 2272 questionnaires were sent out to a sample calculated in exactly the same way (it was impractical to try and target the very same people who had been included at time 1 since the questionnaire returns were anonymous).

Stratification took place as to whether staff were field workers, residential and day care staff, occupational therapists, or other[7], in order to ensure representation for each category. Calculations to obtain a representative sample size were made separately for each participating department with four separate considerations (see Monette *et al.*, 1989; Oppenheim, 1992) namely: number of variables being investigated; level of population homogeneity present; precision level required (95% confidence level); and an appropriate sampling fraction to avoid overestimation.

A 42-item questionnaire (see Table 1 overleaf) was sent to participants with a guarantee of confidentiality based on code numbers[8], and a brief description of the purpose of the study. A maximum of three mail outs took place to ensure a good return rate, but no arm-twisting by Directors was involved (honest).

Analysis

For the purposes of analysis by occupational status, qualifications and job titles were used to categorise participants as social workers (holding a DipSW, CQSW, or CSS), occupational therapists (holding a Diploma or BSc in Occupational Therapy) and 'other social care professionals' (mainly care or case managers who may or may not hold these qualifications, or who may have relevant but different ones).

Responses to the closed questions were coded and then entered into the statistical package SPSS, version 10. Data from the open-ended questions were coded and analysed thematically. Answers to open-ended questions were analysed independently by two researchers and a (more than satisfactory) inter-rater reliability level of 85% was obtained. Chi-square tests were used to determine associations between categorical variables, and independent t-tests were used to assess differences on interval data. Both chi-square and t-tests were used to assess differences in responses from time one to time two.

Table 1
Topics covered in the questionnaire.

Topic	Information included:
Demographic information	Age, gender, length of employment, post title, type and level of qualification, and the client group with which respondents mainly worked.
Departmental influences on the availability and use of research findings	Extent to which research findings were discussed in supervision and departmental meetings, availability of and satisfaction with facilities such as library, summaries, etc., perceived support for evidence-based practice within the department.
Existing reading habits and preferences	Identification of relevant publications seen by respondents, opportunities for reading, preferences for different reading materials, opportunities (or the lack of them) for keeping up-to-date with research findings.
Familiarity with research publications	Identification of a randomised controlled trial, a quasi-experimental study or client opinion study known to the participant.
Existing levels of knowledge of research issues and terms	Current understanding of common research terms and issues such as statistical significance and factors influencing positive findings in a client opinion study other than the intervention.
Attitudes to evidence-based approaches	Perceived relevance of research in day-to-day practice, and perceived usefulness of greater access to research in practice.
Priorities for CEBSS project	Ranking of most important activities for CEBSS to undertake to achieve its aims and objectives.

Results

At time one, a total of 1226 respondents (a 53.7% response rate) took part in the study, of whom 67 % were social workers, 9% were occupational therapists, and 24% were 'other social care professionals'. At time 2, a response rate of 58% was obtained, however, 233 responses had to be excluded, mainly because they had been filled in by people for whom the questionnaire was not intended (e.g. non-professional grade staff or non front-line staff). The same problem occurred at time 1 with 115 responses having to be dropped – but precautionary over-sampling reduced the potential statistical distortions created by this. In total, 1089 responses were included in the time two analysis. 65% of the respondents were social workers, 7% were occupational therapists, 9% were classified as 'other social care professionals' and 19% as frontline managers (mainly team leaders). Further details of the sample are provided in Table 2.

There were no statistically significant differences between the respondents at time 1 and time 2 on any of these demographic variables: gender (χ^2 = 2.99, df = 1, ns); age (χ^2 = 1.95, df = 1, ns); time in social services employment (t = 0.86, df = 2282, ns). This means that the two groups of respondents in 1998 and 2002 are comparable on principal demographic variables. Table 3 illustrates the professional qualifications held by respondents in both 1998 and 2002.

Demographic comparisons with the national workforce survey (see LGMB/ADSS, 1997) indicate that these findings are in line with national figures except for those regarding ethnicity. So, social services staff are predominantly women, predominantly middle-aged, with considerable experience behind them, and not, as the tabloid press would have it, 'earnest young people lacking in life experience' who flit from stressful job to (hopefully) less stressful job.

Departmental influences on the use of research

Both questionnaires investigated possible opportunities for, and obstacles to, the application of research findings to cases, and the level of consideration of such matters in supervision

Table 2
Characteristics of respondents

	1998 (N = 1226)		2002 (N = 1089)	
	n	%	n	%
Job title:				
Social worker	817	67	709	65
Occupational therapist	115	9	77	7
Other social care professional	294	24	303	28
Gender:				
Female	881	72	746	75
Male	345	28	247	25
Missing	0		96	
Age:				
21-30	78	7	77	7
31-40	303	25	231	21
41-50	523	44	428	40
51-60	282	24	317	29
Over 60	16	1	30	3
Missing	24		6	
Ethnicity:				
British, European or Caucasian	1201	98	1056	97
Asian or Black	25	2	33	3
Missing	12		11	
Mean (sd) time in Social				
Services employment in years	13	(7)	13	(8)

Table 3
Professional qualifications held by respondents.

Qualification	1998		2002	
	n	%	n	%
DipSW	228	21.5	441	40.5*
CQSW/CSS	529	49.8	400	36.7
DipCOT (or degree in OT)	107	10.1	85	7.8
Other	198	18.6	163	15.0

* This figure reflects the changing titles of professional qualifications.

Fig. 1
Frequency of discussion of research findings in consultation or supervision meetings (%)

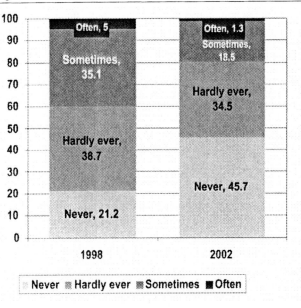

consultation meetings, departmental meetings, or on departmental training courses.

In both 1998 and 2002, staff supervision consultation occurred for most on a monthly basis (61% on both occasions). However, a sizeable minority of respondents had more frequent opportunities (24% in 1998 and 33% in 2002). In 1998, 15% reported having to rely upon less frequent and ad-hoc arrangements, with five respondents reporting that they received no supervision at all. By 2002, the situation had improved, with only 7% having to rely upon such unsatisfactory arrangements. So, more opportunities for supervision over four years, but what do staff think of it and what is its content? In 1998, 85% of respondents rated the quality of their supervision as being 'very' or 'quite satisfactory' and, in 2002, 88% described it in these terms - a finding to celebrate given the pressures on staff time.

Turning next to the question of the extent to which research is discussed within supervision and consultation meetings, it will be seen from Figure 1 above that, by report, in 1998 only

5% of consultations contained regular and routine discussion of research findings and their possible applications and, by 2002 this had fallen to a mere 1%. 35% of respondents in 1998 stated that research was discussed 'sometimes' (which is mildly encouraging, however, if we consider the remaining 'hardly ever' and 'never' categories for 1998, we see that in 60% of consultations the issue was worryingly down the agenda. This concern is compounded by the finding that in 2002 these figures had worsened: now 80% stated that they 'hardly ever' or 'never' discussed research findings in supervision (this difference is statistically significant: $\chi^2 = 185.9$, df = 3, p<0.001).

We say 'worryingly' (above) because all that research is, is the screened and codified experience of others working with similar problems, and so one might have thought it would be, if not the first port of call in such discussions (which is probably risk), then at least the second, and certainly not something to be left out much of the time. However, there is an interesting association in our data, in that those respondents who answered positively to a later question on the perceived relevance of research to their jobs are significantly more likely to be involved in such discussions with their supervisors both in 1998 and 2002 (1998: $\chi^2 = 14.98$, df = 3, p<0.005; 2002: $\chi^2 = 5.95$, df = 3, p<0.05). Therefore, these supervisors are a prime target audience for dissemination events and CEBSS is stepping up its courses on evidence-based practice for staff supervisors on evidence-based practice. These courses (N=21) have been positively evaluated in terms of content, relevance to practice and delivery, and so it looks as if we are up against a displacement effect here. That is, there is the inclination but simply not the time. Conference delegates (CEBSS has carried out 487 conferences and training events to date) tell us that risk monitoring (see Parsloe, 2000) and local and national target attainment and returns are the prime preoccupations.

At time one, discussion of research issues was more prevalent in departmental meetings with 52% reporting that this happened 'often' or 'sometimes', but only 36% saying likewise four years on (see Fig. 2). Again, this is a statistically significant deterioration ($\chi^2 = 79.2$, df = 3, p<0.001) despite our exhaustive work in this area.

Fig. 2
Frequency of discussion of research findings in departmental meetings (%)

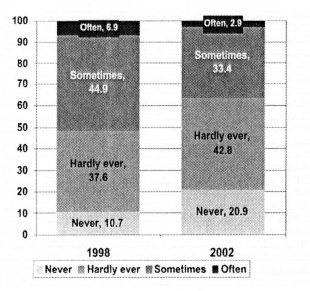

Never ▦ Hardly ever ▦ Sometimes ■ Often

Departmental encouragement to integrate research and practice

In response to a general question on the issue, 66% of 1998's respondents reported having 'little' or 'no' encouragement from their department to keep abreast of the research literature and in 2002 the picture was worse (78%) which is depressing given the provision of 487 conferences and training courses on just this issue by CEBSS and the changing political climate in favour of evidence-based approaches. Evaluation data regarding satisfaction, relevance to practice, and teaching quality averaged 4.2 (out of a possible 5 score) across these events. Therefore it may be that staff do not credit their department's backing for the CEBSS project as part of the support provided to them, or perhaps expectations have risen.

In 1998, staff views were sought as to whether they felt it was primarily a personal/professional responsibility to keep abreast of literature on research trends, or whether it was a departmental responsibility. They were asked to indicate the extent to which they felt it was a personal, professional responsibility on a seven-point scale, with 1 indicating 'a personal, professional responsibility' and 7 indicating 'not a personal, professional responsibility'. Respondents were also asked to mark, again on a seven-point scale, the extent to which they felt keeping abreast of research trends was a departmental responsibility (1 indicated 'a departmental responsibility' and 7 'not a departmental responsibility'). The mean (sd) ratings were 2.8 (1.3) and 2.3 (1.1), respectively. There was a statistically significant difference between these ratings (t = 11.8, df = 1181, p<0.001) demonstrating that respondents felt keeping abreast of research literature was much more a departmental, rather than a personal, responsibility. In 2002, this issue was addressed using a less complicated questioning format and the picture was thus: 9% felt that they personally were responsible for keeping up-to-date with research findings, 11% thought it was mainly their department's responsibility, and 80% saw it, sensibly we think, as a joint responsibility.

Departmental facilities to assist staff in keeping abreast of the literature in the region leave much to be desired (Figs. 3 and 4 overleaf). In 1998, over one third of the respondents reported having no access to library facilities. In 2002, this had improved only slightly, to just over a quarter (26%) reporting no such facilities. There was a minimal increase (65% to 71%) in the proportion of people reporting the availability of journals. The number of respondents reporting having access to computer databases did go up between 1998 and 2002, but at this later date, still nearly half (42%) reported having no access to this tool which is crucial for being an evidence-based practitioner. Retrieving research findings via the Internet is predominantly an activity carried out at home. One can, equally plausibly, take two different views about this finding: (a) that work place conditions do not support such activities – though, as we have argued, they are an essential ingredient of evidence-based practice; (b) that staff now have enough enthusiasm for this idea that they are willing to accept that their professional role is semi-independent of their strict employment obligations and are willing to undertake these opportunities outside working hours.

In 1998, 27% had research discussion groups available to them and 21% had research presentations. The picture is better by 2002, 37% now reporting having evidence-based groups, and

Fig. 3
Reported availability of departmental facilities to assist staff in keeping up to date with research literature in 1998 (%)

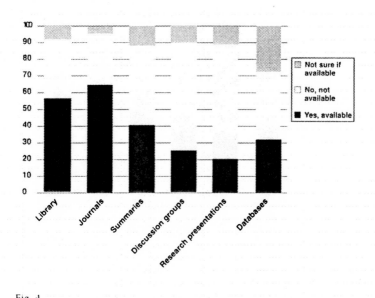

Fig. 4
Reported availability of departmental facilities to assist staff in keeping up to date with research literature in 2002 (%)

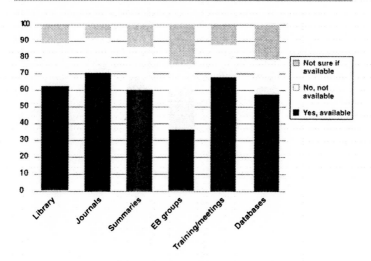

67% describing training courses or meetings with research content conducted within their departments. This is encouraging, particularly since the former events are set up and run by staff themselves. However, it is interesting to note that this increase in research content in training is not credited by respondents to the 'departmental support' account. Therefore, it is likely that they are responding to this question purely in terms of the level of *practical* backing supplied - such as access to computers and the Internet – which facilities are being made available all too slowly in comparison to those granted to colleagues in Health.

In the 1998 survey, respondents were asked to suggest methods that could be used by departments to encourage the practical use of research findings. Over one third nominated increased availability of technical research facilities (36%), with protected study time (20%) and opportunities to attend research meetings (21%) also being listed as important.

Opportunities for reading professionally relevant publications

Evidence-based practice depends upon readers – whether on screens or in articles or books. Therefore we were interested to evaluate the opportunities for this. It may be that at present we have too many writers and not enough readers. Academic researchers are thus largely writing to each other, as encouraged by the Research Assessment Exercise. In 1998, almost 75% of respondents reported having access to, or subscribing to, publications relevant to their work. In 2002 this figure was similar (79%). At both survey points the majority identified the publication to be *Community Care* (65% on both occasions), not a research journal, but an interesting publishing opportunity for people with strong messages to pass on. In 1998, only 19% of the respondents mentioned access to research or academic publications and this group was mostly made up of occupational therapists (55%) with the *British Journal of Occupational Therapy* and *Therapy Weekly* being the main publications mentioned (but then they drop onto the mat as a benefit of membership). There was a statistically significant association between respondents being members of a professional organization and having access to such literature (χ^2 =

128.7, df = 1, p<0.001). The issue being that so few social workers can be bothered with such affiliations, the problems that they confront in their day to day work being so politically neutral that there is no need for independent, representative bodies such as the BMA or the RCN (!). This 'learned helplessness' state urges us to remind readers of the advice given to depressed patients by the cognitive psychologist, Aaron Beck:

If you don't have plans for yourself, then you will very quickly become part of someone else's. (Beck, 1976, p.127)

Although nearly half the respondents reported having read literature pertinent to their work in the week prior (48% in 1998 and 46% in 2002), in the 1998 survey 45% reported that such reading took place at home and this had increased to 62% by 2002. In line with these findings, time pressure (98% in both surveys) was mentioned as a key obstacle to keeping abreast of the literature with lack of access (84% in 1998, slightly improved to 77% in 2002) and cost of journals and books (75% and 68% in 1998 and 2002 respectively) also being highlighted by many respondents. Figures 5 and 6 outline these obstacles.

Knowledge of research findings and critical appraisal skills

On the whole, reported knowledge of relevant studies such as client opinion studies, and particularly randomised controlled trials was low in 1998 (Table 4) with 455 stating that they had not read, nor could they identify or describe, a qualitative client opinion study (against very sub-Paxman acceptance rules).

There was also a worrying gap between self-perceived knowledge and actuality. Our findings show that, when asked, only 22% of the sub-sample of 432 respondents who said that they had read such materials, could *actually* name or describe such a study. Squeeze or reinterpret these data as you will, they are rather dire for a professional workforce largely with university qualifications.

In the 2002 survey, the percentage of people who reported that they had read a piece of evaluative research had reduced to 36%

Fig. 5
Obstacles to keeping abreast of the professional literature in 1998 (%)

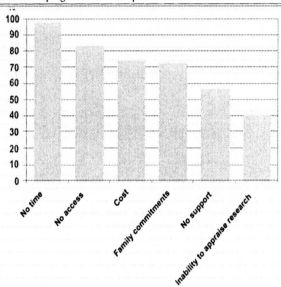

Fig. 6
Obstacles to keeping abreast of the professional literature in 2002 (%)

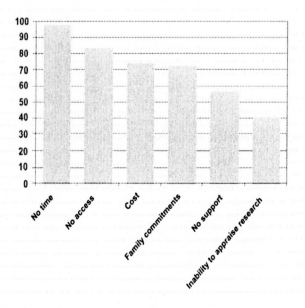

Table 4

Reported knowledge of evaluative research in general; client opinion studies, and randomised controlled trials.

	Evaluative (General)	Client opinion	Randomized control trials
	%	%	%
Have read such material	43.0	35.7	5.0
Have not read such material	39.6	45.3	83.2
Not sure	17.4	18.9	11.9

(N=382). However, the 'hit' rate had improved. We compared the type of evaluative studies that were accurately identified in 1998 and 2002. The actual numbers remain low, but in 2002, 2% (24 people) correctly identified a fully experimental piece of research (ie a randomized control trial), 7% (75 people) a quasi-experimental study (including pre-post designs), and 5% (52 respondents) a client opinion study. This was a statistically significant improvement from 1998, when only 1.5% (18 respondents) gave a correct name of a quasi-experimental study and 2% (29) a client opinion study ($\chi^2 = 85.1$, df = 3, p<0.001): see Fig. 7 below.

In identifying findings which might account for a positive result in a client opinion study other than the professional intervention; in 1998 only 13% of the respondents were able to give accurate responses: such as effects of participating in the study, the passage of time, simple attention, or other collateral changes in circumstances – otherwise, somewhat unwisely, clumped together as 'placebo effects' – which factors are in urgent need of further investigation in their own right.

A further 26% of respondents gave broadly plausible responses such as new government policies or media influences, hence showing some *general* familiarity with the issues. 57% supplied no information. Of those who gave a clearly correct or plausible answer, further analysis showed that, surprisingly, there was no significant association between respondents' level of academic qualification and reported understanding of factors that might account for positive change in a client opinion study apart from the intentionally-helpful intervention ($\chi^2 = 5.3$, df = 2, ns). Also, there was no significant association between this variable and

Fig. 7
Ability correctly to identify an evaluative study by research design (%)

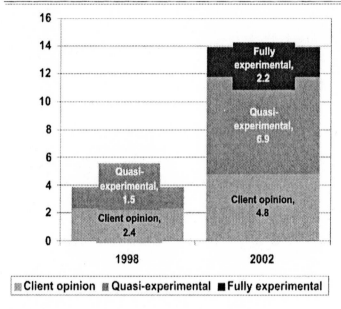

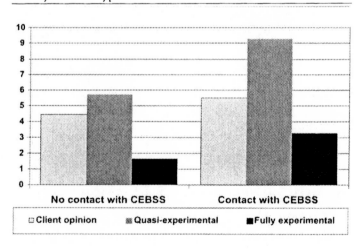

Fig. 8
Association between contact with CEBSS and ability correctly to identify different types of evaluative research (%)

respondents having attended *internal* training courses on interpreting research findings (χ^2 = 0.571, df = 2, ns).

However, we were interested to discover whether there was an association between respondents' abilities to define different types of research study and whether or not they had been in contact with CEBSS. Contact with CEBSS is defined as having attended at least one CEBSS event (such as an evidence-based practice day or a critical appraisal skills course). As will be seen from Figure 8, respondents from the 2002 survey who *had* attended CEBSS events were significantly more likely to be able to define research terms such as 'randomised controlled trial' (fully experimental study), 'quasi-experimental study' and 'client opinion study' than those who had not (χ^2 = 9.3, df = 3, p<0.05).

Although in the first survey 38% reported prior knowledge of this term, only 4% showed substantial understanding when asked. This gulf in reported and actual knowledge was likewise found in the second survey. 63% said they were 'very', 'quite', or 'tentatively confident' about the term, but only 14% could give a clear definition. Although this might be seen as the tip of an iceberg, there was a statistically significant increase from 1998 to 2002 in respondents' abilities to define this term (χ^2 = 28.9, df = 2, p<0.001): See Fig. 9.

Those who had attended CEBSS events were significantly more likely to be able to define and explain the concept of statistical significance (see Fig. 10). These findings have obvious implications for the current impact of research methods teaching on qualifying courses – if the subject is taught at all, that is.

The above findings show a low baseline of basic research knowledge and skills in the general sample. They also indicate, however, that when given access to suitable training, staff respond well (CEBSS have undertaken 56 of these critical appraisal skills courses to date). Available pre-post data for our critical appraisal skills courses indicate a statistically significant improvement in knowledge of research terms and concepts, such as 'standard deviation' (p<0.0001), 'randomised controlled trial' (p<0.0001), 'quasi-experimental research' (p<0.0001) and 'systematic review' (p<0.0001) (see Spittlehouse, 1999). We are thus reporting an 18%, 31%, 30% and 23% degree of positive change on these four indicator tests respectively. These figures are climbing in subsequent, more tailored critical

Table 5
Respondents' understanding of 'statistical significance'

Level of understanding	Criterion	Examples
Limited or no understanding	Inaccurate answer with limited understanding of chance/ collateral factors.	'Something can be said to be statistically significant if it reaches in repeatable studies a certain large percentage recurrence, usually 5% or 15%' (respondent 355). 'That the sample used was large enough to reflect a real trend' (respondent 805).
Some understanding	Mention of the role of chance/ collateral factors but not fully explicit.	'The difference in outcome is accounted for by the factor(s) under research' (respondent 717). 'Something could be due to other factors, not always what was done' (respondent 116).
Full understanding	Results/findings, or a difference in the data were unlikely to be attributable to chance	'An outcome is statistically significant if, according to some accepted level of probability, it is unlikely to be due to chance alone' (respondent 99). 'The greater the statistical significance the lesser the likelihood of chance' (respondent 346).

appraisal skills courses provided by CEBSS.

Overall satisfaction with CEBSS 'appraising the evidence' courses is high; in a recent evaluation (N=118), 32% evaluated them as being 'very good', 51% stated that they were 'good' and 17% that they were 'average' (CEBSS, 2003). Qualitative data indicated that participants valued the opportunity to learn more about research and enjoyed the workshops. These data are included to underline the view that these two surveys were undertaken for intelligence-gathering purposes as well as evaluative purposes, so as to enable us more accurately to tailor our interventions.

Fig. 9
Ability correctly to identify statistical significance (having indicated familiarity) (%)

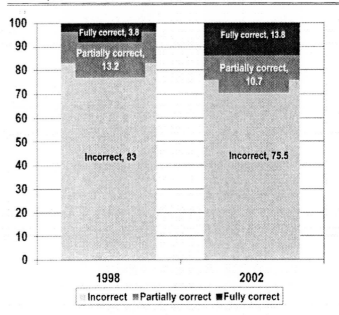

Incorrect ░ Partially correct ▓ Fully correct

Fig. 10
Association between contact with CEBSS and being able to define term 'statistical significance' (%)

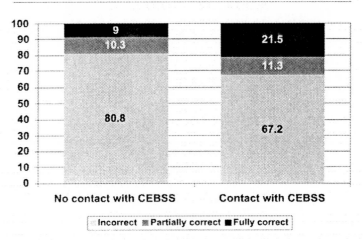

Incorrect ░ Partially correct ▓ Fully correct

Perceived relevance of research to professional practice

The vast majority of the respondents (90% in 1998 and 94% in 2002) viewed research to be of relevance to their jobs, with the figures increasing significantly between 1998 and 2002 (χ^2 = 38.7, df = 3, p<0.001; see Fig. 11.).

Note that in 1998 just under half reported that research findings informed day-to-day practice 'rarely' or 'not at all', but by 2002 there had been significant changes (see Fig. 12). In 2002, only 25% stated that research findings informed their day-to-day practice 'rarely' or 'not at all' (χ^2 = 103.2, df =3, p<0.001).

The extent to which research findings were seen as influencing day-to-day practice was significantly associated with perceived encouragement from departments to keep up to date with such findings in both the first (χ^2 = 71.6, df = 3, p<0.001) and the second survey (χ^2 = 70.2, df = 6, p<0.001), with respondents who reported that research regularly informed their practice also stating that they received 'a lot' or 'some' encouragement from departments. There were also significant associations between this factor and reported access to library facilities (χ^2 = 20.8, df = 3, p<0.001), circulated journals (c^2 = 12.8, df = 3, p<0.001) and research summaries (c^2 = 44.9, df = 3, p<0.001). Figure 12 shows substantial reported increases in the use of research in practice over the four year period.

Respondents' perceptions as to how reading more research publications might influence practice

In the 1998 survey, the vast majority of respondents stated that increased access to research literature would, on the whole, lead to improvements to practice. A majority of the respondents (60%) reported that reading more research publications could assist them in the better selection of appropriate helping methods. Half of the respondents in 1998 reported that practice had changed as a result of previously reading research materials, with some referring to publications such as *Child Protection: Messages from research* (DH, 1995), the CEBSS *Buying Time* Study (Trappes-Lomax *et al.*, 2002) and *What Works in Child Protection* (Macdonald & Winkley, 1999).

Fig. 11
Perceived relevance of research to practice (%)

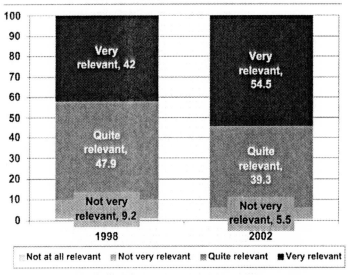

Fig. 12
Extent to which research findings inform day-to-day practice (%)

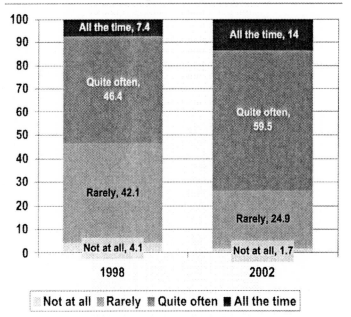

Conclusions

1. This is the largest, and most representative study of the obstacles to, and opportunities for, evidence-based practice yet undertaken. Also, given the attention paid to random sampling and the stratification of key factors, and given comparisons with demographic and other relevant data from national surveys of workplace conditions, we feel confident that these findings have relevance beyond our region.

2. There are encouraging, statistically significant differences in levels of knowledge of effectiveness research present in the comparison study, particularly if staff have had access to CEBSS events. However, it should not be forgotten that these improvements in knowledge are reported by only a minority; the practices of the majority are more likely to have changed their attitudes than their behaviour – which is conditioned, as qualitative data inform us, by circumstances in the workplace. Departments prize departmental accountability exercises and record keeping, and, not always rational, risk-prevention strategies, and so, as revealed by Health dissemination research, reviewing evidence for use in practice is often squeezed out. Thus, no or only a few 'magic bullets' (Oxman *et al.*, 1995), but some promising trends indicating steady change, for example, a near 50% increase in knowledge of effectiveness studies (albeit from a low baseline), lack of which we think is the prime obstacle to more effective service-provision, have to be a cause for modest celebration. Please also remember that these numbers, given our methodology, are representative of many more people in the study population, and probably beyond.

3. At an attitudinal level, the most encouraging finding of these two surveys is the sustained level of enthusiasm for the *idea* of evidence-based practice. Contrary to expectation, there were no ideological debates about the place of scientific rigour in practice, no ethical concerns, no worries about research findings distracting from engagement with clients – in fact, no trace of the worries expressed regarding this approach by some of the post-modernly inclined over the last decade or so (see Webb, 2001; Sheldon 2001). Most staff are convinced by the idea; they are just looking for more departmental support

to enable them to put it into practice. The study has found a positive association between perceived departmental encouragement of keeping up to date with research and actual reported use of research by staff in daily practice. Note that research is increasingly referred to on training courses and debated in evidence-based groups, but not in supervision (a key, statistically significant influence on practice as revealed at time 1). Such findings are well in line with what staff tell us at conferences and on training courses.

4. Library facilities and Internet access are improving, but all too slowly in comparison to the Health staff with whom we are supposed to 'integrate'. Lack of ready access to databases is a major obstacle to evidence-based practice since the idea depends fundamentally upon reading. There is a clear (yet unsurprising) association between the likelihood of staff using research in everyday practice and their department's provision of support facilities including access to journals, research summaries and databases. Such support facilities are essential if staff are to make use of the growing amount of accessible research literature in our field; informed readers concentrating first on systematic reviews – which obsessive-compulsive summaries will shortly come to meet most of our information needs, we predict – and then on good quality trials. But this is a complex field, where we are dealing with processes not substances, and so we need also to pay attention to promising quasi-experimental, pre-post, and qualitative client opinion studies - which form the ingredients of the 'soup' from which more refutable propositions can be ladled out and subjected to further tests. Our guides should be, of course, the nature of the research question.

5. It is perfectly arguable that many research and development centres such as CEBSS spend most of their time conducting remedial Social Work education exercises. It is the case that the qualifying courses that probably need us least are the ones that use us most within this project. The courses that have, e.g., little or no research methodology training; no critical appraisal training; provide little or no education on trends in effectiveness research, no closed circuit television-based training on interviewing techniques (the only effective way to teach them, research tells us); that provide no lectures on developmental psychology (how

else are proper assessments to be made if there is no template of normal/average development in place?); teach their students that mental ill health is a socially constructed phenomenon, etc., etc., are often unwilling to invite us lest their students develop an appetite for something more rigorous. This problem is in our view the overriding obstacle to evidence-based practice, since often there is little upon which to build and one has to start all over again. Perhaps the new degree protocols (see TOPPS, 2000) will solve this problem, though they are a bit of a Rorschach test and so everyone is likely to see in them what they want to. 'A triumph of hope over experience' as Dr Johnson once described second marriages, but hope nevertheless.

6. We cannot claim, given the methodology of these two studies, that any gains reported are exclusively due to the influence of the CEBSS project. However, since the respondents who provided us with the information are in the south west of England where the project is located; since they are unlikely to have got their improved research knowledge from BBC Radio 4 or from *Community Care*, or from governmental or even local policy statements (they don't read them much, the survey itself tells us that) then even allowing for greater discussion of the idea of evidence-based practice nationally, then there is a plausible association between our extensive efforts and the changes reported above, particularly if one looks at the comparative data discussed.

7. Regarding attempts to bridge the gap between important knowledge and changes in practice, we have some findings from our 'creating and sustaining an evidence-based culture' initiative, and from our cognitive-behavioural therapy training, (N= 18 conferences and 28 courses to date) showing that c45% of staff come back with data, examples and graphs showing concrete changes in cases.

These two linked studies show dogged progress towards the aim of establishing evidence-based principles in social services departments despite the many governmental and local authority 'target culture' pressures on staff. To quote the American poet Robert Frost, we still have 'miles to go and promises to keep' but at least we now have a map.

Notes

1. This is an updated and comparative version of the first study published in *Social Work and Social Sciences Review*, Autumn 2002, by Sheldon & Chilvers. The authors are all present or past members of the Centre for Evidence-Based Social Services, Peninsula Medical School, University of Exeter. Our thanks are hereby extended to our (beloved – not too strong a word) Centre Secretary, Sue Bosley, who handled the very demanding logistics of both these studies.

2. There is also the example of James Lind to consider however. In 1753 he conducted a shipboard experiment to settle the question as to whether citrus fruit staved off scurvy by giving it to half the sailors. It did, and the term 'limey' became less of a term of abuse as a result (ish). (See James Lind Library at www.jameslindlibrary.org).

3. For further information visit www.ex.ac.uk/cebss and www.be-evidence-based.com.

4. If you have the stomach for it, see Sheldon (1995) p.117 for a transcript of a 'disclosure interview' with one of the children caught up in this Witches of Salem nightmare.

5. The CEBSS websites (www.ex.ac.uk/cebss) and www.be-evidence-based.com) and CareData are now freely available nationally, thanks to the support of the Social Care Institute for Excellence. Detailed advice on searching the Internet-based literature can be found in Macwilliam *et al*, 2003.

6. See Sheldon & Chilvers (2000) for a more detailed discussion of the findings of the first questionnaire, and a copy of the full questionnaire.

7. The 'other' category covered staff in special projects.

8. Interestingly, despite reassurances and 'blinding' procedures, many staff rang in to check out the security of this system: a message to senior managers, we think.

9. Answers were independently assessed by two researchers.

References

Beck, A. T. (1976) *Cognitive Therapy and the Emotional Disorders.* New York: International Universities Press

Butler Sloss, E. (1988) Report of the inquiry into Child Abuse in Cleveland 1987, Cmd. 412. London: HMSO

Byford, S. Harrington, R., Torgeson, D., Kerfoot, M., Dyer, E., Harrington, V., Woodham, A., Gill, J., and McNiven, F. (1999) Cost-effectiveness Analysis of a Home-Based Social Work Intervention for Children and Adolescents Who Have Deliberately Poisoned Themselves: Results of a Randomised Controlled Trial. *British Journal of Psychiatry,* 174, 56-62

Cabot, R.C. (1931) Treatment in social casework and the need for tests of its success and failure. *Proceedings of the National Conference of Social Work*

Centre for Evidence-Based Social Services (2003) *Annual Report to the Department of Health: 2002-2003.* Exeter: Exeter University, Centre for Evidence-Based Social Services

Cochrane, A.L. (1973) *Effectiveness and Efficiency: Random reflections on health services.* London: Nuffield Provincial Hospitals Trust

Dalrymple, J. (1994) Devils Island: What really happened on the Orkneys. *Sunday Times,* 27th February

Daniels, M. and Hill, H.B. (1952) Chemotherapy of pulmonary tuberculosis in young adults: An analysis of three Medical Research Council trials. *British Medical Journal,* 1, 1162

Department of Health (1995) *Child Protection: Messages from research,* London: HMSO

Fischer, J. (1976) *The Effectiveness of Social Casework,* Springfield, Il: Charles C. Thomas

Frost, R. (1978) *Stopping by Woods on a Snowy Evening.* London. Dutton Books

Griffiths Report (1988). *Community Care: Agenda for action.* London: HMSO

Haslev, J. (1921) *The Good Soldier Schweik (Vol.1)* Prague

Howitt, D. (1992) *Child Abuse Errors: When good intentions go wrong.* Hemel Hempstead: Harvester Wheatsheaf

Hunt, M. (1997) *How Science Takes Stock: The story of meta-analysis.* New York: Russell Sage Foundation

Jones, W.C. and Borgatta, E.F. (1972) Methodology of Evaluation. In E.J. Mullen and J.R. Dumpson (Eds) *Evaluation of Social Intervention.* San Francisco: Jossey-Bass

Laming, Lord. (2003) *The Victoria Climbié Inquiry. Report of an Inquiry by Lord Laming.* London: HMSO

Lehrman, L.J. (1949) *Success and Failure of Treatment of Children in Child Guidance Clinics of the Jewish Board of Guardians.* Research Monographs I. New York: Jewish Board of Guardians

Local Government Management Board (LGMB)/ Central Council for Education and Training in Social Work (CCETSW) (1997) *Human Resources for Personal Social Services: From personnel administration to human resources management.* London: LGMB

Macdonald, G. M. and Sheldon, B. (1992) Contemporary studies of the effectiveness of Social Work. *British Journal of Social Work* 22, 615-43

Macdonald, G. M and Sheldon, B. (1998) Changing One's Mind: The final frontier? *Issues in Social Work Education,* 18, 1, 3-25

Macdonald, G.M and Winkley, A. (1999). *What Works in Child Protection?* Barkingside: Barnardo's

Macdonald, G. M. (2000) *Effective Interventions for Child Abuse and Neglect: An evidence-based approach to planning and evaluating interventions,* Chichester: John Wiley

Macdonald G.M. and Macdonald, K.I. (2000) Perceptions of risk. In P. Parsloe (Ed.) *Risk Assessment in Social Work And Social Care.* Research Highlights 36. London: Jessica Kingsley

Macdonald, G.M. (2004). *A Randomised Controlled Trial of a Training Project for Foster Carers.* Exeter: University of Exeter, Centre for Evidence-Based Social Services

Macwilliam, S., Maggs, P., Caldwell, A. & Tierney, S. (2003) *Accessing Social Care Research: An Introductory Guide.* Exeter: University of Exeter, Centre for Evidence-Based Social Services

Marshall, M., Gray, A., Lockwood, A. and Green, R. (2000) Case Management for People with Severe Mental Disorders (Cochrane Review). *Cochrane Library, Issue 3.* Oxford: Update Software

Marshall, M., and Lockwood, A. (2000) Assertive Community Treatment for People with Severe Mental Disorders (Cochrane Review). *Cochrane Library, Issue 3.* Oxford: Update Software

Maynard, A. and Chalmers, I. (1997) *Non-Random Reflections on Health Services Research.* London: BMJ Publishing Group

Mayer, J.E. and Timms, N (1970) *The Client Speaks.* London: Routledge and Kegan Paul

Monnette, D.R., Sullivan, T.J. and De Jong, C.R. (1989) *Applied Social Research: Tools for the Human Services.* [2nd ed] London: Holt, Rinehart and Winston

Moseley, A. (2004) The Internet: Can you get away without it? Supporting the caring professions in accessing research for practice. *Journal of Integrated Care*, 12, 3

Mullen, E.J. and Dumpson, J.R. (Eds.) (1972), *The Evaluation of Social Intervention*. San Francisco: Jossey-Bass

Oppenheim, A.S. (1992) *Questionnaire Design, Interviewing and attitude assessment*. London: Pinter

Oxman, A.D., Thomson, M.A., Davis, D.A. and Haynes, R.B. (1995) No magic bullets: A systematic review of 102 trials of interventions to improve professional practice. *Canadian Medical Association Journal*, 153, 1423-1431

Parsloe, P. (Ed.) (2000) *Risk Assessment in Social Care and Social Work*. Research Highlights 36. London: Jessica Kingsley

Popper, K. (1963) *Conjectures and Refutations*. London: Routledge and Kegan Paul

Powers, E. and Witmer, H (1951) *An Experiment in the Prevention of Delinquency: The Cambridge-Somerville Youth Study*. New York: Columbia University Press

Reid, W.J. and Hanrahan P. (1981) The effectiveness of social work: Recent evidence. In E.M. Goldberg, E.M. and N. Connolly (Eds.), *Evaluative Research in Social Care*. London: Heineman

Reid, W.J. and Shyne, A. (1968) *Brief and Extended Casework*. New York: Columbia University Press

Richmond, M.E. (1917) *Social Diagnosis*. New York: Russell Sage Foundation

Sackett, D.L., Rosenberg, W.M., Gray, J.H.M., Haynes, R.B. and Richardson, W.S. (1996) Evidence-based practice: What it is and what it isn't. *British Medical Journal*, 312, 7203, 71-72

Seebohm Report (1968) *Report of the Committee on Local Authority and Allied Personal Social Services*, Cmnd. 3703. London: HMSO

Sheldon, B. (1978) Theory and practice in social work; a re-examination of a tenuous relationship. *British Journal of Social Work*, 8, 1-22

Sheldon, B. (1980) *The Use of Contracts in Social Work*. Birmingham: British Association of Social Workers

Sheldon, B. (1986) Social work effectiveness experiments: Review and implications. *British Journal of Social Work*, 16, .223-42

Sheldon, B. (1987a) The Psychology of incompetence. In G. Drewry, B. Martin and B. Sheldon (Eds.) *After Beckford: Essays on child abuse*. Egham: Royal Holloway and Bedford New College

Sheldon, B. (1987b) Implementing the findings of social work effectiveness research. *British Journal of Social Work*, 17, 573-586

Sheldon, B. (1994) The social and biological components of mental disorder: Implications for services. *International Journal of Social Psychiatry*, 40, 87-105

Sheldon, B. (1995) *Cognitive-Behavioural Therapy: Research, practice and philosophy*. London: Routledge

Sheldon, B. (2000) Cognitive behavioural methods in social care: A look at the evidence. In P. Stepney and D. Ford (Eds.) *Social Work Models, Methods and Theories: A Framework for practice*. Lyme Regis. Russell House

Sheldon, B. (2001) The validity of evidence-based practice in social work: A reply to Stephen Webb. *British Journal of Social Work*, 31, 801-809

Sheldon, B. and Chilvers, R. (2000) *Evidence-Based Social Care: A Study of Prospects and Problems*. Lyme Regis. Russell House Publishing

Sheldon, B. and Chilvers, R. (2002) An empirical study of the obstacles to evidence-based practice. *Social Work and Social Sciences Review*, 10, 1, pp 6-26

Sheldon, B. and Macdonald, G. M. (1999) *Research and Practice in Social Care: Mind the gap*. Exeter: University of Exeter, Centre for Evidence-Based Social Services

Spittlehouse, C. 1999. *CASP for Social Services: Final Project Report*. Critical Appraisal Skills Programme, Oxford

Stein, J., and Gambrill, E (1977) Facilitating decision making in foster care. *Social Services Review*, 51, 502-511

Thyer, B.A. (1995) 'Effective psychosocial treatments for children: A selected review', *Early Child Development and Care*, 106, 137-147

Thoburn, J., Lewis, A. and Shemmings, D. (1995) *Paternalism or partnership?: Family involvement in the child protection process*. Studies in Child Protection. London: HMSO

Tolley, K. and Rowland, N. (1995) *Evaluating The Cost-Effectiveness of Counselling in Health Care*. London: Routledge

Training Organization for the Personal Social Services (TOPSS) (2000) *Modernising the Social Care Workforce: The first national training strategy for England. Executive Summary*. Leeds: TOPSS

Trappes-Lomax, T., Ellis, A. and Fox, M. (2002) *Buying Time: An evaluation and cost effectiveness analysis of a joint health/ social care residential rehabilitation unit for older people on discharge from hospital*. Exeter: University of Exeter, Centre for Evidence-Based Social Services

Webb, S.A. (2001) Some Considerations on the Validity of Evidence-Based Practice in Social Work, *British Journal of Social Work*, 31, 57-79

Wessely, S., Rose, S. and Bisson, J. (1999) Brief psychological interventions ('debriefing') for treating immediate trauma-related symptoms and preventing post-traumatic stress disorder (Cochrane Review). *Cochrane Library, Issue 2*. Oxford: Update Software.

2
Evidence based social work practice: A reachable goal?

Frank Ainsworth and Patricia Hansen

Introduction

In New South Wales the heads of Departments of Social Work in Teaching Hospitals have a public commitment to evidence based practice in health care. Likewise, in 2002 the Association of Children's Welfare Agencies bi-annual Sydney conference will have the theme 'What-works? Evidence based practice in child and family services'. The call for evidence-based practice that originated in medicine (Sackett et al., 1996) is now clearly visible in social work (Macdonald, 2001; Dunston & Sim, 1999).

In spite of what is sometimes said the core of social work remains services for individuals and families. In the health sector or in child and family services the demand that faces social work practitioners is to demonstrate accountability for the quality of their services and show that their interventions are effective. It is important to demonstrate that these services encourage change and produce positive benefits to the children and adult family members who receive them. Practice based on research evidence about effectiveness is no longer an option to be accepted or rejected according to personal preference. It is critical for the survival of social work as a professional discipline in health care and child and family service settings (Dunston & Sim 1999).

There are debates about what constitutes evidence and how evidence should shape practice interventions. Some community-based services are able to prosper through advocacy about an issue, cause or social problem (i.e. gay rights, poverty or the response to asylum seekers) although these social action type activities are not the exclusive domain of social work. Moreover, these services are frequently shaped by socio-political considerations and to that extent may be less open to evidence based approaches. But this is not so in health care and child and family service settings where health disciplines have already developed empirical evidence of effectiveness to support their activities. Social work must increasingly do the same, as a broad advocacy or social action focus, while important, is not enough in these settings.

Evidence based practice as ethical practice

Professions such as social work that actively intervene in the individual lives of people face crucial questions about what constitutes ethical practice. In the US the National Association of Social Workers (NASW) code of ethics indicates that social workers carry a responsibility for scholarship and research and are bound to develop and utilize this knowledge in professional practice (cited in Blythe et al., 1994, p.17). In recent draft 'standards for direct practice and service management' that draw heavily on a similar code of ethics, the Australian Association of Social Workers (AASW) indicates that social work mangers should ensure a commitment to 'a continuous quality assurance and improvement in practice research' (AASW, standard 2.11, p.14). This includes having in place a strategy to ensure that quality improvement activities occur and that resources are allocated to support these activities. The actual code of ethics is less explicit on the issue of ethical practice and the link to research (AASW, 2000).

Unfortunately, even in the US where social work scholarship is more firmly established, agencies are not always supportive of this activity and organisational cultures all to often confirm negative attitudes towards research (Epstein, 1996). Alongside this, attempts by schools of social work to produce a generation of practitioner-researchers have not been particularly successful (Epstein, 1996). Similarly, social work agencies in Australia, even departments of social work in teaching hospitals where research is highly valued, are usually bereft of formal research studies. Latterly, there has also been a call in Australia for stronger links between schools of social work and service organisations and a combining of the roles of educator, researcher and practitioner, although why this should be successfully accomplished in Australia any more than in the US is far from clear (Lord, 2002).

In fact, many social workers appear to continue to rely on practice knowledge acquired in qualifying programs way after that knowledge has reached its use by date. There is also a noticeable tendency to base interventions on intuition, acquired philosophy (religious and political), or on individual preferences that are rooted in personal values and life experience, rather than contemporary research findings. Practice is not driven by research and theoretical explanations and even when the effectiveness of a particular practice approach (i.e. cognitive-behavioural treatment) to specific circumstances or conditions has been established, it is often ignored.

Regardless of the above social workers are strong exponents of ethical behaviour and vocal critics of the standards of other professions. Yet, it can be argued that much of social work practice, because of the lack of research that demonstrates practice effectiveness of most interventions (i.e. casework with adolescent offenders; group work with teenage fathers), is of debatable ethical standing. Even worse, is the apparent reluctance of many social work academics to take seriously the need for this type of effectiveness research (Thyer, 2001).

The social work profession advocates that regardless of whether you are, rich or poor, young or old, healthy or sick, educated or illiterate you have a right to be treated with dignity. But apparently, it is acceptable to use interventions that have not been subject to testing to show that they are effective and produce the best possible outcome in relation to a given circumstance or condition. Frequently, people who use social work services are poorly educated or are on low incomes, and some are old and sick, but this is no reason why they should be subjected to practice interventions which have not been shown to be effective and which at best are based on elements of practice wisdom, anecdote or poorly distilled past experience. Indeed, it can be argued that only practice that has been subject to rigorous effectiveness research can truly claim to be ethical practice.

What is evidence?

This brings us to the controversial issue of what is evidence. Clearly, some social work scholars favour scientific standards of evidence derived from random control type (RCT) or the less rigorous quasi-experimental (QE) type research studies (Campbell & Stanley, 1973; Thyer, 1993; Macdonald, 2001). These types of studies are favoured as they can contribute to an understanding of causality in relation to particular circumstances or conditions. Such scholars are always under attack from those who, for various reasons, reject quantitative methods and the underlying positivist paradigm that they argue is an inappropriate way to research human issues (Smith, 1987; Adamson, 2001). Yet studies based on this scientific methodology have made a major contribution to social work by advancing our knowledge of human development and individual well-being through an understanding of person-environment transactions (Bronfenbrenner, 1979).

Equally, those who promote qualitative and participatory forms of research and who ascribe to interpretive and critical paradigms (Sarantakos 1998), that they consider more accurately captures the complexity of the human condition, will be criticised by those who favour the scientific approach. Rigorous qualitative research does provide important insights and it does build knowledge albeit of an alternative kind to that produced by quantitative approaches. But inevitably qualitative research will be subject to criticism as it can only produce time and context specific findings, and unlike quantitative research is unable to offer replicable studies and generalisable results (Sarantakos, 1998). Qualitative research informs practice as it provides a way of examining issues and developing understandings that throw light on individual experience and important aspects of the human condition. But it cannot provide evidence about the effectiveness of a particular social work intervention in general nor does it help to build best practice models for intervention upon which social work practitioners can rely.

The fact is that social work practice requires both quantitative and qualitative approaches to practice research. At a point in time when social work practice research is miniscule and the profession is facing demands that it demonstrates effectiveness, arguments between researchers from different schools of thought are counter productive and sterile. This should not be an ideological battle for one side to win and the other to lose as both approaches have much to contribute. It is a battle to be joined so that those who provide a social work service as well as those who seek a service can be confident that what they offer or receive is the best and most effective service given current knowledge. Alas, few social workers are currently able to say that this is the type of service that they routinely provide. But this is what those who use social work services have a right to expect and richly deserve to receive.

Social work has passed the stage where it is acceptable for practitioners to claim 'each case is different' and use this simplistic approach to individualisation as a justification for not mastering the available research knowledge about 'what works' and 'what works best' in cases that display similar characteristics. That each case is different is self-evident, as every profession and practitioner knows.

Variations on a theme

Another aspect of evidence-based practice that is closely linked to the above, but which is foreign to many social workers, is the expectation that evidence based interventions will reduce the amount of 'unexplained variance' in practice outcomes. For example, in cases where service recipients are comparable on a range of socio-economic variables the outcome of a social work intervention designed to address a set of circumstances or conditions will vary in only a limited number of cases. The outcome sought is that the social work intervention will be predictable and beneficial in most cases and energy and effort will be put into making the intervention even more reliable. Many social workers do not seem to accept that it is possible to define an intervention or to identify the key steps to be followed to achieve a specified outcome of this type. Instead, they resort to a variation of the 'each case is different' argument and claim that the social worker-client transaction involves the individual social worker utilizing a unique constellation of knowledge, skills and practice wisdom that is not replicable to achieve an unspecified outcome. In extreme instances this devotion to individualism provides the ideological foundation for a plea for complete worker autonomy and rejection of the scientific approach. There may be a rejection of any notion of organisational accountability and a refusal to use even the most basic form of analysis that is categorisation. Evidence-based practice substantially challenges this position since it demands accountability and the examination of all aspects of practice.

Another variation on this theme, but one that runs contrary to the notion that 'each case is different', is where social workers work from a favoured theoretical or ideological perspective regardless of the type of situation presented to them. This can be behavioural, psychodynamic, feminist, narrative or a structural approach or any other framework that became a favourite while engaged in professional studies. Macdonald (2001) captures this position with her example 'family therapy is the answer ... now what is the problem' (p.35) quotation. Regrettably, this tendency to do the same thing all the time regardless of circumstances or conditions was confirmed in a recent study by Berry, Cash and Brook (2000). In this study of families served by a US metropolitan child protection agency these authors found that irrespective of the findings of comprehensive assessment of each family made by social workers when it came to planning the social work intervention each family was offered exactly the same combination of services. Yet, these social workers would no doubt still argue that each case is different. What goes unnoticed is that by using the same theoretical framework or way of working on all occasions the claim that each case is different is undermined.

The call for evidence-based practice is a dilemma for social workers who choose to use the 'each case is different' argument, for those who always work from a preferred framework or use the same intervention method. Evidence based practice asks questions about the comparative effectiveness of one intervention by comparison to another (i.e. a behavioural approach versus a feminist approach with victims of domestic violence or casework versus group work). And the evidence, once collected, may mean that you will have to change your mind and your way of working! (Macdonald & Sheldon, 1998)

But understanding about practice interventions can be developed, typologies or classification systems can be created, factors influencing particular case outcomes can be identified and analysed, and theories and hypotheses can be constructed and empirically tested and generalisations can be made. In fact, if this cannot be done there is no justification for the social work education and training enterprise. The results from research studies can also be applied in sensible ways to particular circumstances and to recognisable conditions. Other professions have shown this does not have to undermine sensitivity to human needs or an individual approach to practice. It is time for social work to accept the challenge and demonstrate that research based practice is both ethical and superior to that which is based on personal beliefs, preferred ways of working or political ideologies.

Evidence and social work advocacy

Some aspects of direct social work practice in health care and child and family services involve advocacy (i.e. establishing a families eligibility for income support, negotiating educational services for a disabled child). This type of intervention constitutes individual and service systems level advocacy. Data about interventions in this type of circumstance is certainly open to qualitative analysis to establish the most effective methods for achieving a desired outcome. It is equally feasible to chart the use of social worker's time and quantify the benefits achieved for the service participant (i.e. gain in income, services obtained). The resulting evidence might then be turned into in-house training to increase the effectiveness of this form of intervention. The quality and reliability of practice would be improved if advocacy activities were based on the best available evidence about 'what works' and 'what works best'.

There is also societal level advocacy where a cause, issue or social problem (i.e. gay rights, poverty or the response to asylum seekers) is the focus of social and political action. Some social workers argue that the pursuit of these and similar social justice goals (i.e. legislative changes, income redistribution or the granting of permanent residency visas) should assume a more prominent role in social work education and practice (Bardill 1993; Mendes 2001). They argue for a social work curriculum that teaches skills in political action and social change and a professional code of ethics that obligates social worker to support these activities. In that context a social work code of ethics should 'define a core set of beliefs and values that are incumbent upon all social workers ... publicly state their commitment to a number of concrete social justice objectives, and provide specific guidelines for community activism including moral principles to judge the ethical legitimacy of civil disobedience strategies' (Mendes 1998).

This type of practice is well beyond the purview of evidence-based social work practice and is unsupported by many social workers (Mendes 2001). This is the territory of the politician and the priest where being a 'true believer' and 'having faith' is more important than any earthly evidence. It is not relevant for social work practice in health care and child and family service settings where other health disciplines have already developed empirical evidence of effectiveness to support their activities. Social work must increasingly do the same and should not be diverted away from this professional task by activities that are unlikely to enhance the standing of the profession in these important service venues.

An evidence based research agenda

A research agenda for social work practice in health care and child and family service settings inevitably focuses on a series of questions about service effectiveness. To itemise a few of the questions is both illuminating and scary as it shows how far social work has to travel before even the most basic intervention elements are established as effective with given populations. For example, we need to know:

- Which type of intervention (i.e. casework, group work, community or health education programs) works best with clients who present a particular set of circumstances (i.e. child neglect, failure to comply with a treatment regime) and display similar demographic characteristics (i.e. education, age, income level)?

- Which type of condition or circumstance (i.e. adaptation to illness, coping with a child's disability) is best addressed through group or community or health education programs rather than individual interventions and how is this affected by demographic characteristics (i.e. education, age, income level)?
- How many intervention sessions are needed to produce changes in child and family function in relation to a specific condition or circumstance (i.e. confirmation of a child's acute health status, parental custody disputes post separation).
- For how long does the effect of a particular intervention last in relation to a particular condition or circumstance (i.e. child neglect, non-compliance with a treatment regime) and how might the effect be enhanced?
- What client characteristics (i.e. education, age, income level) or conditions or circumstances (i.e. child physical abuse, parental mental illness) contra indicate individual, group or community or health program interventions?

These questions cover a range of social and health factors and wide array of medical conditions. They are not new questions and we do have a substantial body of research, albeit US dominated, on which to draw. Recently, Maluccio et al (2001) drew together the child welfare outcome research from the US, UK and Australia. Macdonald (2001) has done a similar comprehensive review of the child protection research. These reviews now need to be complemented by exhaustive Campbell type reviews (Campbell Collaboration, 2001) of social science and social work research that addresses other themes, especially in health care and social work. However, such reviews will be pointless if social work practitioners fail to access these resources and do not restructure their practice to take account of what is known. In medicine, up to two decades may pass before research findings are translated into improvements in practice (Agency for Healthcare Research and Quality, 2001).

In an effort to address this issue clinical practice guidelines and pathways have emerged that aim to optimise the transfer process and improve the quality of practice (Holt et al., 1996). Social work will need to make similar efforts if evidence based practice is to emerge successfully from the current morass.

Routes to evidence based practice

Two routes to evidence based practice are worth consideration. The newest is the potential use of data generated by information technology systems (DiLeonardi & Yuan, 2000). Indeed, by now most social workers in health care and community based child and family social work agencies are established users of information technology for communication, record keeping and statistical data collection purposes. In the process of adaptation to this new technology large administrative databases have been established that contain retrievable information that has the potential to change the way in which agencies are managed and direct practice is examined. Subject to data being collected in a form suitable for evaluation and research purposes this opens up astonishing possibilities that are only now beginning to be recognised. Of course many agencies have not understood the importance of the architecture of computing systems and how a data collection system can be structured and integrated to facilitate its usage in this way. Nor has every practitioner got beyond fear and mistrust of this technology and about how data might be used to hold them accountable for the way they provide services. Nevertheless, across the next decade the move to a positive position where this type of data will be viewed as making a positive contribution to the quality of practice will occur

As this takes place it will open up the potential for services to be data-driven and rigorously evaluated. For example, it should be possible to carefully assemble data about a particular social work intervention and the component parts of that intervention. Processes and activities that were less strictly monitored can be the subject of scrutiny not just at a case level but across a range of comparable case situations. Even between worker or cross agencies comparison of the same intervention in similar cases is a possibility. Thus, it will be feasible to build greater knowledge about particular social work interventions and the components of an intervention that contribute most to its effectiveness. In turn, this should lead to modifications to improve the quality of the intervention and to move the intervention to a higher level of effectiveness (Pecora et al., 1996).

The second more traditional research route is not unaffected by these developments. Computing technology makes the collection and analysis of large data sets for quantitative research studies more feasible then ever before. Advances in statistical techniques, especially model building, also make it possible to consider more complex statistical equations that account for a range of mediating and moderating variables (Gogineni et al., 1995; Holmbeck, 1997). The capacity of these techniques to include a wider range of variables will make attempts to criticise quantitative research results for what was not included less viable. An example, of model building is groundbreaking work on offending behaviour that seeks to explain the link between social and economic disadvantage and juvenile crime (Weatherburn & Lind, 2001). If heeded, this research should cause social work intervention with juvenile offenders and their families to be substantially reshaped.

In addition, in the US the use of standardised data collection instruments by some social workers has been in evidence for more than a decade (Hudson, 1997). In Britain, the promotion by the Department of Health of a set of family assessment instruments (Framework for the assessment of children in need and their families, 1999) is significant. It introduces social work practitioners to the issue of measurement and the use of these instruments as a way of mapping the effectiveness of service interventions (Blythe et al., 1994; Mullen & Magnabosco, 1997). Unfortunately, different views amongst social workers in Australia have so far resulted in minimal developments of this kind.

Data collected through the use of these instruments, provided they are valid and reliable measures administered appropriately will provide evidence of individual and family change that can legitimately be seen as an indicator of service effectiveness. This development means that the next generation of social work practitioners are being acculturated into the use of these type of instruments and this will encourage the use of a broader range of these tools.

On a different note, a recent qualitative study of families served by a family preservation program reported that consumers and social workers were satisfied with the outcome of the service (Walton & Dodini, 1999). While satisfaction is not a measure of effectiveness this study also reported that a positive therapeutic relationship between the worker and child and family, along with skill training and concrete services 'contributed most to the success of the program' (p.3). In this context the development by Bickman and Doucette (2000) of a 'therapeutic alliance' measurement scale is important. The therapeutic alliance scale assesses the emotional bond, between the client and the social worker, agreement on therapeutic tasks, agreement on goals of the intervention, as well as the perceived openness/truthfulness of the social worker-client relationship. Thus the scale assesses the process of treatment or service and provides a way of examining the relationship between the service process and service outcomes. This opens up the possibility of mounting a study to examine the relationship between social worker and client. Social workers have long claimed that this relationship is at the centre of effective service interventions. Research of this type would be a good start in efforts to move social work practice toward a firmer evidential base and away from mere assertion about what works and why.

Reforming social work education

The fact that a noticeable number of social workers in the US, Britain and Australia think that is acceptable to practice primarily from a foundation of personal beliefs, political or religious ideology rather than empirical research evidence suggests that a reform of social work education is long overdue. The following proposals are offered as a starting point for the debate about these reforms. They are based on the joint authors substantial experience of Australian, British and US social work education.

Student selection

- That the selection processes for entry into social work qualifying programs are reviewed and that an emphasis is placed on attracting the most academically able candidates. The anti-intellectual components of this process that favours personal attributes over academic ability to be removed from this process (Lyons, 1999).

Academic appointments

- That schools of social work only consider for appoint to teaching positions candidates who hold PhD qualifications and who have published a minimum number of research articles in referred journals.
- That the alternative approach to achievement of a PhD in social work, as with some other disciplines, through publication in key research journals of a set number of articles be given serious consideration.
- That as with other disciplines the schools of social work create a series of Research Professorships in order to stimulate and highlight social work research activities.

The structure of qualifying education and curriculum content

- That social work education accepts responsibility for teaching the academic knowledge base of social work practice and reduces its commitment to teaching practice skills.
- That consideration be given to specialisation in social work education to enable practitioners who intend to practice in health care and child and family service settings to master the academic knowledge base relevant for this type of setting.
- That a firmer emphasis should be placed on teaching 'critical thinking' skills from day one of social work studies (Macdonald & Sheldon 1998).

- That social work practice skills be taught in an 'articles' or 'internship' year post graduation as in other applied disciplines such as law and medicine. Membership of the professional association to be fully granted only after successful completion of this year of practice.
- That when teaching about social work values, academic staff emphasise and model that knowledge building through research is a core social work value and that practice that is not research based is unethical.
- That research teaching becomes a core item in every year of study that leads to a social work qualification. In order to qualify programs require students to demonstrate skills in research design, data collection and data analysis using both qualitative and quantitative techniques, as well as competence in direct practice.
- That social work academics concentrate on the core university activities of scholarship and research, writing and dissemination of knowledge through publications. The priority of research over continuing practice experience should be asserted (Trotter & Hewitt 2001).

Continuing education

- That after five years of practice all social workers be required to complete a Masters degree by research in order to maintain their eligibility for membership of a professional association and be certified as a practising social worker.

Conclusion

To conclude, it is clear that some Schools of Social Work and the present generation of social work academics have not adequately fulfilled their scholarly responsibility to build the evidence to support the professional activities of social workers. We include ourselves in this criticism. In addition, it is clear that generic models of social work education that claim to equip practitioners for work in all and any social work position do not adequately equip social workers for practice in health care and child and family service settings. It is time to re-address these issues and to accompany these changes with a move to a model of evidence based social work practice. Social work education, as currently structured in many places, is stuffed. Without these changes the progressive disappearance of social work from universities during this decade is a real possibility (Lyons, 1999).

References

Adamson, C. (2001) Social work and the call for evidence based practice in mental health: Where do we stand? *Social Work Reporter*, Winter, 8-12

Agency for Healthcare Research and Quality (2001) *Translating Research into Practice (TRIP) –11, Fact sheet*. Publication no. 01-PO17. Rockville, MD

Australian Association of Social Workers (2001) *Draft, Outcome Practice Standards for Social Workers. Direct practice and service management*. Canberra

Australian Association of Social Workers (2000) *Code of ethics*. Canberra

Bardill, D. (1993) Should all social workers be educated for social change? *Journal of Social Work Education*, 29, 1, 13-17

Berry, M., Cash, S. J. and Brooks, J.P. (2000) Intensive family preservation services: An examination of critical service components. *Child and Family Social Work*, 5, 2, 191-203

Bickman, L. and Doucette, A. (2000) *Therapeutic Alliance Scale*. Nashville, TN: Vanderbilt University, Centre for Mental Health Policy

Blythe, B., Tripodi, T. and Briar, S. (1994) *Direct Practice Research in Human Service Agencies*. New York: Columbia University Press

Bronfenbrenner, U. (1979) *The Ecology of Human Development*. Cambridge, MA: Harvard University Press

Campbell, D.T. and Stanley, J.C. (1973) *Experimental and Quasi-experimental Designs for Research*. Chicago: Rand McNally

Campbell Collaboration Secretariat (2001) http://www.campbell.gse.upenn.edu

DiLeonardi, J. and Yuan, Y.Y.T. (2000) Using administrative data. *Child Welfare*, 79, 5, 437-443

Dunston, R. and Sim, S. (1999) Evidence based projects and social work: Survival and opportunity. *Australian Association of Social Workers, New South Wales Branch, Newsletter*, 4, 15-17

Epstein, I. (1996) In quest of a research-based model of clinical practice: Or, why can't a social worker be a researcher?. *Social Work Research*, 20, 2, 97-100

Gogineni, A., Alsup, R. and Gillespie, D.F. (1995) Mediation and moderation in social work research. *Social Work Research*, 19, 1, 57-63

Holmbeck, G. N. (1997) Towards terminological, conceptual and statistical clarity in the study of mediators and moderators: Examples from the child-clinical and paediatric psychology literature. *Journal of Consulting and Clinical Psychology*, 65, 4, 599-610

Holt, P., Ward, J. and Wilson, A. (1996) *Clinical Practice Guidelines and Clinical Pathways. A status report on national and NSW development and implementation activity.* Sydney: New South Wales Health Department

Hudson, W.W. (1997, *Walmyr Assessment and Scale Scoring Manual.* Tallahassee, FL: Walmyr Publishing

Jackson, S. (1999) Foreword. in K. Lyons *Social Work in Higher Education. Demise or development?* Aldershot: Ashgate

Jones, C. (1996)) Anti-intellectualism and the peculiarities of British social work education. in N. Parton (Ed.) *Social Theory, Social Change and Social Work.* London: Routledge, pp.190-210

Lord, B. (2002) Editorial: Practice and scholarship. *Australian Social Work*, 54, 4, 1

Lyons, K. (1999) *Social Work in Higher Education. Demise or development?* Aldershot: Ashgate

Macdonald, G. (2001) *Effective Interventions in Child Abuse and Neglect. An evidence based approach to planning and evaluating interventions.* Chichester: John Wiley

Macdonald, G. and Sheldon, B. (1998) Changing one's mind: The final frontier?. *Issues in Social Work Education*, 18, 1, 3-25

Maluccio, A.N., Ainsworth, F. and Thoburn, J. (2000) *Child Welfare Outcome Research in the United States, the United Kingdom and Australia.* Washington, DC: Child Welfare League of America Press

Mendes, P. (1998) Social workers, professional associations and social justice. *Northern Radius*, 5, 1, 12-15

Mendes, P. (2001) Social workers and politics: Should there be greater involvement?. *Social Work Reporter*, Winter, 33-36

Mullen, E.J. and Magnabosco J. (Eds.) (1997) *Outcome Measurement in Human Services. Cross-cutting issues and measures.* Washington, DC:

National Association of Social Workers

National Association of Social Workers (1994) Code of Ethics. in B. Blythe, T. Tripodi and S. Briar (Eds.) *Direct Practice Research in Human Service Agencies*. New York: Columbia University Press, p.17

Pecora, P., Seelig, W.R., Zirps, F.A. and Davies, S.M. (1996) *Quality Improvement in Child and Family Services. Managing into the next century*. Washington, DC: Child Welfare League of America Press

Sarantakos, S. (1998) *Social Research*. (2nd Ed.) Melbourne: Macmillan Education

Sackett, D.L., Rosenberth, W.M., Jray, J., Hayes, R.B. and Richardson W.S. (1996) Evidence based practice: What it is and what it isn't. *British Medical Journal*, 312, 71-72

Smith, D. (1987) The limits of positivism in social work research. *British Journal of Social Work*, 17, 4, 573-586

Thyer, B. (1993) Social work theory and practice research: The approach of logical positivism. *Social Work and Social Science Review*, 4, 1, 5-26

Thyer, B. (2001) What is the role of theory in research on social work practice. *Journal of Social Work Education*, 37, 1, 9-25

Trotter, C. and Hewitt, L. (2001) Practice experience and social work education. *Australian Social Work*, 54, 4, 13-18

Walton, E. and Dodini, A.C. (1999) Intensive in-home based services: Reactions from consumers and providers. *Family Preservation Journal*, 4, 1, 39-51

Weatherburn, D. and Lind, B. (2001) *Delinquent-prone Communities*. Cambridge: Cambridge University Press

3
Reframing an evidence-based approach to practice

Stephanie Tierney

Setting the scene

Over the past decade, evidence-based practice has become an established principle in the world of social care, strengthened by organisations such as the Centre for Evidence-Based Social Services (CEBSS), the Cochrane Collaboration and the Campbell Collaboration. We also have the new body, to be at arms length from government, looking at standards, knowledge and evidence: The Social Care Institute for Excellence (SCIE).

Evidence-based practice has been defined as 'an approach to decision-making which is transparent, accountable and based on careful consideration of the most compelling evidence' (Macdonald, 2001, p.xviii). It is underpinned by a philosophy suggesting that decisions of how and when to intervene should be backed up by best current findings from robust research, to ensure the most efficient and effective use of limited resources.

Proponents and opponents debate the theoretical intricacies associated with this approach, hailed as 'one of the success stories of the 1990s' (Trinder, 2000, p.1), while simultaneously being condemned as the plaything of bureaucrats and a poisoned chalice ready to turn practitioners into unthinking technocrats (Webb, 2001; see Sheldon, 2001 for a rebuttal of this charge). Such polarised arguments fail to engage the interest of a large number of those in the profession, who regard these debates as the preserve of academics, far removed from their day to day dealings with clients. For many practitioners, evidence-based practice is a philosophy they aspire towards, rather than an initiative that has been embraced at a practical level. There are some exceptions to this (see CEBSS, 2000, 2001), but a fair summary is to say, in the words of the poet Robert Frost, 'we have miles to go and promises to keep.'[1] This article calls for a rethinking of the nature of evidence-based practice and considers the future steps that might be taken so that those on the ground come to value it as a means of reinforcing both their rapport with service users and carers, their own effectiveness as would be helpers, and indeed, their much compromised professional standing.

Why bother with evidence?

Professionals, on claiming this title (though social workers, in particular, have always been queasy about this term), should be equipped with the knowledge to justify claims to special expertise (Gambrill, 1997). However, knowledge is not a static entity, acquired in training and stopped upon receipt of the certificate or graduation photograph. Our understanding of the world, its problems and their amelioration, changes daily. Professionals must therefore adapt and remain informed of altered trends, based on good quality, up-to-date evidence of 'what works', as well as what appears not to have (see Marshall et al., 2000, or Tolley and Rowland, 1995, for examples of interventions shown not to have worked: there are many others).

Having a sound knowledge foundation, based on the latest findings from research, is more than a professional imperative. It is a moral and ethical obligation of anyone who purports to be employed in a 'caring' job. There is nothing caring about carrying out an intervention that makes no difference to the individual's situation, or, more concerning, makes it worse. Unfortunately, this may be the case of practice that is based entirely on an adherence to expert declarations or past experiences, rather than examining what the evidence says. It is recognised that research findings cannot hope to inform practitioners about all situations, environments and individuals, yet they should comprise a substantial part of a practitioner's knowledge base (Dare et al., 1995), providing empirically supported guidance about how best to deal with specific situations, adapted or appraised to measure their applicability to the case at hand. Searching for evidence to support intervening in potentially complex human difficulties and situations can prove to be an overwhelming proposition to the already over stretched practitioner, who, unfortunately, may be tempted to stick to a form of practice that they feel most confident and comfortable using, regardless of its track record.

An altered mind set

Legislation, guidelines, frameworks, assessments; the busy practitioner may feel they are drowning in a thick soup of national and local initiatives and policies. Tracks of rainforest are being cleared for the paperwork that social care workers are exposed to on a yearly basis. And the use of evidence may seem just another burden to add to this list of things to read (professionals in other public services, such as teachers, nurses and doctors, face a similar situation). But if practitioners took a fresh look at the potential of an evidence-based approach to practice, untainted by previous stereotypes and prejudices, they may come to appreciate its complex and multidimensional nature. This section examines some of the overlooked yet essential elements of evidence-based practice.

Democratising in nature

The professional and ethical obligation to seek out supportive findings calls for open-mindedness when tackling problems, rather than being beholden to a single approach, resulting in a dogmatic style of practice (Sheldon, 1998). Evidence-based practice rejects the notion of senior practitioners holding a monopoly on the knowledge base simply by grace of their tenure in the role. Consequently, a more democratic approach to decision-making and service delivery, in which the opinions of others are respected when empirically substantiated, can be realised. This overcomes the need to kow-tow to the beliefs of those in hierarchical positions, who may have kudos and years in the job, but lack sound justification for their decisions. It also removes the hierarchy in terms of accepted techniques. Once something becomes established within an organisation's culture, it may continue to be applied without question. But questioning and reflecting on practice leads to improved service delivery and innovation. An evidence-based approach should ensure that the potential of all interventions are considered, with those that are empirically supported, acceptable to the recipient, and within the capabilities of the practitioner being implemented.

Dynamic in nature

Evidence-based practice is dynamic in nature. It should not be feared as an approach that will turn practitioners into unthinking information processors (Webb, 2001), who blindly act on what an electronic database or web search churns out. Professionals need to appraise what they read, reflect on what they have learnt and tailor findings to the specific cases of their clients. On occasion, a practitioner may feel that the research is too weak or that general findings are inapplicable to the service user sat in her/his office. Therefore, professional judgements must be made in terms of critically thinking about decision-making. This calls for the input of expertise into this process, although professional acumen should be founded on a reflexive, critical and empirically supported approach to practice, rather than 'on questionable criteria such as tradition ... popularity ... or newness, [which] may harm rather than help clients and victimize rather than empower them' (Gambrill, 1997: xi). If too much weight is given to tradition, experience or familiarity, practitioners might enter into cases with a predetermined perception of how they will evolve, influencing their approach and, possibly, leading to a less concerted effort as a consequence. A critical approach to practice is therefore required, in which opposing views are considered and appraised, with decisions made 'on well-reasoned judgements in which the interests of all involved parties are considered' (Gambrill, 1997: 68). Otherwise, the present, rather implausible situation will continue, where social care practitioners are given a single, allegedly immunising dose of training (and the very occasional booster) to stave off incompetence for life.

Protective in nature

The media crusade to sensationalise failures within social care leads to a state close to 'frozen watchfulness' amongst staff, suppressing risk taking, due professional judgement, and creativity. Yet reviews of the effectiveness of social care indicate that, in general, positive improvements are being made to people's lives through interventions delivered by professionals (Gorey, Thyer and Pawluck, 1998; Macdonald and Sheldon, 1992). These successes need to be advanced, although whilst the journalistic adage of 'if it bleeds it leads' remains, then in the media world no news (or should that be favourable outcomes) is definitely not good news.

An evidence-based approach to decision-making that is 'conscientious, explicit and judicious' (Sackett et al., 1996) should make social care less vulnerable to claims of irresponsibility and incompetence. It is more than a top down policy priority; it is a means of empowering frontline staff in carrying out well-supported approaches in line with empirical findings. In addition, by assessing what has been shown not to work through robust investigation, practitioners can help to protect clients against being subjected to ineffective or damaging interventions. It is essential for researchers and editors to realise the immense importance of negative findings and ensure that they are disseminated as fully and frequently as reports of 'what works'.

Preventative in nature

The notion of preventative measures, at a primary or secondary level, should be a crucial element in debates about evidence-based practice. Preventative measures need to play a greater role in social care (Sheldon, 1986; Macdonald and Sheldon, 1992), so that problems can be ameliorated before they have escalated to a level where only intensive and expensive, and usually less effective, risk-containing measures can be employed. For example, in the case of a young girl showing signs of isolation, perfectionism, low self-esteem and weight loss, is it right for treatment to begin only when she resembles a prisoner from Auschwitz? A glance at empirical reviews should have alerted professionals to the risk of anorexia nervosa in this case, leading to primary or secondary preventative measures in response.[2] Exactly the same argument holds for autism (Richer and Coates, 2001), relapse in schizophrenia (Sheldon, 1994), and suicidal ideation among people with depression (Gilbert, 1992). Studies investigating the onset and nature of problems should be prioritised in evidence-based care, making practitioners aware of early warning signs and ensuring that the intervention provided forms a logical fit with reported causes.

The scientific nature of evidence-based practice

The use of science to investigate human problems has been a major criticism of an evidence-based approach to social care (Sheldon, 1994). Science is rejected as oppressive or inappropriate in this field, based on a positivistic approach, which centres on determinism and neutrality, regarded as diametrically opposed to social care values (Spittlehouse et al., 2000). But this paints a narrow, stereotyped perception of the term 'science', which, in other countries, denotes an 'informed, systematic enquiry, with an eye to whatever evidence is worthy of debate' (Macdonald and Sheldon, 1998, p.10). Unfortunately, in Britain, science is associated with men in white coats (Sheldon and Macdonald, 1999), unethical practices, and is seen as part of the problem rather than the solution (Smith, 1996).

Antibody reactions to the broader application of scientific procedure to social and personal problems accentuate the gulf that exists between users and producers of research. Interesting and relevant findings from scientific papers can get lost amid scientific 'jargon', which is off putting for practitioners unversed in the language of 'chi-square' and 'standard deviation'. Consequently, some individuals reject or negate the importance of empirical findings, due to a lack of comprehension.[3] Therefore, the language employed by researchers (who may be more concerned about peer reviews and academic accreditation than relevancy and applicability of their work to practice) needs to be addressed. For example, the conclusion that

> *independent variables (modes of intervention) [are] associated with dependent variables (change in clients) while accounting for the influence of intervening variables (client and helper characteristics).*
> (Cnaan, 1991, p.139)

would be incomprehensible to many practitioners without the information contained in the brackets. In turn, practitioners need to be taught how to understand terms such as 'p-value' and 'confidence intervals', and the difference between statistical and clinical significance, so they can assess whether findings produced by researchers are great enough to warrant a change in current practice. Without this essential knowledge, practitioners are condemned to inhabit a field where congeniality of conclusion, familiarity, and fashion hold sway.

In summary, an altered mind set is called for, whereby the liberating and democratising potential of scientific enquiry is accepted, in which all alternatives are explored, and unsubstantiated adherence to specific approaches rejected. Scientific enquiry ought to be considered as a means of making practice more accurate, highlighting past mistakes. The divide between producers and consumers of research also needs to be bridged. Publications such as Barnardos' 'What Works' series and CEBSS' reviews illustrate that such a balance can be achieved.

Areas for future consideration

Unfortunately, even when evidence in support of specific interventions is reported, practitioners do not necessarily act on it. Reasons for such resistance include the failure of professional courses to train students in empirically supported techniques and to continue to focus on those that lack such support. There is also a limited awareness of the professional literature and an intractable belief among some clinicians that all therapies are more or less the same in terms of their effectiveness (Nathan and Gorman, 1998). A number of procedures that could help to make evidence-based practice a more realisable goal within everyday professional activities follow.

Improving students' skills base

The gap between empirically supported findings and the skills of social care practitioners is a serious obstacle to evidence-based practice. McGuire and Priestly (1995) observe, in relation to those dealing with offenders, that working on the basis of techniques that have emerged as effective entails a considerable investment in training those within the profession. Training bodies and academic departments need to take steps to overcome this problem by ensuring that the content of courses reflects messages from research. It may prove difficult for academic institutions to incorporate further modules into an already overcrowded curriculum, hence an annual appraisal and culling of what students are taught, with more emphasis placed on empirically supported techniques, is needed. Such whole scale alterations to learning programmes will, understandably, be seen as an additional burden by teaching staff, who may prove particularly reluctant to introduce training in interventions that vary substantially from the received wisdom of years in the trade. However, this is an ethical as well as a pedagogic priority.

Accessing information

A survey carried out by Sheldon and Chilvers (2000) highlighted the extent and consequences of practitioners' limited access to information. In their study, involving 1226 randomly selected, professional grade social care staff, less than 50% of respondents said they had read evaluative research. Limited access to information was the second most quoted reason given to explain this lack of professional reading (Sheldon and Chilvers, 2000).[4] The potential of Information Technology, for example on-line databases, journals and research from organisations, should make the process of accessing and keeping abreast of empirical findings an easier task. But this requires new skills of practitioners, such as how to search effectively on the web without being bogged down by a mass of irrelevant information. Such skills need to be carefully incorporated into the academic curriculum and should also be regarded as an important area for those already in the profession to develop.

The increasing use of computers in gathering and retaining information in social care has met with resistance from some professionals who fear a 'loss of confidentiality, depersonalization, and the mechanization of the basically human process of social work...' (Rafferty, 1997, p.263). But the use of technology should not be seen as a threat to autonomy or as an example of the 'contemporary technocratic culture' (Webb, 2001, p.58), nor does it indicate a desire to create 'information processors', to replace social care professionals, 'operating within a closed system of decision making' (Webb, 2001, p.67). It does not imply that practitioners can or should be able to make decisions relating to practice by tapping a series of keywords into a database and having a computer generated recipe for working with clients. What it does mean is that empirically supported data is more readily accessible to frontline workers, who must then use their professional expertise to assess how readily the findings of studies can be applied to the specific circumstances of clients on their caseload.

Appraising and applying research findings

An overturn in practice will not emerge simply through an increased access to data, although this will be a significant help. Practitioners require protected time for assessing and reading research, the findings of which ought to be discussed regularly during supervision. They also need the skills to effectively evaluate what has been written about the nature, course and amelioration of problems they are faced with and encouraged not to take everything they read as read. If they are not taught to judge the robustness of findings, then a situation in which 'knowledge is merely stored, rather than sifted or redefined' (Sheldon, 1978, p.10) may occur. As a consequence, information overload can arise. To prevent such an event, it is increasingly recognised that critical appraisal skills play an imperative role in professional training,[5] with a focus on assessing studies' methodology and execution. Through such training, practitioners learn to assess how relevant a study is to their own world and gain the confidence to challenge weakly supported proclamations delivered by authorities, by becoming experts themselves in obtaining and evaluating evidence to back up their arguments.

Adequate and appropriate psychosocial enquiry

Motivation for investigating treatment efficacy is partly an attempt to ensure that scarce resources are used in the most appropriate manner. However, concern has been expressed that this means only empirically supported interventions will receive financial backing, limiting service innovation and the range of solutions that can be applied to a problem (Davison and Lazarus, 1995). In the field of mental health in particular, it is feared that more emphasis will be given to the use of pharmacological treatments, subjected to stringent trials, funded by drug companies wanting to prove the safety and efficacy of their products, whilst psychosocial treatments will take a backseat, not having the same financial backing to demonstrate their effectiveness (Geddes, 2000). Such a concern highlights the need for adequate funding to investigate non-pharmacological interventions, possibly coming from governmental or charitable sources. In addition, whilst RAE status rests on the production of research papers, quantity rather than quality of studies may come to dominate. A change is in order in which 'a small number of important, practice-relevant, knowledge-building studies should be well rewarded, whereas a large number of disjointed, vita-building studies that do not make a valuable contribution to the cumulative building of practice-relevant knowledge should not be so well rewarded' (Rubin, 2000, p.12).

Beyond the qualitative/quantitative divide

An enduring, uneasy stand off exists between qualitative and quantitative researchers, which is unfortunate because the two approaches could be embraced as complementary means of investigation. Quantitative techniques are still approached with caution and some scepticism in social care, which has more of a tradition for using qualitative designs, especially in gathering client opinion, as a means to improve services. The value of clients' views should not be underestimated, but, instead, supported by quantitative measures of progress (and vice versa; see Sheldon, 1984, p.637).[6] Instead of polarising ourselves, we should consider not only what kinds of useful change we are pursuing (qualitative), but how much and at what cost and how far outcomes can be attributed to the intervention itself and not to other collateral factors (which means some sums and quantitative work).

Qualitative work could be seen as the bread in a research sandwich, with the quantitative element acting as the filling. Initially, qualitative researchers contextualise problems, increasing knowledge of how and why they occur which, in turn, increases knowledge of how best to alleviate them (Gambrill, 1997, p.177). Upon quantitatively measuring the effectiveness (or otherwise) of a specific technique, qualitative methods again ought to be employed to answer why research participants thought a specific approach succeeded or failed (Sheldon, 1986) and how satisfied they were with its delivery.

Critics of evidence-based practice argue that its advocates are too narrow in their view of research methods, regarding them as 'RCT junkies' and 'number crunchers'. But such stereotypes are an unfair representation. Take the following words from Macdonald and Sheldon (staunch supporters of an evidence-based approach in social care):

> ... Hilary Graham's in-depth, qualitative study on women's smoking sheds more light on the ineffectiveness of anti-smoking campaigns, and on the likely parameters of effective interventions than many scientific outcome studies in the field (Macdonald and Sheldon, 1998, p.12).

Rather than rejecting other methods, advocates simply

suggest that different designs lack the same attributional confidence offered by experimental methods, accepting that qualitative designs can offer illuminating insights into people and their problems, if carried out with rigour (Rubin, 2000).

Service users and evidence-based practice

A fundamental area for developing evidence-based practice is for this approach to adopt a more user focused perspective, as a means of improving collaborative decision-making and equipping those involved in social care with the techniques and resources to make use of the best available evidence.

One of the three main tenets of such an approach to practice, highlighted by Sackett and colleagues (1996) was explicitness, which involves being clear about motivations for action, entailing a showing of 'workings out', alongside answers, and a degree of accountability (Macdonald and Sheldon, 1998). Those who use services provided by social care have a right to know on what basis professionals have made decisions affecting their lives, so they can draw their own conclusions as to the relevancy and appropriateness of such decisions. By having the research evidence to hand, the practitioner is able to lay open to clients reasons for the approach taken to their situations. Client and professional are then able to examine and explore possible means of treating the case, based on the existing evidence (Gambrill, 1999). This should enhance the relationship between service users and practitioners, with negotiation playing a central role, rather than an approach that is dominated by professional procedure (Fisher, 1997).

Advances in Information Technology have and will continue to empower service users in relation to their care, giving them greater access to what has been shown to work in their situation and enabling them to be more confident about challenging decisions made by service providers (Geddes, 2000). For patient advocacy and empowerment to become a substantial force, steps to ensure equitable access to technology (e.g. a computer with a modem) must be made. Libraries now have publicly accessible internet use and local authorities could also make terminals available to service users. But since many social care staff still do not enjoy adequate computer facilities, this is unlikely to become a widespread phenomenon. And for service users to employ such resources in a discriminating manner, with an appropriate understanding, they would need training not only in accessing, but also in critically evaluating evidence. This area of user empowerment is being explored by CASP (Critical Appraisal Skills Programme), which has developed the tool DISCERN to be employed by service users wishing to appraise research (http://www.phru.org.uk/~casp/userinvolve/discern.htm). It may be beneficial for each local authority to have service user advocates, trained in either accessing and/or appraising research, who can act for all those who are served by social care practitioners.

Some commentators have warned that the implementation of an evidence-based approach to practice will further erode the face to face work carried out with clients (Webb, 2001). But if this form of practice is to be explicit, as discussed above, it will require direct contact to ensure that the intervention proposed is acceptable. If the client is unwilling to participate in the intervention suggested, any chance of a successful outcome will be seriously hampered (Gambrill, 1997). Developing a service that meets the demands of its users and the findings from research may call for more time to be devoted to initial assessments and decision-making. However, if carried out successfully, such an approach will demonstrate practically the empowering, democratising and collaborative potential of an evidence-based workplace and workforce.

Conclusion

The democratising, empowering and protective elements of evidence-based practice outlined above have been overshadowed by rather defensive concerns in some quarters about its threat to professional autonomy and creativity. The time has come for the debate to move forward and for the positive nature of such an approach to be acknowledged by key stakeholders in social care, including managers, practitioners, service users, researchers and teaching staff.

Acknowledgements

I would like to thank Brian Sheldon and Alice Caldwell for the useful comments they made about the draft version of this chapter, which were greatly appreciated.

Notes

1. For an empirical study of exactly what the obstacles to the forgoing are, see Sheldon and Chilvers, 2000.
2. This is a particular concern of mine, having experienced this condition as a teenager and having mortgaged my free time to carrying out a systematic review on this topic as part of a PhD.
3. Practitioners' inability to understand scientific language relates to a deficiency in undergraduate social studies (science) courses, in which statistics are overshadowed by attention given to qualitative designs. This problem was recently alluded to by the Chief Executive of the Economic and Social Research Council (Marshall, 2001).
4. Over 80% of respondents reported that lack of access was a difficulty. The number one response to this question was a pressure of time and, therefore, a lack of time (98.3%).
5. CEBSS has responded to this need by commissioning CASP (Critical Appraisal Skills Programme: http://www.phru.org.uk/~casp/) to carry out workshops in critical appraisal, provided free of charge to all social work practitioners, managers and practice teachers in the South West. Results from pilot events of this initiative have demonstrated clear improvements in the participants' knowledge (Spittlehouse et al., 2000).
6. However, it must be recognised that, as research suggests, clients are prone to value the service they receive, regardless of its impact on behaviour or circumstances (Gibbons et al., 1978).

References

CEBSS (Centre for Evidence-Based Social Services) (2000) *Annual Report*. Exeter: University of Exeter

CEBSS (Centre for Evidence-Based Social Services) (2001) *Annual Report*. Exeter: University of Exeter

Cnaan, R.A. (1991) Applying clinical trials in social work practice. *Research on Social Work Practice*, 1, 2, 139-161

Dare, C., Eisler, I., Colahan, M., Crowther, C., Senior, R. and Asen, E. (1995) The Listening heart and the chi-square: Clinical and empirical perceptions in the family therapy of anorexia nervosa. *Journal of Family Therapy*, 17, 31-57

Davison, G.C. and Lazarus, A.A. (1995) The dialectics of science and practice. in S.C. Hayes, V.M. Follette, R.M. Dawes and K.E. Gardy (Eds.) *Scientific Standards of Psychological Practice: Issues and Recommendations*, Reno: Context Press

Fisher, M. (1997) Research, Knowledge and Practice in Community Care. *Issues in Social Work Education*, 17, 2, 17-30

Gambrill, E. (1997) *Social Work Practice: A Critical thinker's guide.* Oxford: Oxford University Press

Gambrill, E. (1999) Evidence-based practice: An alternative to authority-based practice. *Families in Society: The Journal of Contemporary Human Services*, 80, 4, 341-350

Geddes, J. (2000) Evidence-based practice in mental health. in L. Trinder with S. Reynolds (Eds.) *Evidence-Based Practice: A critical appraisal*. Oxford: Blackwell

Gibbons, J.S. et al., (1978) Evaluation of a social work service for self-poisoning patients. *British Journal of Psychiatry*, 133, 111-118

Gilbert, P. (1992) *Depression: The evolution of powerlessness*. Hillside: Lawrence Erlbaum Associates

Gorey, K.M., Thyer, B.A. and Pawluck, D.E. (1998) Differential effectiveness of prevalent social work practice models: A meta-analysis. *Social Work*, 43, 3, 269-278

Macdonald, G. (2001) *Effective interventions for child abuse and neglect: An evidence-based approach to planning and evaluating interventions.* Chichester: Wiley and Sons

Macdonald, G. and Sheldon, B. with Gillespie, J. (1992) Contemporary Studies of Effectiveness of Social Work. *British Journal of Social Work*, 22, 6, 615-643

Macdonald, G. and Sheldon, B. (1998) Changing one's mind: The final frontier? *Issues in Social Work Education*, 18, 2, 3-25

Marshall, M., Gray, A., Lockwood, A. and Green, R. (2000) Case management for people with severe mental disorders (Cochrane Review). in *The Cochrane Library*, Issue 3, Oxford: Update Software

Marshall, G. (2001) Addressing a problem of research capacity. *Social Sciences*, January

McGuire, J. and Priestly, P. (1995) Reviewing 'what works': Past, present and future. in J. McGuire (ed.) *What Works: Reducing reoffending: Guidelines from research and practice*. Chichester: John Wiley and Sons

Nathan, P.E. and Gorman, J.M. (1998) Treatments that work: And what convinces us they do. in P.E. Nathan and J.M. Gorman (Eds.) *A Guide to Treatments that Work*. Oxford: Oxford University Press

Rafferty, J. (1997) Shifting paradigms of information technology in social work education and practice. *British Journal of Social Work*, 27, 6, 959-969

Richer, J. and Coates, S. (Eds.) (2001) *Autism: The search for coherence*. London: Jessica Kingsley

Rubin, A. (2000) Editorial: Social work research at the turn of the millennium: Progress and challenges. *Research on Social Work Practice*, 10, 1, 9-14

Sackett, D.I., Rosenberg, W.M., Gray, J.H.M., Haynes, R.B. and Richardson, W.S. (1996) Evidence-based practice: What it is and what it isn't. *British Medical Journal*, 312, 7203, 71-72

Sheldon, B. (1984) Evaluation with one eye closed: The empiricist agenda in social work research – A reply to Peter Raynor. *British Journal of Social Work*, 14, 635-637

Sheldon, B. (1986) Social work effectiveness experiments: Review and implications. *British Journal of Social Work*, 16, 223-242

Sheldon, B. (1994) The social and biological components of mental disorder: Implications for services. *International Journal of Social Psychiatry*, 40, 2, 87-105

Sheldon, B. (1998) Evidence-based social services: Prospects and problems. *Research Policy and Planning*, 16, 2, 16-18

Sheldon, B. (2001) The validity of evidence-based practice in social work: A reply to Stephen Webb. *British Journal of Social Work*, 31, 801-809

Sheldon, B. and Macdonald, G. (1999) *Research and Practice in Social Care: Mind the gap*. Exeter: University of Exeter, Centre for Evidence-Based Social Services

Sheldon, B. and Chilvers, R. (2000) *Evidence-Based Social Care: A study of prospects and problems.* Lyme Regis: Russell House Publishing

Smith, A.F.M. (1996) Statistics and an evidence-based society. *Journal of the Royal Statistical Society,* 159, Series A, 368-382

Spittlehouse, C., Acton, M. and Enock, K. (2000) Introducing critical appraisal skills training in UK social services: Another link between health and social care? *Journal of Interprofessional Care,* 14, 2, 397-404

Tolley, K. and Rowland, N. (1995) *Evaluating the Cost-Effectiveness of Counselling in Health Care.* London; Routledge

Trinder, L. (2000) The context of evidence-based practice. in L. Trinder with S. Reynolds (Eds.) *Evidence-Based Practice: A critical appraisal,* Oxford: Blackwell

Webb, S. (2001) Some considerations on the validity of evidence-based practice in social work. *British Journal of Social Work,* 31, 57-79

Part Two

Critical reflections

4
What works about what works? Fashion, fad and EBP

Carolyn Taylor and Susan White

Introduction

In the last few years, the concept of *evidence-based practice* (EBP) has come to prominence within the health and welfare professions as a proposed foundation for good practice, even if it has yet to become firmly embedded in everyday routine. To be sure, EBP could be described as 'old wine in new bottles', since there is nothing new, or remotely controversial about suggesting that professionals should measure the effectiveness of their interventions and modify their work accordingly. For example, Brian Sheldon, a leading UK proponent of EBP in social care, refers approvingly to work undertaken in the United States from the 1930s (see for example Lehrman, 1949; Powers and Witmer, 1951) and in the UK since the 1960s (reviewed in Sheldon, 1986; see also Sheldon and MacDonald, 1999) to evaluate systematically the effects of social work interventions. In more critical vein, Wendy Hollway (2001) draws parallels between the development of Taylorism and scientific management in the early twentieth century as a means to control manufacturing production and current attempts to control professional practice through EBP.

What is new, perhaps, is the espousal and promotion by the UK government of the concept of EBP across the public services generally. There is growing reference made to EBP, or knowledge-based practice, in government publications (see for example Department of Health *et al*, 2000; Department of Health, 2001; TOPSS, 1999) and we have also seen the creation of the National Institute for Clinical Excellence (NICE) and the

Social Care Institute for Excellence (SCIE). The remit of both these organizations is to review and make available in their respective fields rigorously assessed research findings and best practice guidelines. The role of SCIE, for example, is described thus:

> SCIE will make a unique contribution to improving the quality and consistency of social care practice and provision through the creation and dissemination of best practice guidelines in social care. . . SCIE will rigorously review research and practice, and the views, experience and expertise of users and carers. It will identify what works in social care, and produce best practice guidance, and will work to ensure their implementation at a local level. SCIE will create a knowledge base of what works through:
> · rigorous methodology to assess evidence and knowledge from academic research, user and carer expertise and existing practice
> · assessment of the strength and quality of the evidence
> · a transparent review process
>
> (www.scie.org.uk/aboutscie.about.htm)

It is clear then that EBP has the backing of the current government and investment is being made in the process of knowledge acquisition and dissemination through the funding of various centres for EBP, for example, the Centre for Evidence-Based Social Services at Exeter University and the Centre for Evidence-Based Nursing at York University (for a list of related websites and so forth see Reynolds, 2000, p.18). Just as clearly, from our discussions with candidates on a post-qualifying child care award, there is growing awareness among childcare practitioners of the imperative to underpin decision-making with evidence. However, those charged with disseminating EBP are clearly worried about the scope and scale of their task, Brian Sheldon and Rupatharshini Chilvers (2000, 2002) report a lack of research literacy and limited knowledge of research findings among social care staff. From such a standpoint, there is clearly an urgent need to press on with the implementation of EBP and it is perhaps understandable that criticism may be treated as an unwelcome and unnecessary diversion (Sheldon, 2001, in response to Webb, 2001).

However, before we rush to embrace EBP as the latest good

thing for social work, it is appropriate to take stock of what EBP has to offer and to pose questions about its key assumptions and the likelihood of it achieving its aims. Such scrutiny can assist practitioners to understand better both EBP and its implications. After all, if we want critical and reflective practitioners, and it would appear foolhardy to propose otherwise, then we need to ensure that they are able to appraise the limitation of EBP as well as its strengths. What follows is a contribution to this process of appraisal. We begin by briefly outlining the key premises of EBP and its underlying assumptions before considering what are its limits and how it may usefully be supplemented by other approaches. In particular we argue for a more methodologically inclusive reframing of what is meant by EBP.

EBP: what it is, what it is against and what it promises to deliver

Readers may, of course, wish to refer to other articles on EBP in this volume for definitions of EBP. Yet, we must begin by outlining what *we* understand by the concept. There is widespread consensus that evidence- based practice means:

> *The conscientious, explicit and judicious use of current best evidence in making decisions about the care of individual patients [or service users], based on skills which allow the [practitioner] to evaluate both personal experience and external evidence in a systemic and objective manner.*
> (Sackett et al, 1997, p.71)

It is noteworthy that this definition has been truncated by proponents of EBP within social care. Sheldon (1998) for example refers only to the application of evidence to decision making and ignores the reference to skills and the role of experience. He has further explicated his definition by seeking to clarify what is meant by 'conscientious, explicit and judicious'. To be conscientious is to eschew subjectivity and to 'resist falling in love with favourite ideas and theories' (Sheldon, 1998, p.16); to be explicit is to show not simply what has been decided but how that decision has been arrived at and why it is the correct one; judicious means basing 'our helping recipes on best available evidence and applying them cautiously within their known scope' rather than more indiscriminately according to prevailing trends (Sheldon, 1998, p.16). Significantly Sheldon does not define 'evidence-based', a point to which we return later.

To what question or problem is EBP the solution? There is a clear motif running though the EBP literature of a 'crisis in the professions' and the parlous state of past and present practice. It is suggested that practitioners are (or at least have been) insufficiently accountable for their practice and fail to utilise or draw upon research findings to determine or guide their actions. Instead practitioners depend in their decision making upon other, less reliable indicators such as knowledge gained during initial training, opinion and prejudice, prevailing fads and fashions, collegial advice and the outcomes of previous cases (Trinder, 2000a). Practitioners' work is, therefore, too often based on outmoded thinking, personal opinion and dubious common sense. The consequence of this situation, according to advocates of EBP, is that 'practitioners continue to utilise interventions that have been shown to be ineffective or harmful, that there is a slow or limited adoption of interventions that have been proven to be effective or more effective, and that there continue to be [unacceptable] variations in practice' (Trinder, 2000a, p.3-4). Within medicine, several examples are offered of 'ritual-based practice', for example: the ongoing use of grommets to treat glue ear in children despite evidence to the contrary (Appleby et al, 1995) and the failure to use newer, more effective treatments such as clot-busting drugs to treat heart attacks (Department of Health, 1998a)

EBP thus seeks to sweep away outmoded practice and ideas past their sell-by date. In opposition to ritual-based practice, EBP extends the promise of overcoming the gap between research and clinical practice. It can, it is claimed, assist practitioners to sift out what is directly relevant in terms of evidence and it can provide a 'simple set of rules for evaluating research evidence' (Reynolds, 2000, p.19). In so doing, it provides an objective basis on which to make sound decisions in health and welfare practice. Only then will we avoid situations where interventions of no known benefit are offered and, better still, practitioners will 'avoid doing more harm than good'. Its champions posit EBP as the single solution to the malaise of poor practice:

> In the 21st century, the healthcare decision maker, that is, anyone who makes decisions about groups of patients or populations will have to practise evidence-based decision-making. Every decision will have to be based on a systematic appraisal of the best evidence available. (Gray, 1997, p.1)

Proponents of EBP thus advocate the production of 'really useful knowledge' for health and welfare organisations and practitioners. They argue that a more rational approach to research can result so that the emphasis is placed on key areas of need (for example cancer care and heart disease in health) and not the whims and fancies of researchers who may be much more interested in more esoteric subjects (for example rare brain disease), preferring to research the rare rather than the mundane. Where practice has been previously rather disorderly and ad hoc it can now be made orderly and rational. Two aspects are vitally important elements of EBP: the hierarchy of evidence and the use of clinical questions.

The hierarchy of evidence

Shaw has expressed some scepticism about the definition of EBP:

> What do we mean by 'evidence'? What do we mean by 'practice'? How is one 'based' on the other? Far too much is assumed. But of course one does not describe a Holy Grail – one simply searches. (Shaw, 1999, p.3)

It is true that phrases such as EBP become so well assimilated into our vocabularies that we cease to ponder their meaning and instead take them entirely for granted. Although a relatively new phrase, EBP is in danger of becoming naturalised in this way. It is important, therefore, to consider what 'evidence-based' means in practice. Within EBP 'evidence' seems to equate to research findings but not all research data carry equal weight. A hierarchy of evidence has been proposed that runs like this:

1. Strong evidence from at least one systematic review of multiple well-designed randomised control trials (RCTs)
2. Strong evidence from at least one properly designed RCT of appropriate size.
3. Evidence from well-designed trials without randomisation, single group pre-post, cohort, time series, or matched case-control studies.
4. Evidence from well-designed non-experimental studies from more than one centre or research group.
5. Opinions of respected authorities, based on clinical evidence, descriptive studies or reports of expert committee.
   (Gray, 1998 reproduced in Geddes, 2000, p.78)

Developed in the medicine and health care context, this hierarchy is nonetheless being reproduced within social work and social care, for example Gomm argues:

The properly conducted, correctly interpreted RCT (randomised controlled trial) is superior to any other method for producing evidence about cause and effect. This includes evidence about the effectiveness of health and social care interventions. (Gomm, 2000, p.51)

Whilst SCIE (www.scie.org.uk/aboutscie.about.htm) does intimate that it will take into account the opinions, experiences and expertise of service users these sources of information will clearly have to take their place within the hierarchy of evidence and will not carry equal weight to the rigorous methodology of the RCT. This method is rapidly achieving iconic status as the gold standard for assessing the efficacy of treatments because it eliminates (allegedly) all sources of bias and error. Evidence, once gathered and reviewed in a rigorous manner, can then be applied to a variety of aspects of practice for example in relation to assessment/diagnosis, intervention/ treatment, prognosis and cost effectiveness.

Clinical questions: Applying EBP

The application of evidence to practice is clearly crucial to the success of EBP and the use of *clinical question* lies at its core (Sackett *et al*, 1997). In order to deal effectively with patients/service users, either singly or collectively, practitioners need to conduct a staged process, beginning with the construction of a specific question concerning patient/service user care. They should then seek to answer the question by appraising the best available evidence about what works in such a situation (and we should note that only recently has information technology enabled this process to be possible across a range of health and welfare settings). These findings should then be applied and the outcome evaluated. Clinical questions might ask which drugs are most (cost) effective or whether surgery is more effective than chemotherapy in cancer treatment. Whilst they are often aimed at treatment/intervention this need not necessarily be the case as the examples in figure 1 indicate.

Re-evaluating EBP

As we have noted elsewhere (Taylor and White, 2000) the main strength of EBP is surely its appeal to rationality. In the current climate of intense scrutiny and vociferous criticism of health and welfare professionals and their practice it is difficult to resist the argument that current practice is unsatisfactory in many respects. There are far too many instances of inadequate practice (or worse) within social work and social care, medicine, nursing, health screening services and so forth (as readers you will be able to make your own list of examples) for us to contemplate contradicting the 'poor practice' thesis of EBP. Although, we should note that not all practice is poor and it is not always easy to determine how representative are the headline-hitting examples we can think of. EBP, then, strikes a chord with public disquiet about professional competence and care in the late twentieth and early twenty-first centuries. It promises not only better treatments/interventions but also

Figure 1

Treatment	
Patient:	In *children with depression*
Clinical action:	does *cognitive therapy*
Comparison:	when compared *with trycyclic antidepressants* alone
Outcomes:	lead to *fewer symptoms* of depression?
Diagnosis	
Patient:	In *non-symptomatic adults*
Clinical action:	does *routine screening* for colorectal cancer
Comparison:	compared *with no routine screening*
Outcomes:	*increase diagnosis* and lead to *reduced mortality*?

(Reynolds, 2000, p.24)

greater fairness in the distribution of scarce resources both at local and national levels. We have heard much in recent times of resources allocated on the basis of age, ability to pay or the vagaries of postcode rather than on the basis of need and/or equal right to treatment. The EBP movement and its various satellite organizations such as NICE and SCIE hold out the promise of equity, consistency and up-to-date methods of treatment and intervention. It is hardly surprising then that it accords so well with the modernizing agenda of the current government (Department of Health, 1998b, 1998c).

As a result of this apparent 'fit' with the problems affecting health and social care practice, it is easy to portray any criticism of EBP as the height of folly and irrationality. From this perspective, to disagree with its claims, is to ensure that practice remains dominated by ad-hocery, commonsense and personal opinion (Sheldon, 2001). Notwithstanding this resistance to criticism, we cannot and should not simply rush to embrace EBP without considering in more detail its underlying assumptions and questioning whether it has the potential to achieve its goals. First, we want to state plainly that we are not opposed to the use of research findings in practice. In situations where it is possible to make a clear assessment or diagnosis and determine the most efficacious treatments then, like other people, we would want to receive that treatment rather than something less efficacious. If TPA (tissue plasminogen activator) works better than streptokinase in the treatment of myocardial infarction then that seems the more reasonable choice (Gray, 2001). However to acknowledge the potential of EBP in certain aspects of practice is not to argue that it is amenable to being unproblematically applied to practice, nor that it could or should assume a monopoly position as the cornerstone of health and welfare policy initiatives.

There have been several criticisms made of EBP (see inter alia Harrison, 1998; Hunter, 1998; Trinder with Reynolds, 2000; Webb, 2001). One focus of these has been the concern that EBP will be used as a tool of managerialism to promote further technical-procedural control over health and welfare practice (Hunter, 1998; Trinder, 2000; Webb, 2001). This is perhaps to be expected given that a major impetus for EBP within medicine has been the recognition of scarce health care resources and the consequent need to address the issue of the most efficient and effective deployment of resources (Cochrane, 1972). Similar resource constraints bedevil the delivery of social care. We recognize these concerns about the utility of EBP to an 'audit society' (Power, 1997) but this is not the thrust of our argument here. Our intention is to problematize the hierarchy of evidence and the processes of applying evidence to practice. We further suggest that EBP fails to recognize and attend to the complexities of knowledge production in health and welfare practice by proposing a particular version of science and method. It is these issues that we now address.

Rationality or misplaced concreteness?

At first glance the process of EBP and the use of clinical questions seem entirely appropriate. They are geared to establishing 'what works?' and agreeing preferred methods by comparing and contrasting alternative approaches. They avoid the trap of plumping for a preferred option as part of routinized and unthinking practice. This process of evaluating the evidence in a rigorous and scientific manner should lead to sound answers about how to proceed in practice. And yet there are difficulties with the approach that, certainly within social care, remain unacknowledged.

First we are being asked to accept a very narrow and rigid definition of science that has been seriously under fire for many decades, and indeed centuries (as the Duhem-Quine debate demonstrates; see also Kuhn, 1970). Put simply, it is assumed by EBP that: '[s]cience is concerned with the formulation and attempted falsification of hypotheses using reproducible methods that allow the construction of generalisable statements about how the universe behaves' (Greenhalgh, 1999, p.323). Second, as part of this scientific project we are being asked to accept a 'hierarchy of evidence' that privileges certain research techniques and, by default, renders others as less consequential and less likely to generate 'scientific' knowledge. Sheldon's intemperate dismissal of the potential contribution of sociological knowledge (Sheldon, 2001), to which we return later, is indicative of just how entrenched this hierarchy may become. Third, specific parallels are being drawn between science and health and welfare practice: social care practitioners (and their counterparts in health) are being asked to behave as impartial investigators who base their assessments on the formulation and falsification of competing hypotheses about service users or patients. Certainly within social work this view pervades most thinking on assessment, which is presented as a logical sequence of fact gathering, hypothesis generation, and deciding among options (see *inter alia*, Sheppard, 1995; 1998, for an alternative view see Milner and O'Byrne, 1998). The insertion of clinical questions (or their social care equivalent) is entirely consistent with this staged approach. As Trinder notes:

> . . .*there is an unshakeable belief in the capacity of science, and the rational, and systematic application of science, to bring about effective, accountable practice . . . [EBP] is presented as a radical approach, where the neutrality of science and the transparency of the process provides the opportunity for both practitioners and*

consumers to participate. Knowledge, rather than authority or position, is privileged, and access to knowledge is available to anyone willing to learn the techniques or with access to the evidence. (Trinder, 2000b. p.215)

Fourth, EBP implicitly accepts a biomedical approach to health and welfare underpinned by strict adherence to a particular set of rules about how knowledge (evidence) should be gathered. Even within the context of medicine this approach is open to criticism, indeed from the leading proponents of evidence-based medicine:

Evidence-based medicine is not 'cook-book' medicine. Because it requires a bottom-up approach that integrates the best external evidence with individual clinical expertise and patient choice, it cannot result in slavish cook-book approaches to individual patient care. External clinical evidence can inform, but can never replace, individual clinical expertise and it is this expertise that decides whether external evidence applies to the individual patient at all and, if so, how it should be integrated into a clinical decision...Clinicians who fear top-down cook-books will find the advocates of evidence-based medicine joining them at the barricades. (Sackett et al. 1997, p.4)

Moreover, Hunter (1998), as a health policy analyst, argues that EBP runs counter to the methodological challenges presented outside acute medicine. Rather than focusing on what works to make people better when they get ill (as EBP does), Hunter argues that we need to focus much more on developing an understanding of 'the forces that keep people well, not only those that make them ill' and 'a refocusing of public health research on the root causes of ill-health and disease' (Hunter, 1998: 5). In other words we would prioritise preventive healthcare strategies. This would have important methodological implications since it would require a move away from a formal hierarchy of evidence privileging quantitative methods and a focus on outcomes of acute interventions towards a pluralistic approach acknowledging the equal contribution of qualitative methods.

The assumptions underpinning EBP cannot be simply

accepted without challenge. What is science, how it is conducted, whether the natural sciences have intrinsic elements in common or intrinsic difference is a matter of profound debate (that should not be equated with the banalities of the 'Science Wars'). It is surely noteworthy that this appears to achieve much greater acknowledgement within medicine and health care than in social work. The latter seems to need to cling to narrow and formulaic versions of science, that is scientism rather than science. For example, Sheldon seems to advocate a version of science exclusively based on deductive reasoning, concerned not with the generation of ideas, but with testing them. We can see the attraction of this rather arid reading of science. If we start from a falsifiable hypothesis and pare down our questions accordingly, we may indeed produce a neat answer to our question. Of course, this activity can have considerable value - it is the mainstay of much pharmacological research - but its value depends on the appropriateness of the question and without inductive reasoning driven by data or experience, there would quite simply be few ideas to test. Moreover, professional practice is itself often dependent on inductive reasoning, as Downie and MacNaughton note:

> The concept of evidence, as it is used by scientists, is logically related to that of an hypothesis. Information, data, observations and experiments become 'evidence' when they are for or against a specific hypothesis...The concept of evidence as used by detectives or forensically differs in two respects: the data and observations suggest a hypothesis...about a specific or particular state of affairs. The concept of evidence that applies to medical research is like that of the scientist, and the concept that applies to clinical consultations is like that of the detective (Downie and MacNaughton, 2000, p.183).

Thus, both induction and deduction, often as part of a productive, recursive process, are important aspects of professional knowledge production - but induction is messier and rather than answering questions, it often generates them.

As we have suggested elsewhere (Taylor and White, 2000) an understanding of the philosophy of science and the sociology of scientific knowledge would not go amiss in social work. It would help us to understand the complexities of knowledge generation in the natural sciences and to appreciate that within science itself 'the impossibility of making theory-free observation ... has long been understood ... Duhem, Quine, Goodman and Kuhn are but a few of those who have challenged the traditional views of empiricism and argue against the possibility of simple, 'objective' observations in science' (Harari, 2001: 725).

If science and medicine can cope with having more sophisticated understandings of the processes involved why cannot social work? We should be particularly wary of buying into the hierarchy of evidence proposed by EBP. It makes no sense to put RCTs at the pinnacle and others in descending order of worth. Methods are just that, methods. A whole panoply of methods should be available for us to use. Which one we will choose will depend on the questions we want to ask and the sorts of answers we want to come up with. RCTS will do fine for certain kinds of questions (for example to compare the efficacy of drugs among broad populations) but patently be useless for others. It would seem ridiculous to want to restrict ourselves to asking the sorts of questions that RCTs are suited to, particularly in the field of social work, where problems do not come neatly packaged.

Moreover, evidence from RCTs cannot be treated as the unvarnished truth. For example, strong criticism has been made of the Cochrane review of case management for people with severe mental disorders. This study concluded that case management did not improve mental state, social functioning or quality of care (Marshall et al, 1996). Rosen and Teesson (2001) argue among other things that the review: a) utilized a very narrow definition and set of principles of care management; b) excluded all RCTs involving other, more active models of care management; c) excluded all RCTs of acute patients who were case managed; d) the outcome objectives (negative outcomes were linked to contact with services and admission) might be interpreted as being 'underpinned by political and philosophical motives'. In other words we cannot assume that RCTs automatically possess scientific purity. Any method has to deal with issues of rigour, validity and reliability (see Silverman, 2000). From their close scrutiny of the Cochrane review and other studies Rosen and Teesson (2001, p.739) conclude that, despite its credentials as an evidence-based review for an internationally esteemed organization, the findings were 'astoundingly passionate and parochial'. Parker (1997) too was critical of this review, arguing that the control condition, 'standard care', was ill defined and insufficiently different from the experimental intervention, 'care management'. Indeed he was moved to comment rather acerbically:

> *A number of their [i.e. Marshall et al's] conclusions illustrate how evidence-based researchers can (once freed of their strict protocols) spring from the bedrock of the evidence base into subjective musings. In this context it might be of benefit for the Cochrane Collaborators to incorporate another set of variables (ie the reviewer's a-priori biases or beliefs: did the evidence change such beliefs; if so, or if not, why?) into their protocols.* (p.263)

The unquestioning acceptance of RCTs and the hierarchy of evidence would thus be wrong. Wrong, too, is the assumption of practitioners as technicians, if by that we mean those who derive formal, propositional knowledge from outside their day-to-day work and apply it straightforwardly to practice. This technical-rational view of the relationship between knowledge and practice (Schön, 1983, 1987) has been strongly critiqued in recent years (see Taylor and White, 2001). Practice, many would argue, just isn't like that. And this is not because of error and incompetence on the part of practitioners. Practice is more than the application of formal knowledge. Research knowledge may play its part but other things are also involved. Practitioners are not simply making rational choices between competing hypotheses in order to assess/diagnose or intervene. They are involved in complex interactions with service users and professionals in which they arrive at partial understandings of complex and ambiguous situations and draw on other forms of knowledge, particularly moral judgements, in order to decide what to do.

Sheldon (2001) derides sociology, equating it with the crude version of structural Marxism popular in the 1970s, but as we show below, it is precisely certain forms of sociological or anthropological inquiry that can assist us in the process of understanding the taken-for-granted aspects of practice. For example ethnomethodology, conversation analysis and discourse analysis (see Taylor and White, 2000, 2001 for a detailed exposition of these approaches and their relevance to health and welfare) can enrich our understanding of the minutiae of decision-making and clinical judgement.

Making sense of decision making

A major drawback of EBP is its focus on interventions and outcomes. Not in the sense that these are unimportant but in the sense that in so doing it seriously underestimates the difficulties of diagnosis, assessment and case formulation. Deciding what sort of a problem the practitioner faces is a rather taken-for-granted part of the process in EBP whereas in everyday practice it is far from straightforward. The treatment example in Figure 1 above hints at this: 'Children with depression' is taken to be an unproblematic categorization and yet other studies on decision making evidence would suggest that this is by no means the case (Kahneman et al, 1982; Greenhalgh, 1999; White, forthcoming; White and Stancombe, forthcoming).

Focusing all the attention on what to do when the diagnosis has been made obscures the fact that diagnosis (or assessment) is a complicated and contentious process. Sackett *et al* (1991), for example, acknowledge that doctors struggle to reach clinical agreement in routine clinical procedures such as detecting the presence/absence of pulses in the feet, classifying diabetic retinopathy as mild or severe, assessing the height of jugular venous pressure. Moreover cardiologists agreed more often in diagnosing angina from patients' descriptions of chest pain and often failed to reach agreement when interpreting 'the abstracted, hard reality' of electrocardiographic tracings (Greenhalgh, 1999). Atkinson (1995) shows how the interpretation of laboratory slides in haematology requires that the observer select from a vast range of available descriptions to account for what they see and there are frequent disagreements between clinicians. That is, to do the work of diagnosis, the descriptions of the cells under the microscope are actively selected and negotiated in the talk. Of course, the cells themselves do not change, but how they are classified is subject to negotiation in interaction. This should not surprise us. Work in the sociology of science has shown how esoteric scientific domains are in fact characterised by high levels of uncertainty, tentativeness and equivocation (Fleck, 1979). Incidentally, Fleck was himself a microbiologist and his comments were certainly not intended to be pejorative about science and its contribution to human life.

Thus, the clinical questions promoted by EBP promise to eradicate disorderly decision-making by imposing an ordered process of rational thinking, but by focusing on the 'what to do when this occurs?' part of the question they seriously underestimate the difficulty of deciding what it is that is occurring. If this is difficult within the arena of medicine with its supposed greater certainties about symptoms and diagnoses and its use of technology in these processes (X-rays, CAT scans and the like), then the problems are magnified within social work, notably in childcare where deciding whether child abuse and neglect has occurred is highly problematic, as we know from inquiries into child abuse and the controversies about child sexual abuse (see for example London Borough of Brent, 1985, Department of Health, 1988 and the Climbie inquiry available on line). *Making* knowledge is damned hard work and it is *making* knowledge, or crafting formulations about their cases that is the primary pre-occupation of practitioners. Should this domain simply be left unexplored? We think not.

Interrogating the tacit dimension: An exemplar

We have argued that there are some serious omissions in the current incarnation of EBP. We suggest that the concept of 'evidence' be broadened to include methods more suited to examining those aspects of practice that must rely on other forms of reasoning. Let us work with one of Sheldon's own examples. In his response to Stephen Webb, Sheldon notes:

> *The popular idea (who dared challenge it?) that child sexual abuse*
> *was absolutely rampant in Britain in the 1980s, fed by bad medicine,*
> *and politically inspired feminist methodology, led to the catastrophes*
> *at Cleveland and Orkney .... I propose that evidence-based training,*
> *supervision, management and practice are the most promising*
> *correctives to all this. (Sheldon, 2001, p.804).*

We share Sheldon's concerns about the influence of fashion and
fad in social work, but disagree that experimentally-based inquiries
are likely to provide adequate means by which such taken-for-
granted ideas may be defamiliarized and opened up for debate.
Sheldon is referring to events in the 1980s in Cleveland, UK
(Department of Health, 1988) when a large number of children
were removed from their families because of suspected sexual
abuse. The principal evidence in their cases was not a disclosure
from the children, but a since discredited diagnostic procedure
'reflex anal dilatation', favoured at the time by a local paediatrician,
Dr. Marietta Higgs. If a child's anus dilated in response to the test,
the theory was that they had been subject to sexual abuse. This
may now seem a preposterous assertion, but that is the benefit of
the critical eye lent by history. At the time Higgs' persuasive
rhetoric, presumably invoking all kinds of scientific evidence, was
sufficiently potent to persuade members of the judiciary to grant
court orders in respect of the children. This took place at a time
when population figures for sexual abuse in childhood as high as
one in four were routinely invoked to justify such interventions
(Lloyd, 1992).

Sheldon thinks experimentally based EBP would have prevented
this, but how? Clearly, the production of reliable and valid
population indices on the prevalence of child sexual abuse is, and
always will be, deeply problematic. EBP would certainly have
provided social workers and medics with training in scepticism,
which is no bad thing, but it would not have been enough.
Sheldon is disparaging of the validity and reliability of sociology,
but it is precisely the methods originating in that discipline that
can help unmask 'fashion and fad'. Sociology does not equate with
hubris.

For example, White's (1997) ethnographic study of child
care social work, completed a decade after Cleveland, picked
out exactly the taken-for-granted beliefs about child sexual

abuse and the climate of fear associated with questioning them, to which Sheldon refers. She notes:

> *It is .... hazardous [for social workers] to dispute the truism 'believe*
> *the child' ... The competent individual will whisper their doubts in*
> *corners, will swear the accomplice to secrecy. Since the mid to late*
> *1980s (when social work involvement in cases of child sexual abuse*
> *increased), I can recall hearing this orthodoxy explicitly challenged*
> *only once or twice* (White, 1997, p.150).

However, whilst social workers normally privilege the child's voice, a child's account is less likely to be believed if they are asserting that all is well at home, when social workers' suspicion has been aroused that it is not, either by a referral, or by a previous statement from the child. Under these circumstances, the scepticism usually reserved for parental versions is reinstated and the child's account loses its privileged status. Clearly, this may often be absolutely the right way to proceed to protect children, but the taken-for-granted assumption about its intrinsic, always and forever correctness potentially makes allegations of sexual abuse virtually incorrigible - which is precisely what happened with some of the cases in Cleveland.

At a more micro-analytic level, Lloyd (1992) used conversation analysis to study the linguistic practices of therapists and social workers in the USA during forensic interviews with children in cases of suspected sexual abuse. His data illustrate how denials from children that abuse had taken place were dispreferred by the adult interviewers, who would respond to such denials with subtle censure or with further questions. Lloyd summarises his findings as follows:

> *The adults elicit children's confirmations by producing candidate*
> *response initiations [suggesting the answer], ratifying confirming*
> *turns, censuring children's non-confirming responses, producing*
> *subsequent versions of initiations [suggesting the answer again] and*
> *treating children's weak agreements as strong agreements.* (1992,
> p.109).

The techniques in vogue at the time for eliciting children's involved the use of puppets and play acting. The following is an example of an adult censuring a child for producing a non-confirming response:

> *(Adult treats Nicole as animating the Houndy puppet)*
> *Adult: Do you remember that part?*
> *Child: No I don't*
> *Adult: Oh Houndy. You were doing so good. I think you're losing your memory. How about...* (Lloyd, 1992, p.115).

Lloyd does not pass judgement on whether abuse had actually taken place. He does not have the data to support such an assertion. Does this make his analysis irrelevant to practitioners? No it does not. Lloyd's data illustrate perfectly the local reproduction of certain ideas that were dominant at the time, which were treated by practitioners working with sexual abuse as the only right and proper way to think. It makes this process transparent - it makes the familiar strange. Making the familiar strange is important in professions which rely to a large extent on moral reasoning. Thus, we contend that Sheldon is mistaken on two counts. First, he gives no adequate account of how EBP in its current incarnation may have prevented Cleveland, and second he fails to recognise the value of sociological inquiry in rendering the taken-for-granted explicit and therefore open to debate and challenge (White, 2001). Social work is intrinsically interactional and is saturated with moral and cultural influences. If we are properly to understand their impact we need some analytic tools to help us to interrogate them. We agree that the version of structural Marxism, adopted by social work in the 1970s is not perhaps the most promising candidate, but discourse analysis and the sociology of everyday life meet the job specification very nicely.

Summary and conclusions

EBP holds much promise, but before deciding on its particular shape in a social care context, we need to have a much better picture of what social workers do. We suggest that certain forms of sociological inquiry which eschew prescription in favour of description are perhaps best suited to this task. Moreover, we need to acknowledge that in their decision-making and in crafting their categorizations of clients social workers work up versions of events which are often based on moral assumptions about the rights/adequacies of service users. With this in mind, we need to think carefully about how we can improve skills in reasoning and critical analysis. In order to develop such skills, social workers will need to become more explicitly aware of what they take for granted.

In seeking a more inclusive version of EBP, we need to avoid irate and acrimonious exchanges, which caricature and ironize opposing positions (see for example Sheldon, 2001). Good knockabout fun they may be but, in reality, they generate more heat than light. They are unlikely to aid practitioners and are no substitute for reasoned, rigorous argument. Sheldon himself exhorts us to recognize the need 'to resist falling in love with favourite ideas and methods – stopping our ears to anything compromising said about them . . .' (Sheldon, 1998, p.16) This injunction applies just as much to proponents of the current, rather narrow version of EBP as to those who are more sceptical of what it has to offer. EBP invokes (its own version of) 'science' or 'rationality'. Valued cultural artefacts these may be – but this should not render the assumptions, presuppositions and promises of EBP immune from constructive critical analysis. By knowing its limits, we may be helped to see EBP's strengths.

References

Appleby, J., Walshe, K. and Ham, C. (1995) *Acting on the Evidence: A review of clinical effectiveness. sources of information, dissemination and implementation.* Birmingham: University of Birmingham, Health Services Management Centre / National Association of Health Authorities and Trusts

Atkinson, P. (1995) *Medical Talk and Medical Work.* London: Sage

Cochrane, A. (1972) *Effectiveness and Efficiency: Random reflections on health services.* London: Nuffield Hospitals Trust

Department of Health (1988) *Report of the Inquiry into Child Abuse in Cleveland 1987,* [Cm 412] London: HMSO

Department of Health (1998a) *A First Class Service*. London: The Stationery Office

Department of Health (1998b) *Modernising Social Services: Promoting independence, improving protection, raising standards*. London: The Stationery Office

Department of Health (1998c) *The New NHS, Modern and Dependable: A National Framework for Assessing Performance*. London: The Stationery Office

Department of Health (2001) *Assessing Children in Need and their Families: Practice Guidance*. London: The Stationery Office

Department of Health, Department for Education and Employment and Home Office (2000) *Framework for Assessment of Children in Need and their Families*. London: The Stationery Office

Downie, R.S and Macnaughton, J. (2000) *Clinical Judgement: Evidence in practice*. Oxford: Oxford University Press

Fleck, L. (1979) *Genesis and Development of Scientific Fact*. Chicago: University of Chicago Press

Geddes, J. (2000) Evidence-Based Practice in Mental Health in L. Trinder with S. Reynolds (Eds.) *Evidence-Based Practice: A critical appraisal*. Oxford: Blackwell Science

Gomm, R. (2000) Making sense of surveys. in R. Gomm and C. Davies (eds) *Using Evidence in Health and Social Care*. London: Sage

Gray, J.A.M. (1997) *Evidence-Based Healthcare*. London: Churchill Livingstone

Gray, J.A.M. (2000) Evidence-based public health. in L. Trinder with S. Reynolds (Eds.) *Evidence-Based Practice: A critical appraisal*. Oxford: Blackwell Science

Greenhalgh, T. (1999) Narrative based medicine in an evidence based world. *British Medical Journal*, 318, 323-325

Harari, E. (2001) Whose evidence? Lesson from the philosophy of science and the epistemology of medicine. *Australian and New Zealand Journal of Psychiatry*, 35, 724-30

Harrison, S. (1998) The politics of evidence -based medicine in the United Kingdom. *Policy and Politics*, 26, 1, 15-31

Hollway, W. (2001) The psycho-social subject in 'evidence-based practice'. *Journal of Social Work Practice*, 15, 1, 9-22

Hunter, D. (1998) The new health policy agenda: The challenge facing managers and researchers. *Research, Policy and Planning*, 16, 2, 2-6

Kahneman, D., Sloveic, P. and Tversky, A. (1982) *Judgement Under*

Uncertainty: Heuristics and biases. New York: Cambridge University Press

Kuhn, T. (1970) *The Structure of Scientific Revolutions.* Chicago: Chicago University Press

Lehrman, L.J. (1949) Success and failure of treatment in child guidance clinics of the Jewish Board of Guardians, *Research Monographs I.* New York: Jewish Board of Guardians

Lloyd, R.M. (1992) Negotiating child sexual abuse: the interactional character of investigative practices. *Social Problems,* 39, 2, 109-124

London Borough of Brent (1985) *A Child in Trust: Report of the Panel of Inquiry Investigating the Circumstances Surrounding the Death of Jasmine Beckford*

Marshall, M., Gray, A., Lockwood, A. and Green, R. (1996) *Case management for People with Severe Mental Disorders.* Cochrane Library website, 26 February

Milner, J. and O'Byrne, P. (1998) *Assessment in Social Work.* Basingstoke: Macmillan

Parker, G.B. (1997) Case management: An evidence-based review fails to make its case. Anniversary Editorial. *Current Opinion in Psychiatry,* 10, 261-263

Power, M. (1997) *The Audit Society: Rituals of verification.* Oxford: Oxford University Press

Powers, E. and Witmer, H. (1951) *An Experiment in the Prevention of Delinquency: The Cambridge-Somerville Youth Study.* New York: Columbia University Press

Reynolds, S. (2000) The anatomy of evidence-based practice: Principles and methods. in L. Trinder with S. Reynolds (Eds.) *Evidence-Based Practice: A critical appraisal.* Oxford: Blackwell Science

Rosen, A. and Teesson, M. (2001) Does case management work? The evidence and the abuse of evidence-based medicine, *Australian and New Zealand Journal of Psychiatry,* 35, 731-46

Sackett, D.L., Richardson, S., Rosenberg, W. and Haynes, R.B. (1997) *Evidence-based Medicine: How to Practise and Teach EBM.* Edinburgh: Churchill Livingstone

Schon, D.A. (1983) *The Reflective Practitioner.* New York: Free Press

Schon, D.A. (1987) *Educating the Reflective Practitioner: Towards a new design for teaching and learning in the professions.* San Francisco: Jossey-Bass

SCIE (2002) www.scie.org.uk/aboutscie.about.htm

Shaw, I. (1999) *Qualitative Evaluation*. London: Sage

Sheldon, B. (1986) Social work effectiveness: reviews and implications. *British Journal of Social Work*, 16, 223-42

Sheldon, B. (1998) Evidence-based social services: prospects and problems. *Research Policy and Planning*, 16, 2, 16-18

Sheldon, B. (2001) The validity of evidence-based practice in social work: A reply to Stephen Webb. *British Journal of Social Work*, 31, 6, 801-809

Sheldon, B. and Chilvers, R. (2000) *Evidence-Based Social Care: A study of prospects and problems*. Lyme Regis, Dorset: Russell House

Sheldon, B. and Chilvers, R. (2002) An empirical study of the obstacles to evidence-based practice. *Social Work & Social Sciences Review*, 10, 1,

Sheldon, B. and Macdonald, G.M. (1999) *Research and Practice in Social Care: Mind the gap*. Exeter: Centre for Evidence-Based Social Services

Sheppard, M. (1995) Social work, social science and practice wisdom. *British Journal of Social Work*, 25, 3, 265-293

Sheppard, M. (1998) Practice validity, reflexivity and knowledge. *British Journal of Social Work*, 28, 5, 763-781

Silverman, D. (2000) *Doing Qualitative Research: A practical handbook*, London: Sage

Taylor, C. and White, S. (2000) *Practising Reflexivity In Health and Welfare: Making knowledge*. Buckingham: Open University Press

Taylor, C. and White, S. (2001) Knowledge, Truth and Reflexivity: The Problem of Judgement in Social Work, *Journal of Social Work*, 1, 1, 37-59

TOPSS (1999) *Modernizing the Social Care Workforce*. Consultation Document. Leeds: TOPSS

Trinder, L. (2000a) Introduction: the Context of Evidence-Based Practice. in L. Trinder with S. Reynolds (Eds.) *Evidence-Based Practice: A critical appraisal*. Oxford: Blackwell Science

Trinder, L. (2000b) A Critical Appraisal of Evidence-Based Practice. in L. Trinder with S. Reynolds (Eds.) *Evidence-Based Practice: A critical appraisal*. Oxford: Blackwell Science

Trinder, L. with Reynolds, S. (eds) (2000) *Evidence-Based Practice: A critical appraisal*. Oxford: Blackwell Science

Webb, S.A. (2001) Some Considerations on the Validity of Evidence-Based Practice in Social Work, *British Journal of Social Work*, 31, 1, 57-79

White, S. (1997) *Performing Social Work: An Ethnographic Study of Talk and Text in a Metropolitan Social Services Department.* Unpublished PhD. thesis. Salford: University of Salford

White, S. (2001) Auto-ethnography as reflexive inquiry: The research act as self-surveillance. in I. Shaw and N. Gould (Eds.) *Qualitative Social Work Research: Method and content.* London: Sage

White, S. (forthcoming) Accomplishing the case in paediatrics and child health: Medicine and morality in interprofessional talk. *Sociology of Health and Illness*

White, S. and Stancombe, J. (forthcoming) *Clinical Judgement in the Health and Welfare Professions: Extending the evidence base.* Buckingham: Open University Press

5
The limits of positivism revisited

David Smith

Evidence-based practice

The title of this chapter alludes to a paper (Smith, 1987) in the *British Journal of Social Work* called 'The limits of positivism in social work research'. At the time it was written, it was not unusual to hear academic colleagues argue that there was something inherently conservative about positivist approaches to social research, and that such approaches inevitably served the interests of the powerful and maintained the status quo. I was never clear about the stages involved in this argument and remained unpersuaded by it, and this was not the line followed in the article (though I might be more readily persuaded now, for reasons discussed later in this paper). Instead, the 1987 article was mainly taken up with a critique of the work of Brian Sheldon, as the leading advocate over the previous ten years - and, as it turned out, over the next fifteen - of what would now be called 'evidence-based practice'.

The paper argued that Sheldon's traditional version of positivism, and his rejection of other research approaches, were epistemologically and methodologically limited and limiting, since if we were to take Sheldon's advice a number of other useful research approaches would be lost to the social work community, whether of practitioners or of researchers. It also suggested that Sheldon was wrong to argue that social workers were unique among comparable professional groups in neglecting the evidence of evaluative research, since much of the evaluation literature would be incomprehensible if it were the case that teachers, for example, attended as a matter of course to evaluations of educational practices and modified their own practice accordingly. The article argued for attention to processes as well as to outcomes, on the grounds that measuring and counting outcomes was of little use unless one knew what had produced them (a naïve version of the 'realistic evaluation' more recently advocated by Pawson and Tilley (1997)), and it was this part of the argument that received most attention and gave the article whatever influence it had (Cheetham et al., 1992).

Now that positivist outcome-oriented evaluation has made a dramatic reappearance in the guise of advocacy of 'evidence-based practice', and, in the field of criminal justice social work at least, in managerial and political demands that practice should be based on 'what works', it may be useful to try to take the arguments of the 1987 paper on a stage, and take a critical look at just what it would mean to take seriously the expectation that practice should be evidence-based, and what we might make of the claim that there is something wrong, and in need of managerial correction, with any practice that cannot demonstrate that it has this quality.

On the face of it, it is very hard to argue with the proposition that practice in social work should be 'evidence-based'. The same demand has recently been stressed in relation to medicine, and most of us are likely to find that reassuring. What else could practice be based on? Intuition, gut conviction, habit, whim, obsession, mania?

But in the language of politicians and of many social work - and, in England and Wales, probation - managers, the demand that practice should be based on evidence reveals an over-simplified and over-certain view of what evidence does or might consist of, and of how it should be interpreted and used. In trying to justify this claim and suggest a more nuanced, more modest, but also more helpful approach to evidence in the field of social work I shall move from the general to the particular, arguing first that the demand for evidence-based practice often rests on a misconception about the nature of the social sciences, and then drawing on my own experience and the work of other evaluation researchers to support the argument that knowing what counts as evidence, what it is evidence of, and how we should use it rationally is more complicated and also more interesting and creative than managers and politicians would like to believe.

One way of beginning to look at the question of the nature of social science knowledge is to note that social work seems recently, and perhaps for the first time, to have embraced a most uncritical version of positivism just as the most closely related academic disciplines are tending to move away from it (for a very polarised exchange on the implications of this see Webb (2001) and Sheldon (2001); Webb's anti- or post-modernist critique of the evidence-based practice movement is not the position I want to argue for here). In my use of the term, as in Sheldon's, positivism means the assumption that social science should proceed on the model of the natural sciences, and that the more it resembles them the better (more rigorous, more valid, more useful and so on) it will be.

It is intelligible that social work should suddenly embrace evidence as a source of practice, because there is truth in the charge (Sheldon and Chilvers, 2001) that it has done without it for too long (not that this makes it unique among the helping professions), and it is now being told that its very existence is at risk if it does not mend its ways. But there is no need for the social work professional community to adopt a view of evidence which encourages exactly the misconceptions about what it means and how to use it which are dear to the hearts of bureaucrats and politicians.

The nature of the social sciences

The philosopher Alasdair MacIntyre (1985) puts the matter thus:

> *What managerial expertise requires for its vindication is a justified conception of social science as providing a stock of law-like generalisations with strong predictive power. (p.90)*

This is, according to MacIntyre, exactly the conventional image of social science over the past 200 years, the period of positivist domination. But MacIntyre argues that this position is based on a misunderstanding of the nature of the social sciences and the kinds of generalisation they can produce. In practice, theories can survive in the social sciences alongside plenty of instances in which their predictions fail to be confirmed, and still be found useful, which is not the case in the natural sciences. An example given by MacIntyre is Oscar Newman's (1973) theory of defensible space. Based on impressive and extensive research, this predicts, among other things, that crime rates will rise with the height of buildings up to a height of thirteen storeys, and then level off. This is a risky prediction, and positivist criminologists were not slow to test it, find disconfirming cases, and claim that the theory was wrong. But, with some modifications, the theory has survived, and now routinely informs decisions in architecture and town planning.

This suggests that the logic of theory in the social sciences is different from that of theory in the natural sciences, and, according to MacIntyre, this is inevitable because the social world is ineradicably unpredictable; Machiavelli knew this, and called the element of chance, of unpredictability, *fortuna*. Those positivist social scientists, like their bureaucratic counterparts, who want to remove all sources of uncertainty are yearning for a God-like omniscience (God knows everything that will ever have happened)"–"and of course they keep failing to achieve it (MacIntyre's main examples are economics and demography).

Empirical social science, which is just as old as the natural sciences (the Greeks did both) relies on induction from research to produce its generalisations, and these take the form not of universal laws but of statements which begin with something like 'Characteristically and for the most part...', not 'If x is the case then, given that certain conditions hold, y will always follow'. This is so because social science generalisations are rooted in the form of human life, and the practice of social science reveals that its ancestry and tradition are different from those of the natural sciences. Positivists, or some of them, forget this when they aspire to total control of all that is unpredictable; and the same is true of some managers and politicians.

The realist tradition

One source of unpredictability for social work is the context, changing with time and space, in which it is practised. This is crucial for the main alternative to the positivist tradition, evaluation within the philosophical tradition of realism. Realist evaluators (e.g. Pawson and Tilley, 1997) are right to stress that context (and not outcomes alone) is crucial in the evaluation of any social programme. So are the 'mechanisms' which generate change - the choices and capacities which are made available to participants - and their operation is always contingent on context: 'subjects will only act upon the resources and choices offered by a program if they are in conducive settings' (Pawson and Tilley, 1997, p. 216). Understanding the contexts that are needed for the mechanisms for change to work is essential for understanding how outcomes are produced. Pawson and Tilley write of context-mechanism-outcome configurations, which are propositions stating what it is about programmes that works for some people in some circumstances. The same programme will work in different ways in different circumstances, and sometimes it will not work at all. So rather than trying to replicate programmes which seem to work in the hope that they will work everywhere and always, we should try to generalise about programmes by developing middle range theories about context-mechanism-outcome patterns which will allow us to interpret differences and similarities among groups of programmes. This is the realist alternative to the aspirations of the experimental method of positivism, which, hypnotised by method to the point where theory is forgotten, has rarely managed to tell us anything helpful about the questions that matter: what is it about this programme that works for whom in what specifiable conditions and given what contextual features?

This is because positivist ways of thinking about evaluation ignore contexts and (despite some claims to the contrary) generally also ignore processes, or mechanisms in Pawson and Tilley's terms. Its decontextualised preoccupation with outcomes inevitably means that most of the results of positivist research are non-significant and inconclusive, because the theories that it is supposed to be testing depend crucially on the specific context in which they are implemented. The philosopher Russell Keat (1981) indicated the ground which a realist philosophy might occupy in trying to understand how outcomes are produced, and some of the problems in connecting processes with outcomes. I quoted this in the 1987 article, and still do not know of any clearer statement of the problem. Keat is referring to the relationship between the truth or falsehood of psychoanalytic theory and the success or failure of psychoanalytic practice:

> *the failure of therapeutic techniques is compatible with the truth of this theory, whilst the success of those techniques may provide little support for it ... this is primarily due to the fact that in deriving predictions about therapeutic outcomes from psychoanalytic theory, a number of auxiliary statements must typically be assumed, whose own truth or falsity may display various degrees of independence from the explanatory claims made within this theory. Such auxiliaries may usefully be said to comprise a 'theory of technique': that is, an attempt to specify and explain the effects upon the patient of various elements of the therapeutic process. Thus even in those cases where predicted therapeutic success is achieved, it is possible that neither psychoanalytic theory nor its associated theory of technique are significantly supported, since it may be that this success is better explained by another theory of technique (Keat, 1981, p. 159).*

So the relationship between outcomes and the theory on which the programme is based (and some kind of theory or theories necessarily lie behind any social work intervention) is nothing like as straightforward as the managerial culture which demands single right answers requires it to be.

The positivist programme of theory falsification is thus not only ill-founded philosophically, since it misunderstands the nature of social science generalisations, but usually unhelpful to practitioners and policy-makers. John Braithwaite (1993), writing about criminological positivism, has suggested that what is important is to develop a range of theories that are sometimes useful. These will often be theories which positivists say explain less variance than others across sets of decontextualised cases: that is, they will be theories which have less predictive power. Braithwaite suggests that a useful way of thinking about theory is to see it as metaphor. Practitioners concerned with a particular problem in a local context can then scan lists of theories to see which supplies a helpful or interesting metaphor. 'In the world of problem solving that matters, it is contextualised usefulness that counts, not decontextualised statistical power' (Braithwaite, 1993, p. 386). In social work too, what is likely to be helpful is to use theory for the generation of interesting hypotheses about what might work in a particular local context, not to search for a universal one best way of responding to a given problem.

Difficulties in evaluation research

There are other reasons why what appears to be evidence is less straightforward to interpret and use in practice than we are being encouraged to believe. One is that a great deal of evaluative research is not very good. Positivism deserves some of the blame for this: as Co-Editor for four years of the *British Journal of Social Work* I read more papers than was good for me, some by quite distinguished social work academics, that showed a preoccupation with statistical testing combined with very little understanding of what statistical tests are for and in what circumstances they are useful. Even without any statistical expertise, it was not difficult to recognise that the way statistics were used in some of these papers was nonsensical. The preoccupation with scientific method meant that tests were used on data for which they were sometimes literally meaningless.

As an aside on statistics, whose application to social data is one of the main achievements of positivism, one piece of learning in the editorship was that this is not the exact and settled science that I had taken it to be. People who clearly knew what they were talking about often disagreed radically about what statistical procedure should be used when, and for what purpose. The fact of having been around for a long time, and looking scientific, does not, apparently, make statistical analysis any more beyond argument than any other approach in the social sciences.

Another indication of the quality of much evaluative research comes from Andrew Underdown's (1998) review for the Home Office of groupwork programmes in probation services in England and Wales. This is, of course, preceded by a management summary, but if the managers were to go on and read the body of the report, described by the Chief Inspector of Probation as the most important he had ever written an introduction to, they would find that from the 267 replies on programmes received in the initial trawl, 210 were judged to have been evaluated in some way, 33 had produced enough evaluation material for analysis, and eleven were identified as having some value as indications of good evaluative practice. (And this at a time when the evidence-based, or 'What Works', agenda was well established in probation, and the old orthodoxy of 'Nothing works' had been firmly rejected by managers and policy-makers.) Of the evaluations obtained by Underdown, the clearest model for imitation was that by Raynor and Vanstone (1996; 1997) of the STOP (Straight Thinking on Probation) project in mid-Glamorgan, a careful and rigorous piece of external evaluation covering process as well as outcomes and examining implementation issues, levels of compliance and completion, and attitudinal change as well as reconvictions after one and two years, compared with those for several similar groups of offenders as well as against a statistical predictor. This was an evaluation of practice which was itself already evidence-based, since the STOP programme was designed as an adaptation to local conditions of the Reasoning and Rehabilitation programme developed by Robert Ross and his colleagues in Canada, and the conditions for its successful implementation and maintenance seem to have been near to ideal.

So it is as well to remember that while the one-year reconviction rates were promising for those who completed the programme (though not for those who did not), the two-year rates were much less so (though they were still better in terms of offence seriousness than for the comparison groups). The researchers concluded that the falling-off in performance was attributable to the absence of relevant reinforcement and support after people had left the programme. That is, for continued good results the programme would have needed to be supplemented by opportunities to build on the learning and solving of problems participants had achieved; it should have been part of a broader network of resources integrated with the programme's aims and methods (Raynor and Vanstone, 1996). I will come back later to the importance of strategies that are contextual, integrated and multi-modal, and that, necessarily, draw on more than one strand of theory.

The reason why there are so few adequate evaluations of practice, and therefore so (relatively) little evidence to base practice on, is that evaluation is difficult. My own work, undertaken with colleagues, on two projects for persistent juvenile offenders in Scotland provided a strong reminder of this (Lobley and Smith, 1999; Lobley *et al.*, 2001). The collection of rich process data that allow confident conclusions to be drawn about what the important aspects of a programme are, associated with success or failure, requires close, time-consuming observation and analysis of what is observed. It needs to be able to chart changes over time, and to incorporate the understandings and theories of both staff and participants. For quantitative data, it is necessary to have or develop systems of collection which are reliable and consistent, and give access to data sources that are reliable and complete. A particularly sharp reminder concerned the limitations of reconviction data as a measure of change (though reconvictions are often treated as 'harder' data than what is usually available in evaluating social work interventions in other fields (Cheetham *et al.*, 1992)).

In both projects we had access to details on the number and nature of charges faced by the young people in the twelve months before they started at the projects. This material on charges stopped being collected when the young people reached the age of sixteen, after which the only source for a record of offending was the Scottish Criminal Records Office, covering only offences for which the young people were convicted. While of course the young people may not have committed some of the offences with which they were charged, it is still the case that the SCRO record gives a much attenuated account of the volume and rate of offending, and that the time lag between charge and conviction, or at least the appearance of the conviction on the official record, is often very long. It also proved far from straightforward to find a suitable comparison group.

After a good deal of effort on the part of Scottish Office colleagues and two time-wasting false starts, we identified a comparison group which was useful, though not ideal, for evaluative purposes, but the data on the comparison group were of course subject to the limitations of the SCRO record. Mair *et al.*

(1997) among others have discussed the limitations and problems of using reconviction rates, and a health warning about their limitations customarily accompanies research reports using reconvictions as the main outcome measure. But the warning could do with being strengthened, and issued more than once. It is probably rare for a persistent offender to avoid convictions altogether, at least in the long run, though there is plenty of anecdotal evidence to suggest that it can happen over a year or two, but there is no certain fit between recorded convictions and amount of crime actually committed. Thus some of the hardest-looking data available in social work evaluation become noticeably softer when subjected to close inspection.

Another area in which there is currently a strong demand for evidence is on cost-effectiveness. Since this was a prescribed element of the evaluation of the two Scottish Office projects, I tried to read the relevant literature conscientiously, get my head round the maths, and understand the assumptions which are characteristically built into such analyses in the field of criminal justice interventions about what would have happened without the intervention (it is possible that fewer assumptions are required in other fields, such as the evaluation of health services, in which cost-benefit evaluation seems to be more firmly established). Most writers in this area advocate comprehensiveness, but the more comprehensive the evaluation gets the more complex it is likely to become, and the more assumptions need to be built into the analysis.

For instance, there have been various attempts to assess the cost of a 'typical' crime (itself a difficult concept) some of which have tried to measure only criminal justice system costs, while some have tried to assess the cost to the victim, to insurance companies, to employers, and so on ... because once you start down the road of inclusiveness the possibilities multiply. Even studies which consider only criminal justice system costs typically have to make assumptions about the marginal cost saving of each offence prevented, and, still more fundamentally, seem almost universally to consider all criminal justice costs as net social costs, whereas one could easily argue that the creation of jobs, and therefore wealth, and the avoidance of unemployment among criminal justice personnel count as overall social and economic benefits (and the private sector in criminal justice is of course a notable current case of economic success). Finally, it is worth noting that in a recent Rand Corporation (Karoly *et al.*, 1998) report on the effectiveness of early intervention with children the researchers decided that there were only two studies which provided sufficiently high quality and long term data to use in their effort to assess cost savings (their preferred term).

We could all wish that cost-benefit or cost-savings analysis were an exact science, as those who seek to control the social world require it to be; but it is not. This is not to say that nothing sensible can be said about these issues, and (too late for their suggestions to be incorporated in the Scottish Office evaluations) the Home Office produced guidance on them that was a good deal more sophisticated than previous efforts (Dhiri and Brand, 1999; Colledge *et al.*, 1999), but what is said will generally be - and certainly ought to be - tentative and qualified, and the assumptions behind the conclusions should be explicit (it is reasonable to say, for instance, that someone who has been free of convictions for two years at the age of eighteen is less likely to get into a criminal career as an adult than someone who has 20 convictions over the same period, but the unpredictability of social life means that this assumption will sometimes be false).

Conclusions

In this chapter I have dealt briefly with the nature of generalisations in social science, the importance of context and processes in making sense of outcomes, the inevitability of theoretical pluralism, and various more mundane and technical matters which have a bearing on the production and interpretation of evidence. Given that the status of any evidence is therefore qualified and ambiguous, how should practitioners and policy-makers use it? I think that Braithwaite's (1993) argument for what he calls 'contextual, integrated strategies' (p. 395) in tackling crime problems can be adapted to apply to the social work field more generally, and, combined with my own and colleagues' experiences of the Scottish projects for juvenile offenders, can be used to suggest a number of pieces of prescriptive advice for evaluators.

The first of these might be to put positivism in its place. In criminology and in social work, positivist evaluations have been vital in enabling the detection of nonsense; but the positivist (and managerialist) claim that such evaluations can produce - or have produced - law-like universals should be rejected. Secondly, remember that context matters, and that it makes little sense to try to understand any kind of intervention without reference to the local environment which sustains it (or fails to do so); and this means (Tilley, 1996) that replication is strictly speaking impossible. Thirdly, and despite some current orthodoxies about 'programme integrity', it is unhelpful to practitioners to encourage them to rely on a single type of theory, and therefore on a single form of intervention; nothing should be expected always to work on its own, and integrated approaches that are responsive to changes in the social, political and policy environment are preferable to static approaches based on the supposition that all the available evidence points in a single direction. Fourthly, theoretical pluralism and tolerance, within limits set by positivist achievements in identifying nonsense and making it manifest, are virtues, not vices. Finally, take seriously the realist stress on processes or mechanisms, on what it is that makes a difference (in either direction).

If evaluators were to think and work along these lines, the claims they would make, and what they would encourage managers and bureaucrats to believe, would be more modest, but also more realistic, than the most confident claims of positivism.

References

Braithwaite, J. (1993) Beyond positivism: Learning from contextual integrated strategies. *Journal of Research in Crime and Delinquency*, 30, 4, 383-99

Cheetham, J., Fuller, R., McIvor, G. and Petch, A. (1992) *Evaluating Social Work Effectiveness*. Buckingham, Open University Press

Colledge, M., Collier, P. and Brand, S. (1999) *Programmes for Offenders: Guidance for Evaluators*. London, Home Office

Dhiri, S. and Brand, S. (1999) *Analysis of Costs and Benefits: Guidance for evaluators*. London, Home Office

Karoly, L.A., Greenwood, P.W., Everingham, S.S., Houbé, J., Kilburn,

M.R., Rydell. C.P., Sanders. M. and Chiesa, J. (1998) *What We Know and Don't Know about the Costs and Benefits of Early Childhood Interventions.* Santa Monica, CA: Rand Corporation

Keat, R. (1981) *The Politics of Social Theory.* Oxford: Blackwell

Lobley, D. and Smith, D. (1999) *Working with Persistent Juvenile Offenders: An evaluation of the Apex CueTen Project.* Edinburgh, Scottish Office

Lobley, D., Smith, D. and Stern, C. (2001) *Freagarrach: An evaluation of a project for persistent juvenile offenders.* Edinburgh: Scottish Executive

MacIntyre, A. (1985) *After Virtue: A study in moral theory.* London, Duckworth

Mair, G., Lloyd, C. and Hough, M. (1997) The limitations of reconviction rates. in Mair, G. (Ed.) *Evaluating the Effectiveness of Community Penalties.* Aldershot, Avebury, pp.34-46

Newman, O. (1973) *Defensible Space: Crime prevention through urban design.* London: Architectural Press

Pawson, R. and Tilley, N. (1997) *Realistic Evaluation.* London: Sage

Raynor, P. and Vanstone, M. (1996) Reasoning and rehabilitation in Britain: The results of the Straight Thinking on Probation (STOP) programme', *International Journal of Offender Therapy and Comparative Criminology,* 40, 279-91

Raynor, P. and Vanstone, M. (1997) *Straight Thinking on Probation (STOP): The Mid-Glamorgan Experiment.* Oxford: Centre for Criminological Research

Sheldon, B. (2001) The validity of evidence-based practice in social work: A reply to Stephen Webb. *British Journal of Social Work,* 31, 801-09

Sheldon, B. and Chilvers, R. (2001) *Evidence-based Social Care: A Study of prospects and problems.* Lyme Regis: Russell House

Smith, D. (1987) The limits of positivism in social work research. *British Journal of Social Work,* 17, 401-16

Tilley, N. (1996) Demonstration, exemplification, duplication and replication in evaluation research. *Evaluation,* 2, 1, 35-50

Underdown. A. (1998) *Strategies for effective offender supervision.* London: Home Office

Webb, S.A. (2001) Some considerations on the value of evidence-based practice in social work. *British Journal of Social Work,* 31, 57-79.

6
A problematic relationship? Evidence and practice in the workplace

Nick Frost

Introduction

In recent years in the United Kingdom, and elsewhere in the world, we have witnessed a shift towards the promotion of what is variously referred to as an 'evidence-led' or 'evidence-based' approach to practice and policy in a range of professional fields (see Pawson, 2001, Solesbury, 2001). This paper aims to develop a critique of this approach with particular reference to social work practice with children, young people and their families.

The emphasis on evidence as the key determinant of professional practice has been encouraged by the U.K. government through research funding, by State sponsored educational initiatives and a stated political commitment to ensure that policy is informed by evidence (see Blunkett, 2000, Solesbury, 2001). This movement has become associated with the phrase 'what works', which is used in both government and academic circles (see McGuire, 1995, for example).

The origins of the evidence model are to be found in the field of medical practice"–"most notably through the work of the Cochrane Collaboration (see Oakley, 2000). An oft-quoted definition comes from McKibbon and colleagues:

Evidence-based medicine is an approach to health care that promotes the collection, interpretation, and integration of valid, important and applicable patient-reported, clinician-observed, and research-

*derived evidence. The best available evidence, moderated by patient
circumstances and preferences, is applied to improve the quality of
clinical judgements.* (McKibbon, et al, 1995)

I will simply note at this stage that this definition includes
the important phrase 'moderated by patient circumstances and
preferences': this issue will be come central to our argument
later in this paper, as it is a qualification not always recognized
by advocates of the evidence school within social work.

The evidence-based approach has become widespread across
a number of professional practices in the United Kingdom in
recent years. Solesbury identifies a contemporary movement to
what he calls 'the ascendancy of evidence' (2001, p.4).

How is this approach being applied to social work? First of
all it is important to note that within what we might call the
'evidence' school there exists a continuum of views. These
range from 'hard line' advocates of 'evidence-led' approach to
a softer 'evidence-based' approach. It would need a paper in
its own right to properly distinguish the gradations of position
within this spectrum. However, whilst this paper addresses
the issues in a way that can be applied throughout this
complex spectrum, the force of the critique applies mainly to
what we may describe as proponents of evidence-led practice.
The fundamental argument of this paper is that the move
towards evidence-led practice tends to over simplify the
complex issues and challenges facing professional social
workers in their day-to-day practice.

First of all it is necessary to establish that I am simply not
developing a 'soft target'. What exactly is being advocated by
the 'evidence' school and which concrete initiatives demonstrate
that it is currently in good health? I wish to quote directly from
some of the leading proponents of the evidence school and
thus, hopefully, escape any claims that the critique I develop is
aimed at an imaginary target.

Probably the leading advocate in the U.K. of such an
evidence-led approach is Professor Ann Oakley, of the Social
Science Research Unit. She argues, with colleagues Newman
and Roberts that:

Practitioners who adopt a particular approach must be able to

*describe what evidence has led them to do so, what the intended
outcomes will be and what the probability is of such outcomes
occurring'* (Newman et al, Guardian, 10.1.96)

This is a very eloquent and pithy definition which I will take
this as a core definition of the approach taken by the evidence
school. I have chosen this in particular as it was published in a
forum which specifically aimed to popularize the approach
amongst human services professions – the Society supplement
of the Guardian newspaper.

There are however a range of similar definitions which are
proposed by other major proponents. Professor Brain Sheldon
has been a champion of the evidence school for many years. His
Centre, drawing on the medical model definition used above,
utilises the following definition:

*Evidence-based practice in social care is the conscientious, explicit
and judicious use of current best evidence in making decisions
regarding the welfare of service-users and carers.*
(www.exeter.ac.uk/cebss)

It is these two definitions, developed by the advocates of the
evidence school, which will be critically addressed in this
paper. The reader may wish to note that both the definitions we
have used demonstrate links between the promotion of an
evidence-based approach and the establishment of institutional
forms aimed at promoting forms of evidence-based practice.
Professor Oakley has helped to establish the Evidence for
Policy and Practice Information and Co-ordinating Centre
(EPPI), funded by the Department for Education and
Employment, which focuses on educational and research.
Professor Sheldon is associated with the Centre For Evidence-
Based Social Services at the University of Exeter, which is partly
funded by the Department of Health. A different, but related
organizational form is that demonstrated by the child welfare
organisation, Barnardo's. They have particularly advocated the
'What Works' approach through their series of publications,
the titles of which commence with that key phrase.

At this stage the paper aims to have established two key
points"–"first that the emphasis on evidence as a key determinant

of professional practice has become an influential movement in the U.K. and second that this takes an institutional form. I now want to move on to the more critical element of the paper, which questions the validity of the emphasis on the link between evidence and practice which is proposed by the champions of all forms of 'evidence-led' practice, 'evidence-based' practice or the 'What Works' school. The paper concludes by proposing what the author suggests is a more realistic model of the link between evidence and practice.

Developing a critique of the evidence school

At first glance the claims of the evidence school may seen to be perfectly plausible. It seems that there should be a clear link between evidence and practice. Further one would think that such a development would be welcomed by the academic community – at last our research is being listened to and utilised.

Initially I need to establish what is not being argued in this paper. The paper is not taking what might be called a 'post-modernist' approach – it is not being argued here, for example, that no truth claims at all can be or that we all have a unique narrative relationship to social reality. Nor is it being argued that the process of gathering evidence is a futile exercise and that there can be no impact on policy and practice. The model at the end of the paper demonstrates a more realistic approach to the utilization of evidence. The aims of the paper are perhaps modest – to contribute to what might be called a 'pragmatic' opposition to the evidence school.

It will be argued that the evidence movement is flawed and represents a false promise for professional policy and practice and for researchers alike. In this paper it is argued that there are four key problems with the approach advocated by the 'evidence' school. These four problems can be identified as follows:

- the problem of 'evidence'
- the problem of applying 'evidence' to practice
- the relationship between 'evidence' and values

- the relationship between providers and users of services

Each of these four issues will be examined in turn, before an alternative model is proposed (see also Frost, 2002).

The problem of 'evidence'

First of all it needs to be asked exactly what is the evidence referred to by the 'evidence' school and what status should social scientific evidence, in general, be granted?

The proponents of the evidence-based approach set themselves high standards. They often call for practice drawing on research of the highest scientific standards and based on the 'gold standard' of a randomised controlled trial (RCT), and have a tendency to refer to 'robust' and 'high quality' evidence (MacDonald, Sheldon and Gillespie, 1992). According to the evidence school these high quality research and evaluation projects in turn produce the highest quality evidence˝–˝which should then in turn be applied by professional practitioners.

If only the world was this simple. First, this approach presents knowledge as if it is static and therefore reaches some unproblematic standard at which it should then be 'applied' to professional practice. However it is argued here that knowledge rarely reaches this unproblematic standard and tends to be enhanced through critique and development. Knowledge is produced which is then debated and challenged and this in order turn produces new forms of knowledge. Knowledge in social science thus is rarely unproblematic or unchallenged.

Second, research and knowledge generation tends to be carried out within particular theoretical frameworks or paradigms. Thus Sheldon, for example, a leading proponent of evidence led practice in social work, takes a cognitive behavioral approach.

Those of us who come from differing theoretical schools would tend to be critical of Sheldon's findings, as a result of their fundamental epistemological position. For example, someone from a psychoanalytical school would argue that the cognitive approach underplays the role of the unconscious.

Thus presentations of evidence are usually subject to what Pawson and Tilley (1997) call 'paradigm wars' – fundamental disputes over theory, methods, concepts and so on. Given these differences it is hard to assess at which point any given form of knowledge reaches a status at which it can then be applied.

Third, much social scientific evidence, particularly that gathered through evaluation, tends to be situational. Pawson and Tilley argue this forcibly in their text 'Realistic Evaluation' (1997):

> *Evaluators will always construct their explanations around three crucial ingredients of any initiative: context (C), mechanism (M) and outcome (O). There will always be contextual variation within and between programs, a corresponding variation in the effectiveness of causal mechanisms triggered, and a consequential variation in patterns of outcomes. (Pawson and Tilley, 1997, p.77).*

Thus they argue that any evaluation has to measure how a mechanism leads to an outcome in a particular context. It is not possible simply to transfer this mechanism to another context and assume that it will 'work'. For example, one might produce rigorous evidence on a given topic in year x – inevitably given the pace of legislative, policy and social change the context for this work will have changed, sometimes fundamentally, even by year $x + 2$. Thus evidence is essentially situational and contextual – making the application of evidence a complex process.

The problem of applying 'evidence' to practice.

Let us assume for the sake of argument that there were indeed no problems in gathering evidence. Let us assume that researchers are able to gather robust and reliable evidence, which then achieves universal acclaim. Even given this assumption it is still not clear how such evidence could be applied in practice.

To illustrate this argument I will take an example from social work practice. First, let us accept that, generally, children looked after by relatives seem to do better in terms of outcomes than children looked after by foster careers they have never met before (Rowe et al, 1989). This seems to be a perfectly acceptable and unproblematic finding. However, how can this be translated this into practice?

All we can say is that a given child is likely to do better if placed with a relative than another foster carer. It does not mean that placement with, say, her actual grandmother will be necessarily be successful, or even better than placement with a different foster carer. Thus whilst the research evidence can be contextual and informative it cannot be determinative in a given situation. Hammersley quotes a similar example from medical practice:

> *There are also problems surrounding the application of information about aggregates to particular patients. The authors of key text in clinical epidemiology .... report a senior doctor as opining that it is immoral to combine epidemiology with clinical practice.*
> *(Hammersley, 1997, p.152)*

Already the case for becomes ELP is severely limited. How can we decide when evidence can be applied and when in cannot?

Second, and this is a purely pragmatic point, but nonetheless a serious one, the pure volume of evaluation and research is problematic. If I might be allowed a personal example: as an academic specialising in the child welfare field, I know there are always journals, books and research reports in my area which I have not read. The explosion of the information age makes it difficult for any of us to claim expertise in any particular field. Whilst academics and the Department of Health in the U.K. have recently made serious efforts to disseminate research evidence in summary and in 'popular' form the scale of this issue for busy practitioners and managers should not be under-estimated. Professionals take many hundreds of 'micro' decisions per day and it is not feasible to imagine that these could be 'evidence-based' in any realistic sense.

Third, the pleas for practitioners to privelege research and evaluation findings in practice seem to ignore the distinction between what leading theorists of education and practice such as

Oakeshot, Eraut, Schon, Tanjoru, Leadbetter and others have variously identified as 'codified' (explicit) and 'tacit' (implicit) knowledge (see Frost, 2001, and Leadbeater, 2000, for discussions of these distinctions). Basically codified knowledge is that which is written down, can be taught and assessed. In contrast tacit knowledge is that we pick up from doing the job, and is more difficult to communicate, measure and transfer.

Take the example of a (mythical) team leader who chaired the team meeting last week. She has 'tacitly' picked up that the staff seem to be unmotivated and generally uninterested by the meeting. The team leader makes a mental note to be more upbeat next week"–"perhaps to start and end the meeting a positive note. Whilst there is some professional guidance on chairing meetings and some limited research, this is an example which crucially relies on 'tacit' knowledge, which is central to professional competence. Even if the topic has been extensively researched the knowledge is clearly situational and specific. It can be argued therefore that such 'tacit' knowledge is not peripheral but central to professional practice"–"yet seems to be fundamentally undervalued by the evidence-led practice school.

The relationship between 'evidence' and values

The evidence school also seems to have what we may define as a technicist approach to social problems. Thus social problems and issues seem to be presented as if they are:

1. neutrally defined;
2. responded to with best possible 'knowledge' in response to the seemingly neutral question;
3. amenable to a 'what works' approach

It will be argued here that at stages 1, 2, 3 are implicitly value questions. If this can be shown to be the case it is a serious blow to the evidence-based practice project.

First of all let us examine how social problems are identified and defined. The vast literature on 'moral panics' and the amplification of social problems has demonstrated that this process is indeed far from neutral. Famously, Stan Cohen has identified how social problems are identified partially through series of moral panics which identify and amplify these problems (see Cohen, 1985).

In the social work field take the example of 'home alone' children. Sporadically the media pick up on this issue and report a number of cases over a few days – and then the story seems to reach an end before emerging again after the passage of some time. This pattern follows the classic description of 'moral panics' by Cohen. As any fieldwork social worker reading this article will know this is actually a regular occurrence in Britain's inner cities and housing estates. The media pick up on one case and apply the 'home alone' label from a Hollywood movie. This process happens time and time again, not least in the fields of child abuse (Parton, 1985) and youth crime (Muncie, 1998) areas of practice which are particularly vulnerable to 'moral panics'. Thus we know that the process by which social problems are identified is actually a political and social process"–"and not a neutral, scientific process.

Second, the 'knowledge' to be mobilised in relation to these problems is not neutral. As we have seen the evidence school in social work, for example, tends to privilege evidence from the cognitive behavioural school (see MacDonald, Sheldon and Gillespie, 1992). Sheldon defends this position as follows:

> *the reason for the appearance of cognitive-behavioural references in (Sheldon's research centre) work on childcare, mental health, learning disability and rehabilitation of frail elderly people, is that most rigorous (that is, the most bias-reducing) studies in these fields and many related ones, show that nothing ever does better. (Sheldon, 2001, p.807)*

Far from being a neutral or rigorous position, this like all other 'schools' is a value-based school. Many would argue that cognitive-behavioural approaches reduce people to response mechanisms, ignores the reflective element of the self, underplays the social context and so on. Thus in the human professions we have value conflicts between the various schools"–"feminist, behaviourist, radical, task-centred, psychotherapeutic and so on (see Adams et al. 1998). Whilst we maybe able to back up our case with evidence, these are ultimately competing ideological positions and should not be presented as neutral claims to expertise. As Braye argues:

> *To assume that it (evidence) will show us the 'one best way' is to devalue the complexity of professional decision-making. Ethical practice requires us to respond to the unique features of the situation ... (2000, p.30)*

Third, the 'what works' question cannot be posed neutrally as the evidence-based practice school seem to wish. Let us take an example from outside of the human professions. A motor company, let us say, have discovered that 'what works' for them is a new fuel which would make their cars cheaper to run. 'What works' for the motor company therefore is the new fuel, which will make their cars more popular. However, environmentalists may argue that the new fuel will lead to increased mileage and therefore is even more polluting than current fuels. Therefore 'what works' for the environmentalist is entirely different that what works for the motor company. I hope to have illustrated here that 'what works' is indeed not a neutral question, and cannot be presented as an 'answer' to social problems.

Indeed it is theoretically plausible that we may find some rigorous, 'gold standard' evidence on a particular issue and decide not to apply it on moral grounds. Say, for example, that evidence was found that imprisoning young people for shoplifting was a powerful deterrent. It is still possible that we may wish to reject the implications for professional practice on the grounds that we have an ethical objection to imprisoning young people. Again the call for applying evidence to practice is highly complex and problematic.

If the arguments above are sound it would seem that we have undermine the evidence-led practice case at three crucial points:

1. social problems are not neutrally defined;
2. the best possible 'knowledge' cannot be neutrally defined;
3. 'what works' in the human professions is a value question, not technical question.

The relationship between providers and users of services

Let me at this stage concede some ground. I am willing to believe that evidence led practice is applicable to technical areas such as engineering and medicine (see Sheldon, 2001). The dimension that makes ELP difficult in the *human* professions is precisely that"–"the *human*, relational nature of teaching, social work, counselling and so on. These professional roles are about recognising human subjectivity and, hopefully, responding in some form of partnership and co-operation with service user, student or client. Thus professional practice needs to be negotiated, disputed and where possible agreed.

This again undermines the claims of the evidence school. The practitioner for example may 'know' that approach x is 'what works'. However, the service user may not want to co-operate with x and might prefer y, as a form of intervention. Surely this is the very complexity of the human professions"–"negotiation, conflict and compromise. Without this complexity and situated nature surely the professions could be taught or even carried out by computers.

Thus evidence-based practice immediately dismantles the possibility of any partnership approach to working with service users. For indeed if I, as a professional, am in possession of *the evidence* then I have no choice but to implement it"–"even if you, as a service user, disagree. Thus the claim made earlier by Newman et al (1996) is spurious as they argue that professionals have a duty to base their work on evidence and that a failure to do this is a breach of trust.

A way forward?

The evidence approach is an attempt to present a rational model of decision-making. In proposing an alternative I wish to challenge this as a basis for understanding public policy and professional practice. What then might replace the evidence-based practice model? As I have already stated I do not want to argue a purely relativist or indeed post-modernist position that there is no 'reality' only discourses. Nor do I wish to totally undermine the role of research – which I see as a worthwhile and valuable undertaking. What I want to take is a pragmatic and realist position which locates evidence within a range of other significant factors which form both policy and practice.

I have my identified my provisional model by the acronym 'RIPE', perhaps suggesting that when certain factors come together the time may be 'ripe' for change. The model hopes to demonstrate that policy, practice and professional development are determined by a complex and dynamic process, which combines the influences of research and evaluation findings (R), ideological positions (I), politics disputes (P) and economic realities (E). I will explore each of these in turn.

By ideology I mean the values and perspectives that social work practitioners use to guide and steer their practice. Ideology can sometimes be devalued as a second order set of beliefs which are seen as of lesser value to scientific or evidence-based perspectives. It is argued here that is not helpful. Think for example about motivation: I would be surprised if there is a social worker in the world who entered the profession for 'scientific' reasons, influenced by a perspective which suggested that they eagerly wished to apply 'evidence' to problem-solving with people. Reality suggests that a moral, or indeed ideological motivation, lies at the heart of social work practice. Finsterbusch and Bender Motz argue that the rational model is unable to, 'handle value conflict. Whenever various people desire (value) different policies, there is value conflict. Unfortunately, almost all decisions involve value conflict' (1980, p.26). The proponents of the evidence school seem to want to wish away this value influence, which must surely be at the heart of social work practice.

By politics I mean politics in the widest sense"–"disputes over the distribution of power and decision-making. Politics"–"organisational, local and national – are central to the policy making process, but again the relationship between evidence and politics is contested. 'A major reason why actual policy decisions invariably deviate from the rational model is the intrusion of political factors into the decision-making process. Such intrusion should not be viewed as necessarily undesirable .... democracies must allow groups to act politically on their own behalf' (Finsterbusch and Bender Motz , 1980, p.32).

Sometimes politicians will ignore even the most robust of evidence for political reasons, an often quoted example being former Home Secretary Michael Howard's view that 'prison works', despite evidence to the contrary (Pawson and Tilley, 1997, p.3). Whilst the current (New Labour) government have a rhetorical commitment to 'what works' and 'evidence' one would have to be naïve in the extreme to think that fundamental political beliefs can be changed by neutrally presented 'evidence'.

Economics and resources are also crucial to this debate. Our practice and policy environments are crucially framed by the realities of resources and funding. Robust evidence may suggest a particular policy direction, for which resources are not made available. Equally there may be economic reasons for hanging on to a practice, which evidence has questioned. As Finsterbusch and Bender Motz argue:

A major defect of the rational model is its failure to recognize limits. It fails to take into account the costs of the decision-making process, the limits of human knowledge, and other real world constraints. (1980, p.25)

There is therefore a complex interplay between evidence, resources questions and evidence- to propose that evidence should in some way take a lead role is therefore idealism in the extreme.

The RIPE model proposed here is an attempt to recognise the complex interaction of factors which influence social work, and indeed other forms of, policy and practice. As Weiss argues:

The process is not linear order from research to decision but a disorderly set of interconnections and back-and-forthness that defies neat diagrams. All kinds of people involved in an area pool their talents, beliefs, and understandings in an effort to make sense of a problem (Weiss, 1997, quoted by Eraut, 1994, p.55)

The reality of social work practice is that there is a role for clear and well-disseminated research and evaluation findings, but that they have to exist a world of competing ideologies, of political conflict and of economic possibility and restraints. This complex mix forms the context in which reflective social work practitioners and managers practice. The RIPE model attempts to move away from the unicausal, static and rationalist elements of the evidence model towards a much more complex, real world, dynamic and 'messy' model of decision-making.

Conclusion

This article has attempted to question the increasing dominance of the evidence school. I have examined four key areas in which the evidence school seems to be presented with considerable difficulties. I have concluded by proposing a model of policy and practice formation which takes the role of evidence seriously, but which recognises that in the real world of policy and practice formation evaluation has to take its place alongside ideology, politics and economics. The evidence led model is not adequate to understanding the messy, real world of decision-making, both within and outside of social work practice.

References

Adams, R., Dominelli, L., Payne, M. (1998) *Social Work: Themes, issues and current debates.* Basingstoke: Palgrave

Blunkett, D. (2000) *Influence or Irrelevance: Can social science improve government?* ESRC/DfEE

Braye, S. (2000) Does Research Matter? *Community Care*, 10-18th February, p.30

Cohen, S. (1985) *Visions of Social Control.* Oxford: Basil Blackwell

Finsterbusch, K., Bender Motz, A. (1980) *Social Research for Policy Decisions.* Belmont: CA: Wadsworth

Hammersley, M. (1997) Educational research and teaching. British Educational Research Journal, 23, 2, 141-160

Frost, N. (2001) Professionalism and the politics of lifelong learning. *Studies in Continuing Education,* 23, 1, 5-19

Frost, N. (2002) Evaluating practice. in R. Adams, L. Dominelli, and M. Payne (Eds.) *Critical Practice in Social Work*. Basingstoke: Palgrave

Leadbeater, C. (2000) *Living on Thin Air*. Harmondsworth: Penguin

MacDonald, G., Sheldon, B., and Gillespie, J. (1992) Contemporary studies of effectiveness of social work. British Journal of Social Work, 22, 6, 615-643

McGuire, J. (1995) *What works: Reducing reoffending. Guidelines for research and practice*. Chichester: Wiley

Muncie, J. (1998) *Youth Crime*. London: Sage

Newman, T., Oakley, A., and Roberts, H. (1996) Weighing up the evidence, *The Guardian*, 10th January

Oakley, A. (2000) *Experiments in Knowing: Gender and method in the social sciences*. Cambridge: Polity

Parton, N. (1985) *The Politics of Child Abuse*. London: Macmillan

Pawson, R., and Tilley, N. (1997) *Realistic Evaluation*. London: Sage

Pawson, R., (2001a) *Evidence Based Policy I. In Search of a Method*. London: ESRC

Pawson, R., (2001b) *Evidence Based Policy II. The Promise of 'Realist Synthesis'*. London: ESRC

Rowe, J, Hundleby, M., and Garnett, L. (1989) *Child Care Now*. London: BAAF

Sheldon, B. (2001) The validity of evidence-based practice in social work: A reply to Stephen Webb. *British Journal of Social Work*, 31, 801-9

Solesbury, W. (2001) *Evidence based Policy: Whence it came and where it's going*. London: ESRC

Part Three

Implementation

7

The Social Care Institute for Excellence: The role of a national institute in developing knowledge and practice in social care

Mike Fisher

Introduction

The UK government's drive towards modernisation has brought substantial changes to the infrastructure of UK society, and the welfare state is now a prime focus for reform. The role of public services in particular has been re-examined with a view to whether they offer best value, and what changes are required to make services genuinely responsive. Within this strategy, there has been particular concern about quality and variation - whether the current balance between regulation and professional discretion is the right one to ensure high quality services, whether the workforce has the skills and knowledge to deliver the kind of quality required, and whether there are remedies to the significant variations in services that cannot be justified by local circumstances.

In 1998, *Modernising Social Services* (Department of Health, 1998) announced a new structure for regulating standards of care (the National Care Standards Commission - NCSC), for training (the Training Organisation for the Personal Social Services - TOPSS) and for registering and setting standards for the social care workforce (the General Social Care Council - GSCC). In children's services, a special initiative called Quality Protects is raising standards, and the whole scheme was underpinned by an extra £1.3bn investment in social services over the three years from 1998-2001. In relation to the workforce, the policy outlined the need to improve the commitment of staff and highlighted the need to improve interdisciplinary training to underpin better collaboration between health and social care staff.

This was shortly followed by *A Quality Strategy for Social Care*, a detailed examination of how to enhance the quality of social services (Department of Health, 2000). This policy document established a new Social Care Institute for Excellence - SCIE - as the major means by which quality and excellence would be defined, it set in place a framework within which local service providers and commissioners would be expected to ensure quality, it conferred a major responsibility on the local Director of Social Services to secure quality, and it reformed social work education and workforce planning. National Service Frameworks would provide models of joint service provision by health and social care and agreed ways of measuring their impact.

SCIE was established in October 2001 as a government-funded, but independent body, dedicated to raising standards of practice across the social care sector, through the better use of knowledge and research. It will be based on a vision of social care which empowers users and promotes the independence of the individual. Building on the Government's concern with knowledge and quality, it will review research and practice, and the views, experience and expertise of users and carers; will use the results of this assessment to create guides for social care practitioners; and will disseminate these across the social care field. (SCIE Prospectus, Department of Health, 2001).

Seeking to highlight the particular role of SCIE in the new set of agencies for social care, the then Social Services Minister John Hutton described it in late 2000 as 'the motor in the engine'. It was therefore designed from the outset to be the key source of evidence-based policy for other agencies to employ in their work, a touchstone and a reference point in a social care arena lacking authoritative bodies of knowledge. This inevitably casts SCIE in a mediating role between different stakeholders in social care, and with a key function to make working relationships with a wide range of organisations offering views of what constitutes the knowledge base. I will return to this theme later.

At the practical level, the Department of Health established SCIE in collaboration with the National Institute for Social Work (NISW), which contributed much of the thinking and practical experience of providing evidence-based policy and practice. SCIE is a small organisation, with a core staff of 35, grouped into four sections covering institutional infrastructure, research reviews, information provision and knowledge management, and quality improvement (including the development of practice guides). A 12-strong board of governors is chaired by Jane Campbell, a leading advocate from the service user movement, whose appointment signals some of the important issues SCIE will have to address, including how to incorporate the views, values and expertise of service users and how to mesh the agendas of a wide range of stakeholders. SCIE will also have a Partners' Council, involving a wide range of stakeholders in SCIE's work.

SCIE was set up to serve England and Wales, with a grant of £2.3m in 2000-01, and £3.4m in 2002-03. SCIE's work is due to extend to Northern Ireland during 2002-03, and it is likely that there will be links with policy developments in the Republic of Ireland. Scotland has a different structure for ensuring quality in social care, including a network of regional centres: it will, however, continue to support and benefit from the development of electronic access to social care knowledge (www.researchweb.org.uk, www.elsc.org.uk).

Social care knowledge and knowledge production

As its prospectus makes clear, SCIE has the initial job of identifying and reviewing material that constitutes the knowledge base in social care. This raises far-reaching questions about the nature of social care knowledge and about ways of assessing its quality, questions to which I will turn later. In the first instance, however, it raises questions about whether the infrastructure is in place to deliver the knowledge that SCIE will evaluate.

Although SCIE's reference points to sister organisations are evolving, during the initial planning there was a clear parallel with the recently established National Institute for Clinical Excellence - a special Health Authority established in 1999 to produce guidance in health care. This parallel was used for instance to evidence the need to ensure that SCIE commissioned its research externally, rather than possessing a fully fledged research capacity in its own right, in order to ensure full independence of its review function. This in turn means that such bodies are designed to operate as 'intelligent customers' of research.

NICE's planned expenditure in 2000/01 was £10.7m, or almost 5 times SCIE's initial budget. Although its staff complement is similar, it spent almost £8m on clinical development, i.e. on developing exactly the kind of infrastructure lacking in social care. This allowed it to mount a programme (in 2000/01) of 26 appraisals, and 10 guides. This is evidence that NICE possesses a very different infrastructure for the supply of knowledge from that available in social care. For example, the NHS generates system-wide priorities for R&D through its largely centralised research policy-making, based on identified priorities for the health of the nation, and operates an R&D levy that generates over £450m p.a. for health research. This allows the development of coherent and reliable bodies of research, which in turn feeds a well-established review and synthesis industry, including the Centre for Reviews and Dissemination at the University of York and the 40+ review groups working under the methodological aegis of the Cochrane Collaboration.

In contrast, there is no centralised framework for organising coherent and cumulative knowledge production in social care. Funding for social work research in the university sector is small-scale: for example, the sum of £3.5m was allocated to English universities in 2001, equivalent to under £10K per head per annum for the research active staff in English universities. Moreover, it is distributed through the Higher Education Funding Councils directly to universities as part of their basic funding, not to support specific programmes of research. The Department of Health invests around £30m p.a. into a policy research programme designed primarily to inform central government policy-makers. Within this, it funds and coordinates research programmes on specific issues, such as the Outcomes in Social Care (OSCA) programme. The Economic and Social Research Council (ESRC) has a responsive programme, which recognises social policy but not (yet) social work as a disciplinary subject: its major commissioned programmes are not specifically targeted at social work or social care, although elements of the recent initiatives on Growing Older and on Evidence-based Policy and Practice do contain relevant research (see www.evidencenetwork.org). Substantial funding amounting to around £20m p.a. is directed towards social care research by the charitable foundations (such the Joseph Rowntree and the Nuffield Foundations.) Criteria for funding clearly reflect issues of national importance, and foundations do liaise to ensure complementary rather than competitive priorities: however, funding must primarily reflect the purposes of the charitable foundations and it is difficult to conceive of such funding as comprising a clear and coordinated national programme.

The absence of a nationally coordinated programme and of agreed national priorities, is compounded by the absence of any agreed system of reviewing and synthesising knowledge. The sister to the Cochrane Collaboration, known as the Campbell Collaboration, held its inaugural plenary in February 2001 and addresses criminal justice and education as well as social care. It has a single group overseeing all work in social work and social care, although this group will draw on members of two methods groups, and there may be some overlap with the other groups in education and criminal justice. In social care, there is no equivalent to the Centre for Reviews and Dissemination at the University of York. Several research-into-practice organisations offer access to research reviews and to practice improvement, but these are either subscription-based and therefore limited to subscribers, based on a specific service user group (e.g. Research Into Practice - RIP - focusing on services to children and families) or service a specific region (e.g. the Centre for Evidence-Based Social Services - CEBSS). While the largest group, RIP, has over 40 member agencies and can make some claim to national salience, the lack of coordination between these groups and, critically, the lack of free access to the knowledge base they have developed, means they do not constitute a nationally coordinated programme.

Table 1

Volume and quality of university-based R&D in health and social care, RAE 1996/2001

Unit of Assessment	No. Units 1996	No. Units 2001	No. Staff 1996	No. Staff 2001	% 5 or 4 1996	% 5 or 4 2001	Average size 1996	Average size 2001
Clinical laboratory	32	25	1097	1107	53	88	34	44
Community-based clinical	35	31	1213	1177	37	77	35	38
Hospital-based clinical	34	31	2814	2473	56	81	83	80
Nursing	35	43	397	575	8	23	11	13
Other – allied to medicine	68	75	661	1016	24	37	10	14
Total	205	205	6812	6348				
Social Work	32	30	354	383	34	43	11	13
Social Policy	46	47	642	958	41	54	14	20
Total	78	77	996	1341				

*Note: a full list of university research centres in social work
and social policy appears in the Appendix.*

The problems of coordination that distinguish social from health care research are overshadowed, however, by the differences in sheer volume. As indicated above, social care R&D spending is probably between 1/8 and 1/10 that of health care (with several caveats about the distinctions between social and health care and what gets counted). The effect is that in social care there are fewer research groups, with fewer staff, and fewer centres of national excellence. Table 1 uses data from the 1996 and 2001 Research Assessment Exercises to show the differences between the health and social care research workforce. Although there are difficulties in mapping social care or health research directly onto Higher Education Funding Councils (HEFC) subject areas, the table gives a rough estimate of size differences, and some indications of differences in quality.

The data show that there are roughly 2.7 times as many research centres in health as in social care, and roughly 4.7 times as many research-active staff. The table uses the RAE rating of 4, 5 or 5* as a measure of the presence of substantial, nationally and internationally relevant research in a centre's work, and this indicates that there is generally a higher proportion and a greater absolute number of centres of research excellence in health care. As a subject area, social work possesses 13 centres of national excellence, while there are 25 in social policy. The 13 social work research centres returned 196.1

research staff (average 15) while the social policy centres returned 588.7 (average 24). Size of staff group is important in terms of continuity of excellence, the interdisciplinarity necessary to explore complex social phenomena, and the ability to respond to short-term demands (such as urgent systematic reviews).

Thus the knowledge industry supporting SCIE is very different from that supporting the development of excellence in health care. There are fewer suppliers, fewer centres of excellence, with fewer staff and less flexibility. Critically, the field lacks cumulative and programmatic research designed to throw concentrated light on specific fields. Moreover, social care research often lacks tested theoretical frameworks and reliable and validated research tools. For technical reasons concerning confidence in the results, social care R&D directed at testing interventions needs to be replicated using such theoretical frameworks and tools in cumulative bodies of research.

In other words, it is not just that the main source of social care R&D - the universities - have much less capacity than their health care counterparts to supply the material for which SCIE would be a customer, it is also that technical confidence in social care R&D as a basis for national policy-making requires coordinated and cumulative research programmes, within an agreed national framework, that the field currently lacks. This points to the need for SCIE to operate differently from its health care counterparts, and in particular to the need to consider a role for SCIE in coordinating and sponsoring social care R&D. There are three main reasons to pursue this.

First, there is no other mechanism for achieving the degree of national coordination required if social care R&D is to serve as the basis for national policy-making, and the modest resources for R&D in this field means that it is all the more critical that it should yield maximum benefit. SCIE should thus act as a focus for generating an overview of the social care R&D agenda, working with the central government, service user and provider organisations, regulatory agencies, with Higher Education, and with independent funders, to identify capacity and gaps, to prioritise research topics and to establish the programme specifications that would lead to a cumulative, programmatic approach. This work resembles that undertaken by ESRC when it establishes a programme of research: it involves commissioning acknowledged experts or expert groups in particular fields, but retaining an overview of the overall framework under development. It is vital to underline the term a degree of national coordination: just as in the case of ESRC, the strategic outline developed by SCIE should not dictate the subsequent work undertaken, but rather should provide a framework within which the social care R&D community can respond in a coordinated and cumulative way. In section 3 of this paper I address some of the issues in identifying and accessing the knowledge base for social care, and, in the conclusions to this paper, I will return to SCIE's role in sponsoring a national research agenda.

The second reason for SCIE adopting a coordinating and sponsoring role is that social care R&D lacks capacity in specific, vital fields. Particularly scarce is research on the social care workforce and on knowledge utilisation. Existing research on the social care workforce is fragmented and unable to generate convincing research-based findings to underpin training and education strategies required for empirically-based practice. Current cross-sectional survey work needs to be aligned with strategic longitudinal and qualitative studies in order to provide this foundation. In the area of knowledge utilisation, important strands of work on knowledge mapping, critical thinking, the development of expertise, and on methods of integrating guidance into professional practice need to be woven together into a strategy to inform the work of social care training and education policy-makers and providers. Section 4 of this paper outlines some of the factors SCIE will take into account in promoting R&D into professional change.

Thirdly, there is no simple parallel in social care to the Cochrane-developed hierarchy of research-based knowledge. Four different approaches - evidence-based practice, knowledge-based practice, realistic evaluation and pluralistic evaluation - highlight the difficulty for SCIE in assembling and filtering knowledge without a working consensus. Developments within the Campbell Collaboration will provide another perspective, although key aspects of the social science debate in the UK appear to be underplayed in current Campbell materials (such as the role of user-defined outcomes, the question of the durability of outcomes and issues in achieving professional change). In the absence of academic consensus on the question of quality, SCIE has commissioned important studies of the classification and quality rating of social science knowledge, in order to offer users a quality guide to accompany the knowledge base. This work draws on existing approaches from various organisations, but divisions within the social care R&D community mean that it is vital that SCIE promote its own approach, with sufficient authority and credibility to achieve a working consensus.

Identifying and accessing social care knowledge

It follows from the argument so far that, in many fields, social care knowledge will inevitably lack coherence and comprehensiveness. In order to develop reliable and relevant guidance, social care requires developed bodies of knowledge, rather than a succession of individual studies (however well executed). Prerequisites for such bodies of knowledge are concerted, intensive effort in well-defined fields of investigation, with cumulative, long-term planned research programmes, incorporating a degree of replication, the capacity to test theoretical frameworks and to undertake the methodological development of reliable tools.

The development of such bodies of knowledge will be characterised by tensions between breadth and depth. The funding system for social care research will not permit the progression of all the required fields simultaneously, and the need to ensure the development of agreed national standards for research requires methodological consensus about the tools for reviewing and synthesising knowledge. This tension between breadth and depth is well illustrated in the balance SCIE must seek between producing research reviews, and resolving the questions about what counts as reliable knowledge. For example, one approach to defining empirically grounded therapeutic interventions requires evidence of statistical superiority and moderate effect size favouring the intervention from at least two randomised controlled comparisons (Chambless and Hollon, 1998). To this it might be added that SCIE will give significant attention to users' and carers' views, so that the question is not merely what works, but what is acceptable to and wanted by service users and carers: gaining such perspectives, and designing and executing research with user and carer involvement as a permeating principle, demands time and resources, and adds complexity to the analysis. Such approaches in turn tax the policies of funding bodies, where demands for large scale work, for genuine user involvement and for replication in order to produce nationally reliable knowledge compete with demands for research in new fields. SCIE must therefore work, initially at least, with very imperfect tools. In this context, the use within RIP of the phrase 'best available evidence' constitutes an important recognition of the state of the knowledge base to support practice.

In another sense, the question whether appropriate research is available is a test of the relationship between research producers and key stakeholders in social care. Funders can obtain the research they want, within the constraints of the skills and availability of researchers. The charitable foundations and the ESRC increasingly require evidence of utility to the end-users of research before funding studies, although there are varying definitions of what is meant by end-users. Only foundations such as Rowntree and Nuffield require evidence of involvement by service users in proposals: other funders may see users primarily in terms of the academic, policymaking and commercial sectors. There is thus a key question whether research production currently takes account of the interests of service users. Increasingly, service user groups are demanding involvement in research production, and in the UK the disability movement has led the critique of research that fails to address the need for change in the social circumstances of disabled people and that fails to involve disabled users (see e.g. Oliver, 1992; Zarb, 1992; Lindow and Morris, 1995; Barnes and Mercer, 1997). Out of this grew the demand for emancipatory research, that is, research aligned from the outset with the views of service users about their priorities and with a clear goal to increase the power of service users to enhance their quality of life.

The call for a new kind of relationship between researchers and service users extends beyond the disability field. For example, the Shaping Our Lives group is a user-led organisation working on user-defined outcomes of different kinds of community care, while the Toronto Group is an alliance of users and researchers established to encourage and support user involvement in research generally. The group Consumers in NHS Research is funded by the NHS to act as a stimulus for user involvement in health care research, and its brief has recently been extended to the social care and public health research funded through the Department of Health's Policy Research Programme.

In one sense social care research cannot progress at all without some involvement of service users, but it should be clear that the concept of emancipatory research goes well beyond mere participation. SCIE is founded on the concept that users should be involved in all stages of reviewing the knowledge base for social care, and this includes a role in setting the research agenda that generates knowledge in the first place. There are now examples of research led throughout by service users (Beresford and Turner, 1997; Beresford and Wallcroft, 1997; Evans and Fisher, 1999b; Evans and Fisher, 1999a), and at least a theoretical case that user-controlled research can enhance research quality (Fisher, 2002).

However, it is not only service users who have been marginalised in research production. The lack of a strategic framework for social care research has meant that practitioners have had almost no voice in determining the key questions that research should address. UK social work research in particular has a poor track record of collaborative knowledge building in partnership with practitioners (Fisher, 2001), and research-in-practice organisations such as RIP and Making Research Count (MRC) have had to invest substantial resources in creating a voice for the practitioner constituency in their subscriber agencies. Small groups such as the Social Work Research Association have tried to bridge the gap between the research and practice communities, but their impact has so far been small-scale. This necessarily raises questions about relevance to practice: since practice concerns have not hitherto informed the research agenda, there is unlikely to be research available on key issues. If research relevant to practice is not available, reviews and practice guidance cannot be entirely driven by research findings, and will have to draw on examples of best practice, and inspection and audit material.

This issue about the relationship between research production and marginalized stakeholders in social care is one that requires a long-term perspective. Of immediate concern, however, is the question whether SCIE can identify and access relevant existing research. This is usually achieved by searching cumulative literature databases, such as Medline, CINAHL or ASSIA. One of the first issues is that social work and social care are based on a multidisciplinary knowledge base (Fisher, 1998) and searching within databases designed to service other academic fields is highly problematic (Howard and Jenson, 1999a). Not only does the literature lie in several disciplines, but those disciplines in addition employ different concepts and conventions. A current expert review under way at Kings' College, London, on social assessment of older people with mental health needs is a case in point: the literature stretches across the medical and nursing literature as well as the social sciences (Moriarty, 2001).

Attempting to focus on more closely defined aspects, such as empowering or participative approaches to assessment, it becomes quickly apparent that, although some concepts may be shared with other disciplines, the specific descriptive terms are often not. Moreover, the reporting conventions, and adherence to them, will differ between disciplines: a relatively well-developed system of structured abstracts in health care literature assists searching (which is often, at the initial stage, undertaken on abstracts or keywords alone), but, despite over a decade of use, authors' adherence to criteria for structured abstracts remains patchy (Sheldon et al., 2001). Abstracting conventions in disciplines outside health care are different or remain to be developed. Searching across disciplines is therefore fundamentally problematic.

The UK has no database that is capable of indexing the vast range of interdisciplinary knowledge required in social care. The SCIE CareData database perhaps comes closest, but is inevitably selective in the fields covered, has not employed a quality filter for inclusion, and does not resolve the question of a universal, structured abstract that would ensure reliable retrieval. The future probably lies in creating translators that take search terms in one database and convert them to the corresponding terms in others.

Even within narrowly defined fields, searching can be unreliable. For example, Dickersin et al. explored whether Medline could identify a particular kind of scientific review known as meta-analysis (where data is pooled from various studies and reanalysed to generate more reliable findings). Using handsearching and citation tracking, the research group's knowledge of the field permitted them to identify 119 such studies: a Medline search found just 57 of these, missing over half (Dickersin et al., 1990). Although this problem has since been addressed within Medline, it illustrates the general point that searching using keywords works only if the keywords are used consistently and reliably, both by authors and by information scientists creating and maintaining the databases.

Searching such databases is potentially undermined by publication bias, meaning both the questions whether all the relevant studies have been published in indexed journals, and whether there is any systematic bias towards publishing particular kinds of reports? In the social care field, much R&D is not published in the 'official' literature, and there is no central research register against which published reports may be checked. Since much R&D goes unreported, basing a review of any given field on the published literature risks ignoring important and relevant work.

A more complex problem is that publication tends to favour 'successful' studies, that is, those that report results in favour of the intervention under scrutiny. Simes' groundbreaking study of cancer treatment showed that taking unpublished studies into account removed the statistical significance of patient benefits reported in the published studies (Simes, 1986). Another investigation into the publication of randomised controlled trials (RCTs) compared the reporting of statistically significant favourable outcomes in published and unpublished studies: of the published trials, 55% contained favourable outcomes, compared with 15% of unpublished trials (Dickersin, 1997). Clearly, if we want to know whether research supports the use of particular interventions, we need to access all the reports, whether published or not. This in turn requires the establishment of a register of all research into particular fields, so that reviewers can check whether all studies have been reported in whatever form. It also places an ethical obligation on researchers to make available to the public record reports of all outcome studies.

In the social care field, this creates particular problems for the durability of any research review. The difficulties in accessing social care knowledge mean that any review is likely to be unable to draw on all the knowledge that is - theoretically - available. It is common for health care reviews to be reviewed every 4-5 years, largely because of the volume and pace of new work. In social care, reviews may have a shorter 'shelf-life' simply because they surface knowledge that has hitherto been inaccessible.

Lastly, research is fraught with epistemological and methodological complexity. All studies have flaws of varying importance and different claims to offer valid and reliable accounts. The question whether the research supports the use of particular interventions therefore requires a scientific assessment of the methodological quality of the work. This raises two distinct questions - whether the report contains the methodological detail required to assess scientific quality, and what kind of measure of quality is to be used.

Most authors are familiar with the problem that publishers encourage abbreviation of methodological detail. Although this may reduce the volume of a given report and enhance its chances of being read, it also risks removing precisely the material that would allow the reviewer to evaluate the findings. Two recent methodological studies of reviews in the social sciences illustrate the issue (Long et al., 2000; Sheldon et al., 2001): both contain examples of reviewed studies where elements of the methodological evaluation are either missing or inconclusive. We do not know from such summaries whether the methodological quality was lacking or whether the report simply did not contain the material to permit an assessment. SCIE's development of this aspect of research reviews will need to incorporate two refinements: to distinguish reports where key aspects of methodological quality have not been observed from those where the methodological material is simply omitted; and in the longer term to establish minimum reporting criteria for methodological detail.

Measures of quality concern not only what kind of rating system is to be used but also whether different kinds of research require different systems. The Cochrane and Campbell Collaborations offer a clear perspective of methods of evaluating experimental studies of the effects of interventions, and promise valuable rigour and consistency. However, there are several problems in prioritising this approach above all others. First, experimental designs require a well-developed existing knowledge base about feasible interventions and ways of measuring their outcomes, and a considerable investment in time and funds. A recent review of studies of changing professional behaviour advises caution, for example, in designing expensive experimental evaluations when there may be little a priori reason to consider that the interventions under investigation are likely to effect change (Freemantle et al., 1999). This is one of the reasons why experimental studies remain relatively rare in social care research. This, in turn, raises key questions about the development of systematic methods of synthesising qualitative studies, on which systematic reviews in social care will often depend.

A second problem in the prioritisation of experimental methods is that these studies often fail to generate relevant knowledge, that is, knowledge that can be used in practice. Problems include whether the intervention is replicable in day to day practice, whether eligibility criteria exclude people from the experimental intervention who are nevertheless eligible for a service, and lack of attention to the views of service users on what counts as good outcomes (Fisher, 1998). A related point is made by critics from a realist evaluation perspective, who caution that much experimental research underplays the context in which an intervention takes place: instead of identifying 'what works', we should aim to know what 'works for whom in what specifiable conditions and given what contextual features' (Smith, 2000). A recent experimental study of health promotion concluded that the method was not best suited to testing interventions that require active participation of the respondents in achieving change (contrasted with the passive mode of patients receiving treatment), and the numbers required for secure analysis were beyond the likely reach of sample recruitment strategies (Barlow et al., 2001). Although experimental methods offer, in the right circumstances, with the right safeguards and with the right sophistication, the best way of assessing the effects of intervention, it is rare that such studies are currently available and unlikely that their widespread adoption would be viable within the resources in social care research.

This suggests that the development of a system for assessing the quality of social care knowledge will need a more subtle and inclusive approach than a simple hierarchy in which findings from experimental studies take precedence. At a very basic level, the lack of experimental evidence, and the difficulties in applying experimental approaches in social care evaluation, forces us to look at the issues in synthesising knowledge from different types of studies. In doing so, it will be necessary to take careful account of applicability to day to day practice, acceptability to service users, and - perhaps most importantly - to take account of different criteria for different kinds of knowledge.

Promoting professional change

SCIE will deliver useful knowledge to practitioners and to their organisations. Whether change subsequently ensues, will depend in part on the individual motivation for self-improvement, influenced by organisation structures, but also in part on new bodies such as the Commission for Social Care Inspection (that will require those commissioning services to take account of best practice) and new functions, such as the quality control role of local directors of social services. This means that SCIE will need to address questions about how organisations are structured to facilitate learning (the so-called 'learning organisation'), and about how organisations elicit, codify and maintain the knowledge held by their members ('knowledge management').

In developing this field, SCIE will need to take careful account of the nature of practice knowledge and on the potential impact of guides for practice. The next section draws on current debates about the concept of tacit or implicit knowledge as part of professional practice; on the literature concerning the reasoning of practitioners, and on the differences between novices and experts in their approach to reasoning; on debates about the epistemological status of guides and how they are viewed by practitioners; and on reports from health care about the adoption of guides and of evidence more broadly.

Tacit or implicit knowledge

Collins defines tacit knowledge as referring to 'those things that we know how to do but are unable to explain to someone else' (Collins, 2000). Bicycle riding is the most commonly used example: few know the rules of physics involved in bicycle riding, and even if they could be stated it is highly unlikely that this would help many learn to ride. Bicycle riding thus requires the acquisition and use of tacit knowledge.

The opposite of tacit or implicit knowledge is explicit knowledge: tacit knowledge is closer to learning from experience while explicit knowledge approximates to propositional knowledge (sometimes called knowledge about rather than know-how). Organisational theorists, concerned to maximise the organisational benefit of knowledge held by staff, express great regret over the divorce between these two kinds of knowledge (Senge, 1990), and it is sometimes held that the former strength of the Japanese economy was founded on knowledge creation that overcame this dualism (Nonaka and Takeuchi, 1998).

In social care, Zeira and Rosen suggest that 'tacit knowledge, often referred to as intuition, common sense, or practice wisdom, is the implicit store of knowledge used in practice' (Zeira and Rosen, 2000: 104). This concept is important in social care because there is a widespread assumption that practitioners either know very little or have the wrong kind of knowledge. Often this is based on surveys that request practitioners to name the knowledge they possess, on the assumption that the ability to name knowledge equates with the possession of that knowledge (and that the inability to name knowledge equates with ignorance) (Sinclair and Jacobs, 1994; Sheldon and Chilvers, 2001).

It is undeniable that the social care knowledge of many practitioners may be extremely thin, and that many practitioners are under-trained and lacking access to research-based knowledge or to well-developed ways of using it. However, the assumptions underpinning this kind of survey endanger the process of introducing new knowledge, because they ignore the potential to link new information to existing knowledge, and because they mask the extent to which practitioners may resist new approaches which seem 'old hat' to them in the light of their tacit knowledge. The approach also conveys a sense of 'academics know best', that is directly contrary to most thinking on collaborative knowledge development for social care (McCartt-Hess and Mullen, 1995).

Although it is fashionable to contrast the randomness of practice wisdom with the (potentially) systematic approach of evidence-based practice, those who have researched the use of tacit knowledge in social care suggest it provides a rational foundation for selecting interventions, and a way of maximising the fit between practice and the desired outcomes (e.g. Zeira and Rosen, 2000). Another study found that 75% of decisions were supported by a recognisable rationale, and argued that inarticulacy amongst practitioners should not be mistaken for an atheoretical stance or for an absence of research-based knowledge (Rosen et al., 1995). Practice is probably more coherent and ordered than initial impressions would indicate, and therefore SCIE's approach to practice development must recognise and build on this, rather than view existing practice as best swept away.

Furthermore, knowledge transfer can be undermined by lack of attention to tacit knowledge. Even where there are well-established conventions for knowledge transfer (such as in the reporting of scientific experiments), there remains the possibility of omitting essential knowledge. Collins describes a circuit diagram for a laser that left the position of a component to the discretion of the scientist, whereas (unknown to the original author) the success of the experiment actually required a specific configuration. This is one reason why scientific experiments sometimes prove difficult to repeat (Collins, 2000, p. 109).

The study of expertise and of decision-making suggests that all practitioners employ forms of tacit knowledge, which can be made explicit to varying degrees (Fook et al., 1997; Fook et al.,

2000; Sheppard et al., 2000a; Sheppard et al., 2000b). The lack of a fully developed research tradition, of training and (sometimes) of basic literacy probably means that practitioners in social care are less adept at specifying such knowledge than in other fields. This often leads to an assertion by practitioners either that good practice is too difficult to define or that all you need is common sense.

Where tacit knowledge can be made explicit, it can resemble the kind of rules that might be incorporated into guides. For example, to return to bicycle riding, a set of rules might be generated around riding in traffic. This kind of knowledge mapping has the potential to surface the 'rules' or implicit assumptions that can sometimes amount to a set of principles, and SCIE is likely to invest some resources into developing this field of inquiry. If, in addition to being explicitly stated, such principles can be subject to empirical testing, they are a source of guides directly deriving from practice (Zeira and Rosen, 2000). However, such rules always require improvisation ('traffic sense'), because the range of circumstances varies too widely for rote adherence to rules ('going by the book'). Again, it will be vital to balance emphasis on individual learning with recognition of the organisational factors influencing the application of learning to practice. For example, an Israeli project to improve child care services was based on the assumption that good practice means converting 'the tacit knowledge of a professional community into actionable knowledge' (Rosenfeld and Sabah, 1999). That the existence of tacit knowledge was acknowledged is vital, but conversion into 'actionable' knowledge (meaning with direct practice consequences) requires additional work addressing how the organisation can support and foster practice change.

SCIE's work on practice guides is therefore designed to draw on studies that report the diversity of practice: for example, an intervention such as care management may vary widely in its implementation among different practitioners, and descriptions of the outcomes for groups of practitioners may conceal substantial variation within groups. SCIE will also examine examples of tacit knowledge amounting to practice-derived principles, and whether they have common characteristics. In addition, it is vital to examine descriptions of transfer of learning (in order to focus on the tacit element in practice that requires acquisition through means other than written material or direct influence), and to examine descriptions of practice improvisation ('traffic sense') that inevitably accompany the adoption of any guide.

Clinical reasoning

The evidence-based practice movement draws on a long tradition of studying practitioners' reasoning. The main text here is Gambrill's work on critical thinking (Gambrill, 1990), recently restated in the context of evidence-based practice (Macdonald and Sheldon, 1998; Gambrill, 1999). The concern here is to identify sources of error in the way practitioners think about their work (reasoning). Typical sources of error include:

- getting the facts wrong;
- assuming two things are connected when they are not;
- assuming one thing has caused another, when it has not;
- assuming one thing will cause another, when it will not (Gambrill, 1990: 2).

The connection with practice guides is two-fold: practitioners should have an explicit rationale for the choice of intervention (i.e. be able to reason a case for it) and guides may need to challenge accepted wisdom that contains faulty reasoning or has not been subject to logical scrutiny (for a good example of accepted wisdom in medicine about the relationship between salt and blood pressure, see Freedman and Pettiti, 2001). There is a further connection with evidence-based practice, in the sense that faulty reasoning may prevent adherence to the core definition of such practice as 'the conscientious, explicit, and judicious use of current best evidence in making decisions about the care of individuals' (Sackett et al., 1997: 2).

Lastly, the study of practitioners' reasoning may give clues as to how to structure guides. At a very basic level, for example, guides may be constructed to challenge assumptions commonly held by practitioners. However, if we make a connection between the literature on clinical reasoning and on expertise, we can see several further dimensions affecting the construction of guides.

Gambrill connects the two issues by discussing the differences between novices and experts in their reasoning processes. She argues for example that experts are better at problem-solving and at reviewing their decision in the light of evidence (Gambrill, 1990: 14-15). Reviews of critical reasoning in medicine, nursing and occupational therapy suggest that what differentiates expert from non-expert practitioners is that they use some form of mental schemata or pattern recognition to reach conclusions - that is they draw on past experience to match the current problems with previous patterns they have observed. This fits Wakefield's definition of expertise as

> *the ability to perceive holistic relations between the current problem and a vast array of previously experienced situations. (Wakefield, 1990)*

Eraut makes similar observations when he argues that

> *progression from proficiency to expertise finally happens when the decision-making as well as the situational understanding becomes instinctive rather than analytic; and this requires significantly more experience. (Eraut, 1994, pp.125-126)*

In a study of occupational therapists, Roberts argues that practitioners spend substantial time hypothesis-testing and cue-searching (Roberts, 1996). Studies of clinical assessment in medicine also show that hypothesis testing is a critical part of the reasoning process: typically assessment includes consideration of no more than five initial hypotheses, and one of these is likely to prove the 'correct' interpretation (Elstein et al., 1979). The more experienced the practitioner, the more rapid the cue-searching and hypothesis-testing, because it draws to a greater degree on mental schemata. In social work, Sheppard's recent work on hypothesis-testing suggests a relationship between expertise and the depth and complexity of the hypotheses generated (Sheppard et al., 2000a; 2000b).

It would be a mistake, however, to suggest that experts would always agree about appropriate intervention, or all deliver it in exactly the same way. For example, Fook and her colleagues show that, among several experts, there were a variety of ways of performing the same tasks, and the authors suggest indeed that standardisation risks stultifying expertise (Fook et al., 1997, p.412).

There are several key implications for SCIE's work on practice guides. Firstly, guides should offer different access points and presentation approaches to cater for the wide range of reasoning that will be in use among practitioners consulting the guides. For example, few practitioners with any experience are likely to welcome a step by step primer, whereas such an approach may be more appropriate in qualifying training. Secondly, guides should contain credible case examples (preferably from actual practice), since this will aid practitioner recognition of patterns or mental schemata. Thirdly, guides should name the range of possible hypotheses, and possible supporting cues, in order to assist the hypothesis-testing that is already part of practitioners' reasoning. Lastly, guides should be clear where different forms of intervention are equally valid, and leave scope for practitioners to exercise their expertise in selecting and delivering services: the objective is to assist better decision-making, not to dictate what decision should be made.

Guides

More explicit attention to the role of guides in practice change is available from the US literature, particularly a special edition of Research in Practice, May 1999. In the US, the emphasis on guides increased as it became clear that other methods of enhancing the use of evidence were failing. The profession moved towards practice guides as a means of embedding research in advice without requiring practitioners to have access to the original research or competence in its interpretation (Howard and Jenson, 1999b). In contrast, guides development in the UK has a much stronger basis in the attempt to achieve managerial control over professional discretion (and of course, to the extent that such discretion produces unacceptable variation, this does underpin SCIE's emphasis on guides). Although guides are used in the US to enforce standards of practice, including in litigation, this was not the primary reason for their development.

The US debate highlights several key problems (Howard and

Jenson, 1999b; Howard and Jenson, 1999a; Jackson, 1999; Kirk, 1999; Nurius et al., 1999; Richey and Roffman, 1999; Wambach et al., 1999), including

- the difficulty of building strong stakeholder communities in order to ensure guide development properly reflects different interests;
- the need for economic evaluation, particularly where guides indicate a number of viable interventions;
- the need for a viable literature base from which to derive research-based evidence, and problems in defining the appropriate literature to search;
- whether the published literature is representative of empirical knowledge about what does and does not work (Richey & Roffman cite evidence, supporting the earlier discussion in this paper, that studies reporting positive effects are more likely to be published);
- the difficulty of ensuring effective dissemination and effective access to the literature base for practitioners;
- the dangers of developing guides that are too long or too qualified to be helpful (Kirk illustrates with a guide relating to schizophrenia that is 63 pages long with 518 citations, and which hedges each key questions with reservations such that a practitioner could not possibly gain a clear direction for practice);
- lack of evidence of a positive relationship between the use of guides and better outcomes;
- the fact that implementation in the field requires adaptation ('Implementing clinical guides in the field will always require some tinkering by practitioners who strive to incorporate unique client, agency and community factors': Richey and Roffman, p.316), and that it becomes difficult to know when an intervention has been adapted to such a degree that it is not longer that recommended in the guide;
- the disjunction between the predominant emphasis in guides on individual behaviour in contrast to the potential for change via better use of community support systems;
- the need for guides, like practice, to be multidisciplinary;
- the need to link guides to fundamental value systems held by practitioners.

Perhaps the best statement of guide requirements is by Proctor and Rosen (Proctor and Rosen, 2000), who define guides as 'a set of systematically compiled and organized knowledge statements that are designed to enable practitioners to find, select and use the interventions that are most effective and appropriate.' They call for guides to include

- targets for intervention, and for each target an array of alternative interventions;
- how to choose interventions, and to identify gaps and qualifications in the underpinning knowledge base.
- a positive orientation towards including outcomes that focus on harm reduction or maintenance of current well-being (contrasted with many health care guides that assume problem elimination is the goal). An example would be spouse abuse, which may well be best prevented by shelter placement than by attempting behavioural change in the abusing spouse;
- recognition that there will normally be a number of intermediate outcomes leading towards an outcome that requires long-term change;
- attention to what degree or intensity of intervention is required to achieve what degree of effect ('dose' effect);
- for each intervention, known factors affecting its efficacy should be mentioned (e.g. age);
- recognition that 'practice guides are not immutable and infallible knowledge statements. On the contrary, such statements should make clear that in practically every situation, practitioners will encounter gaps in knowledge' (p.16).

Evidence-based practice and the adoption of guides in health care

If SCIE is to profit from such lessons in the construction of guides, it may also learn from the work in the health care sector on the adoption of guides. This is all the more necessary given that the study of guides and professional change is under-developed in the UK: a Nuffield paper on the implementation of guides shows that only 14 of 91 studies examined were UK based (Nuffield Institute for Health et al., 1994). The potential in this field of study is demonstrated in the finding that 81 of the 87 studies on clinical process reported significant improvements, as did 12 of 17 studies of patient outcomes. However, as in other key fields, SCIE will need to promote and foster a systematic programme of UK-based studies of the adoption of research-based guides.

The starting point for this discussion is the increasing evidence that some interventions to change professional behaviour are so poorly conceptualised that it makes little sense to invest in carefully controlled studies to evaluate their effectiveness (Freemantle et al., 1999). This reinforces the need to undertake exploratory development work to test the plausibility of interventions before undertaking expensive controlled trials. This kind of R&D is most likely to require what are called non-equivalent group designs, in which the unit of analysis is the team, rather than the individual practitioner. Studies of health care professionals more widely confirm the importance of teams as the basis for learning (Hart and Fletcher, 1999). Non-equivalent group designs require large numbers of teams for study (in order to reflect the range of team characteristics and in statistical terms to minimise bias arising from unknown factors within teams), and sampling to achieve adequate representation of the conditions under which the intervention is to be tested. In addition, these designs require extensive pre- and post-intervention measures in order to assess whether observed changes have been influenced by pre-existing trends. The implications for SCIE are that:

1. it will need to foster research characterised by long-term relationships with a wide range of teams, and
2. to ensure research covers the range of teams and their characteristics in order to achieve representative samples.

Professional change is most successful if promoted through a variety of methods: the printed word, coaching, consultation and educational outreach and so on (Freemantle et al., 1999). There is a graded effect, where single interventions (such as information transfer) are less often effective than single interventions plus feedback, which in turn are less effective than multiple interventions: 'information transfer is probably always needed at some point in the process of implementing change, but more interventions are usually needed to achieve real changes in the practice routines of clinicians' (Wensing et al., 1998). Similarly, education is less often cited as a factor in prompting change in clinical practice than organisational factors (Allery et al., 1997). In addition, intervention methods must be closely specified and controlled in order to be replicable, and they must be designed so as to be achievable in ordinary, everyday practice in social care (Fisher, 1998).

Research in this field will also need to recognise that change effects are typically very small: it is not just that professional behaviour is difficult to change, it is that the evidence for any changes is likely to be marginal, and capable of different interpretation (see e.g. Cohen and Fisher, 1987). The solution is to replicate studies so that assessments may be made of the validity and reliability of small effect sizes. This means that SCIE will need to focus R&D effort on particular areas in order to build cumulative and reliable bodies of evidence. This is most likely to be achieved through a combination of in-house effort (in order to test designs and offer authoritative leadership) and focused, collaborative commissioning (in order to promote cumulative knowledge building in specific fields).

Conclusions

The reshaping of social care under the aegis of modernisation brings into focus key questions about what we mean by knowledge, and about its role in creating and maintaining high quality services. The establishment of a national institute with a mission to define, create and promote excellence inevitably raises questions about hubris and control: is it realistic, let alone possible, to reach for excellence, and will the effect be to control and regulate knowledge production and utilisation rather than to foster diversity and dynamism in the R&D community?

These are the major challenges that SCIE is tasked to confront. Modernisation may be construed as the attempt to undermine professional discretion and local judgement, rather than to provide better grounds for decision-making; and to dictate what counts as knowledge, rather than to create consensus and coherence in the epistemology of social care.

Only time will tell, but two factors suggest optimism. First, SCIE has no regulatory powers: its work must necessarily be based on persuasion and collaboration, and on winning 'hearts and minds'. Only if practitioners, policy-makers, and users and carers are convinced, will change follow. Secondly, SCIE starts with an inclusive stance: there are no pre-existing 'regimes of truth' (Shaw and Gould, 2001) that seek to marginalize some voices and to prioritise others. SCIE's initial work included a consultation exercise and commissioned work to seek a wide range of stakeholders' views about what counts as knowledge and as best practice. Certainly, it will be necessary to bring coherence to the field, and to prioritise development in some fields over others, but this must be achieved through accountable, transparent decision-making, rather than through dogma or doctrine. As the prospectus cited in the introduction suggests, SCIE also recognises the knowledge and experience of service users and carers as a key source of change in social policy in recent years, and these voices are assured a prominent role in SCIE's work.

As a national organisation, SCIE must therefore operate according to inclusive principles, aiming to coordinate and foster, rather than to regulate and stifle. In providing a national focus for knowledge production, dissemination and implementation, SCIE's approach must be aimed at providing a framework, rather than a straitjacket, for research, development and practice in social care.

References

Allery, L., Owen, P. and Robling, M. (1997) Why general practitioners and consultants change their clinical practice: A critical incident study. *British Medical Journal*, 314, 870-874.

Barlow, J., Stewart-Brown, S. and Elbourne, D. (2001) *Researching the Effectiveness of Complex Community-based Interventions: Lessons from research*. Oxford: Institute of Health Sciences.

Barnes, C. and Mercer, G. (Eds.) (1997) *Doing Disability Research.* Leeds: Disability Press.

Beresford, P. and Turner, M. (1997) *It's Our Welfare: Report of the Citizen Commission on the Future of the Welfare State.* London: NISW.

Beresford, P. and Wallcroft, J. (1997) Psychiatric system survivors and emancipatory research: Issues, overlaps and differences. in C. Barnes and G. Mercer (eds.) *Doing Disability Research.* Leeds: The Disability Press. 67-87.

Chambless, D. and Hollon, S. (1998) Defining empirically supported therapies. *Journal of Consulting and Clinical Psychology,* 66, 7-18.

Cohen, J. and Fisher, M. (1987) The recognition of mental health problems by doctors and social workers. *Practice,* 1, 3, 225-240.

Collins, H. (2000) What is tacit knowledge? in T. Schatzki, K. Knorr-Cetina and E. von Savigny (eds.) *The Practice Turn in Contemporary Theory.* London: Routledge. pp.107-119.

Department of Health (1998) *Modernising Social Services: Promoting independence, improving protection and raising standards.* London: The Stationery Office.

Department of Health (2000) *A Quality Strategy for Social Care.* London: Department of Health.

Dickersin, K. (1997) How important is publication bias? A synthesis of available data. *AIDS Education and Prevention,* 9, Supplement, 15-21.

Dickersin, K., Higgins, K. and Meinert, C. (1990) Identification of meta-analyses: The need for standard terminology. *Controlled Clinical Trials,* 11, 52-66.

Elstein, A., Schulman, L. and Sprafka, S. (1979) *Medical Problem Solving: An analysis of clinical reasoning.* London: Harvard University Press.

Eraut, M. (1994) *Developing Professional Knowledge and Competence.* London: Falmer Press.

Evans, C. and Fisher, M. (1999a) Collaborative evaluation with service users: Moving towards user-controlled research. in I. Shaw and J. Lishman (eds.) *Evaluation and Social Work Practice.* London: Sage. PP.101-117.

Evans, C. and Fisher, M. (1999b) User controlled research and empowerment. in W. Shera and L. Wells (eds.) *Empowerment Practice in Social Work: Developing richer conceptual foundations.* Toronto: Canadian Scholars' Press. 348-369.

Fisher, M. (1998) Research, knowledge and practice in community care. *Issues in Social Work Education*, 17, 2, 17-30.

Fisher, M. (2001) A Strategic Framework for Social Work Research. in A. Mullender (ed.) *Theorising Social Work Research: Report to ESRC, University of Warwick*. available at http://www.nisw.org.uk/tswr.

Fisher, M. (2002) The role of service users in problem formulation and technical aspects of social research. *Social Work Education*, 21, 3, 305-312.

Fook, J., Ryan, M. and Hawkins, L. (1997) Towards a theory of social work expertise. *British Journal of Social Work*, 27, 399-417.

Fook, J., Ryan, M. and Hawkins, L. (2000) *Professional Expertise: Practice, Theory and education for working in uncertainty*. London: Whiting and Birch.

Freedman, D. and Pettiti, D. (2001) Salt and blood pressure: Conventional wisdom reconsidered. *Evaluation Review*, 25, 3, 267-287.

Freemantle, N., Wood, J. and Mason, J. (1999) *Evaluating Change in Professional Behaviour: Issues in design and analysis*. York: University of York, Centre for Health Economics

Gambrill, E. (1990) *Critical Thinking in Clinical Practice*. San Francisco: Jossey-Bass.

Gambrill, E. (1999) Evidence-based practice: An alternative to authority-based practice. *Families in Society*, 80, 4, 341-350.

Hart, E. and Fletcher, J. (1999) Learning how to change: A selective analysis of literature and experience of how teams learn and organisations change. *Journal of Interprofessional Care*, 13, 1, 53-63.

Howard, M. and Jenson, J. (1999a) Barriers to development, utilization and evaluation of social work practice guidelines. *Research on Social Work Practice*, 9, 3, 347-364.

Howard, M. and Jenson, J. (1999b) Clinical practice guidelines: Should social work develop them? *Research on Social Work Practice*, 9, 3, 283-301.

Jackson, V. (1999) Clinical practice guidelines: Should social work develop them? *Research on Social Work Practice*, 9, 3, 331-337.

Kirk, S. (1999) Good intentions are not enough: Practice guidelines for social work. *Research on Social Work Practice*, 9, 3, 302-310.

Lindow, V. and Morris, J. (1995) *Service User Involvement: Synthesis of findings and experience in the field of community care*. York: Joseph Rowntree Foundation.

Long, A., Godfrey, M., Randall, T., Brettle, A. and Grant, M. (2000)

Feasibility of Undertaking Systematic Reviews in Social Care. Leeds, Nuffield Institute for Health.

Macdonald, G. and Sheldon, B. (1998) Changing one's mind: The final frontier? *Issues in Social Work Education*, 18, 1, 3-25.

McCartt-Hess, P. and Mullen, E. (1995) Bridging the gap: Collaborative considerations in practitioner-researcher knowledge-building partnerships. in P. McCartt-Hess and E. Mullen (eds.) *Practitioner-Researcher Partnerships: Building knowledge from, in and for practice*. Washington DC: NASW Press. pp.1-30.

Moriarty, J. ((2001) *Methodological Issues in Undertaking an Expert Review on Assessing the Mental Health Needs of Older People*. London: NISW.

Nonaka, I. and Takeuchi, H. (1998) The knowledge creating company. in C. Mabey, G. Salaman and J. Storey (eds.) *Strategic Human Resource Management: A reader*. London: Sage. pp.310-324.

Nuffield Institute for Health, University of Leeds, Centre for Health Economics, and NHS Centre for Reviews and Dissemination, University of York, Research Unit and Royal College of Physicians (1994) Implementing clinical practice guidelines. *Effective Health Care*, 8, 1-12.

Nurius, P., Kemp, S. and Gibson, J. (1999) Practitioners' perspectives on sound reasoning: Adding a worker-in-context perspective. *Administration in Social Work*, 23, 1, 1-27.

Oliver, M. (1992) Changing the social relations of research production. *Disability, Handicap and Society*, 7, 2, 101-114.

Proctor, E. and Rosen, A. (2000) 'The structure and function of social work practice guidelines'. Paper prepared for 'Toward the development of practice guidelines for social work intervention'. St Louis, MO: Washington University, George Warren Brown School of Social Work

Richey, C. and Roffman, R. (1999) On the sidelines of guidelines: Further thoughts on the fit between clinical guidelines and social work practice. *Research on Social Work Practice*, 9, 3, 311-321.

Roberts, A. (1996) Approaches to reasoning in occupational therapy: A critical exploration. *British Journal of Occupational Therapy*, 59, 5, 233-236.

Rosen, A., Proctor, E., Morrow-Howell, N. and Staudt, M. (1995) Rationales for practice decisions: Variations in knowledge use by decision task and social work service. *Research on Social Work Practice*, 5, 4, 501-523.

Rosenfeld, J.M. and Sabah, Y. (1999) Organizational Learning and Knowledge Management Project for Social Services in the National Program for Children at Risk: Interim Progress Report: October 1998-October 1999 Discussion Paper, Jerusalem: Ministry of Labor and Social Affairs, Strategic Planning Division, in collaboration with JDC-Brookdale Institute Children and Youth Center and Ashalim.

Sackett, D., Richardson, W., Rosenberg, W. and Haynes, R. (1997) *Evidence-based Medicine: How to practice and teach EMB.* Oxford: Oxford University Press.

Senge, P. (1990) *The Fifth Discipline: the art and practice of learning organizations.* New York: Century Press.

Shaw, I. and Gould, N. (eds.) (2001) *Qualitative Social Work Research.* London: Sage.

Sheldon, B. and Chilvers, R. (2001) *Evidence-based Social Care: Problems and prospects.* Lyme Regis: Russell House.

Sheldon, T., Bradshaw, J., Baldwin, S., Sinclair, I. and Burrows, R. (2001) *Methodologies for Socially Useful Systematic Reviews in Social Policy: ESRC End of Award Report.* York: University of York.

Sheppard, M., Newstead, S., DiCaccavo, A. and Ryan, K. (2000a) *Comparative Hypothesis Assessment, Triangulation and Quasi Triangulation as Process Knowledge Assessment Strategies in Social Work Practice.* Plymouth: University of Plymouth.

Sheppard, M., Newstead, S., DiCaccavo, A. and Ryan, K. (2000b) Reflexivity and the development of process knowledge in social work: a classification and empirical study. British Journal of Social Work, 30, 4, 465-488.

Simes, J. (1986) Publication bias: The case for an international registry of clinical trials. *Journal of Clinical Oncology*, 4, 1529-1541.

Sinclair, R. and Jacobs, C. (1994) *Research in Personal Social Services: the Experience of Three Local Authorities.* London: National Children's Bureau.

Smith, D. (2000) The limits of positivism revisited. in ESRC Seminar Series *Theorising Social Work Research.* http://www.nisw.org.uk/tswr.

Wakefield, J. (1990) Expert systems, Socrates and the philosophy of mind. in L. Videka-Sherman and W. Reid (eds.) *Advances in Clinical Social Work Research.* Silver Springs: NASW. pp.90-101.

Wambach, K., Haynes, D. and White, B. (1999) Practice guidelines: Rapprochement or estrangement between social work practitioners and researchers. *Research on Social Work Practice*, 9, 3, 322-330.

Wensing, M., Van Der Weijden, T. and Grol, R. (1998) Implementing guidelines and innovations in general practice: Which interventions are effective? *British Journal of General Practice*, 48, 991-997.

Zarb, G. (1992) On the road to Damascus: First steps towards changing the relations of disability research production. *Disability, Handicap and Society*, 7, 2, 125-139.

Zeira, A. and Rosen, A. (2000) 'Unraveling 'tacit knowledge': What social workers do and why they do it. *Social Service Review*, 74, 103-123.

APPENDIX

RAE results in Social Policy and Social Work, UK, 1992, 1996, 2001

	Social Work			Social Policy		
	1992	1996	2001	1992	1996	2001
Anglia Polytechnic	-	2	3a			
Bath	2	3a	-	5	5	5
Birmingham	3	3a	-	4	4	4 (PP)
4(SP/SW)						
Bolton				-	-	2
Bradford	3	3a	-			4
Brighton				2	3b	3b
Bristol	3	4	5*	3	5	5
Brunel College	2	3b	3a	4	4	-
Central Lancashire	-	-	3a			
Buckinghamshire			-	-	3b	3b
Cheltenham & Glos			-	-	2	
Chichester				-	-	2
City				-	-	3a
Coventry	-	-	3b			
De Montfort	1	2	3a			
Durham	-	-	4			
East Anglia	5	5	5			
East London	-	-	3b			
Edge Hill				-	3b	3b
Exeter	2	3b	4			
Goldsmiths	2	2	-	3	3a	4
Hertfordshire	-	-	3b			
Huddersfield	2	4	5			
Hull	4	3a	3a	3	4	4
Keele	3	4	-	-	4	5
Kent	3	3b	4	5	5	5*
Lancaster	4	5	5			
Leeds						5
Leeds Met				3	3b	
Leicester	3	4	-	-	3a	3a
Lincs/Humberside				1	3b	3a
Liverpool	1	3a	-			4

Liverpool JM	-	2	3b	-	3b	3b
LSE				5	5*	5*
London Guildhall				-	2	
Luton	-	3b	3a	-	2	
Manchester				-	4	5
Manchester Met.	-	2	3a			
Middlesex	2	3b	-	-	4	4
Newcastle				2	3a	4
North London				2	2	3a
Northumbria				2	3b	3a
Nottingham	-	-	3b			4
Nottingham Trent						3a
Open				3	4	3a
Oxford				-	3a	4
Portsmouth				2	3b	
Plymouth						4
Reading	-	-	3b			
Royal Holloway				3	3a	4
St Martins				-	1	
Sheffield				4	4	5
Sheffield Hallam				2	3b	3a
Southampton	3	3a	3a			5
South Bank				3	4	4
Staffordshire	-	2	3b			
Sunderland				2	2	3a
Sussex				2	3a	-
Thames Valley				2	3b	3a
Warwick	3	5	5			
Westminster						3a
York	3	5	5	5	5	5
Dundee	3	3a	4			
Edinburgh	3	4	-	3	4	4
Glasgow					4	4
Glasgow Caledonian				-	2	
Paisley				-	-	3a
Stirling	5	5*	5			
Glamorgan				-	3b	3a

Bangor/UCNW				3	4	3a
NE Wales Institute	-	2	2			
Wales, Newport				-	1	
Swansea/UCS	2	4	5			3a
Queen's Belfast	2	3a	4	-	3b	
Ulster	-	3b	3b	4	4	4

(Source: HEFCs)

8
Promoting evidence based practice in a child care charity: The Barnardo's experience

Tony Newman and Di McNeish

Pity the poor social worker trapped between a post-modernist blizzard of narratives, discursive space and heurism, and an empirical swamp of randomised controlled trials, systematic reviews, critical appraisal and Bayesian statistics. On one side, an ideology that apparently questions the existence of any objective reality and locates personal experience at the centre of the evidential universe. On the other, one which seemingly proposes that the infinite complexity of humanity can be subjected to natural law, and believes that the unmeasurable can be measured. As an observer in a recent debate between protagonists of both perspectives commented in a conference feedback form:

> There appears to be an academic in-fight going on which wasn't clearly outlined. Interesting, but a bit removed from practitioners' concerns.

Whatever the respective merits of these academic disputes, the view from the shop floor is clear - the people who actually deliver services are asking for practical tools, not complex discussions on epistemology.

What works?

Why 'what works'?. When the authors of this paper, along with other colleagues both within and outside Barnardo's, began an initiative in 1994 to promote evidence-based practice in social care, the term seemed both fresh and challenging. It subsequently became the title of a popular series of 'best evidence' reviews, the first of which was published in 1995 (Macdonald and Roberts, 1995). We asked the question:

> *Experts have a duty not to intervene in people's lives on the basis of whim and intuition. But people at the receiving end of interventions are frequently vulnerable and powerless. How certain can they be that the services offered to them have been properly evaluated, that one service is better than another, or that any service is likely to be of greater benefit than no service at all? (Oakley and Roberts, 1996, p.1).*

While no credit (or blame) is due to us for the growth in popularity of this phrase, the term has entered public and professional discourse, and is asked routinely by politicians when reviewing the possible range of welfare investment options. While inevitably suffering from over-familiarity, asking the question 'what works?' has led to other important questions being posed. What works for whom? Who decides what works? What do we mean by 'works'? And, given the immense richness and complexity of humanity, how realistic is it to seek to compile such a body of knowledge in social care services?

Interventions in social care, health or education, do not work well for all people, in all contexts, all of the time. Even if they did, it is unlikely that they would remain the intervention of choice indefinitely, as policies, practice and people's expectations change over time. In many cases, there may be little to choose from between different types of interventions, or the difference between intervening and just doing nothing may be minimal. In some cases, positive shifts at an individual level may need to be aggregated to detect any overall benefits at a population level, and this may only be visible when the experience of hundreds or thousands of people are analysed. This may be compelling evidence for an epidemiologist, but less persuasive to the average UK parent whose main interest is the welfare of the 1.7 children in her family.

What matters?

There is no single best way of helping a child affected by behavioural problems, no single best treatment for attention deficit disorders and no single best method of preventing youth crime. The chosen intervention will be driven by a wide range of factors; empirical evidence certainly, but also the views of children and families, the ecology of their environment, professional experience, the skills available and any resource constraints. However, by a conscious attention to the evidence base, we can increase the odds that a more, rather than a less effective intervention will result. Evidence-based practice cannot deliver certainties, just increase probabilities, and this is the most that any approach claiming to be 'evidence-based' can hope to achieve. We also need to remember that much of what *matters* to children cannot be provided by professional organisations, however richly resourced. No professional has a magic wand that can make children attractive to their peers, repair their parents' broken marriages or help them pass all their exams. However, some of the things that practitioners and policy makers do *can* make a difference, even in these areas. Being realistic about what we cannot do, will leave us more time and resources to devote to what we can do successfully.

Meeting the information needs of practitioners

The delivery of effective services, and the generation of a knowledge base that can underpin this is what, we would suggest, the public have a right to expect from any human service profession. However, while the ethical qualities of services have historically been stressed by both the UK and American professional social work associations, concern as to their actual *effectiveness* has been less prominent (Myers and Thyer, 1997). It is only recently that this dimension - that is, the extent to which the activities of social care agencies bring about the changes intended - has moved centre stage in the policy arena. Social work research in the UK, and indeed the USA, has been largely pre-occupied - judged, at least, by publication volume - by theory, political discussion and descriptive studies. These are, of course, vital aspects of any dynamic profession. In the USA, publications which examine what social workers *do*, and the corresponding effects on service users of their doing it account, according to a recent review, for only 14 per cent of articles in social work journals (Rosen *et al.*, 1999). In the UK, of the 356 articles appearing in the British Journal of Social Work during the 1990s, only five were outcome studies (Sheldon and Macdonald, 1999). Academic social work, unlike medicine, remains curiously unwilling, or unable, to meet the information needs of its core user group - the ones who actually deliver services. This is surely not a satisfactory situation for a profession whose *raison d'être* is intervention, not observation.

Social care services, in common with health, the probation service and increasingly education, have been directed to base practice on 'the best evidence of what works' (Department of Health, 1998, p.93). Investments in child care programmes, including Sure Start, the Children's Fund and Connexions, have been accompanied by an expectation that strategies adopted will be evidence-based. Interventions that have been validated by research methods featuring 'before' and 'after' measurements and comparison groups (for example, Sure Start, 1999), are especially commended. A growing range of consortia, for example Research in Practice (www.rip.org.uk) Making Research Count (www.uea.ac.uk/swk/research/mrc/welcome.htm) and the Centre for Evidence Based Social Services (www.ex.ac.uk/cebbs), are promoting evidence based practice and disseminating robust research summaries to an increasingly broad range of practitioners. Excellent material relevant to social care, as well as guidelines for finding and using research are also available from a range of websites, including Southampton University (www.soton.ac.uk/rminded), the Wales Office of Research and Development (www.dialspace.dial.pipex.com/word), the Scottish Executive (www.scotland.gov.uk/edru/edrupub.asp), the Home Office (www.homeoffice.gov.uk/rds/horspubs1.html) and, especially in relation to disability issues, the Social Policy

Research Unit website at York University (www.york.ac.uk/inst/ spru/pubs/researchwks.htm). On the international front, the Campbell Collaboration (Petrosino *et al.*, 2001, www.campbell.gse.upenn.edu), an analogue of the Cochrane Collaboration (www.cochrane.org) in health care, has been established to review and disseminate evidence in the fields of educational, criminological and psychosocial interventions. The establishment by the Department of Health of the Social Care Institute for Excellence (SCIE) is a clear recognition that the conscious use of evidence is central to a professional social work service. The information technology revolution has enabled any social worker with a PC to access on-line data bases which cover the full range of social work practice, such as the excellent electronic library of social care (eLSC) maintained by NISW, recently transferred to SCIE (www.scie.org.uk), and now available without subscription. The next generation of data bases will, as has already occurred in medicine, contain abstracts which have screened for methodological quality and are regularly updated, rather than simply being a list of published articles. These developments are already taking place. Barnardo's is helping the Centre for Evidence Based Social Services (CEBSS) at the University of Exeter develop an on-line resource of critically appraised social work studies, which will go live in 2003 (www.be-evidenced-based.com). As the only non-academic institution participating in the ESRC Evidence Network (www.evidencenetwork.org), Barnardo's is working with City and York Universities to develop dissemination and implementation programmes for projects in Yorkshire developed under the auspices of the Children's Fund.

Why evidence based practice?

While a degree of controversy surrounds the applicability of evidence-based practice to social work, with some concern that this will over value technocratic solutions to human problems, the empowering potential for users and practitioners in having interventions based on sound evidence is substantial. Whatever one's perspective, an understanding of the issue has become crucial to practitioners and child welfare organisations. So what do we mean by evidence-based practice? Drawing on a number of other sources (Sackett *et al.*, 1996; Sheldon and Chilvers, 2000), we suggest that evidence-based child care practice may be defined as *'the process of systematically locating, critically reviewing and using research findings as the basis for decisions in child care practice'*.

Promoting evidence-based models of practice in child care organisations is frequently a controversial activity. Social workers are often unhappy with empirically based approaches and raise typical - and often justified - issues.

- Why should we value one kind of knowledge more than others?
- Where do the views of users fit in?
- Who gets to decide which evidence is the 'best'?
- Evidence based practice seems to be about counting and measuring everything - not everything that counts can be counted.
- Human problems are much too complex to be managed on this basis.
- Evidence-based practice will discourage radical ideas by imposing conformity on practitioners.

These points deserve answers. Evidence-based practice in social care has indeed been closely associated with empirical models of investigation and cognitive-behavioural methods of intervention. It has been argued that this approach results in other types of knowledge being under-valued (Lewis, 1998), in procedure driving out creativity (Trinder, 1996; Webb, 2001), in process being sacrificed on the altar of outcomes (Sinclair, 1998) and the day to day experience of practitioners being diminished (Shaw and Shaw, 1997). A more worrying objection suggests that evidence-based practice oppresses users by failing to give equal - or paramount - status to their views and experiences (Everitt and Hardiker, 1996). No single form of discourse, it is argued, has the right to claim precedence over another (Witkin, 1999).

These views have some common features. Firstly, they are sceptical that the principles of natural science can be successfully applied to social care practice, give the intrinsic 'messiness' of human relationships and the impossibility of standardising interventions. This, however, tends to exaggerate the extent to which 'evidence' alone is ever the sole criterion justifying a social care intervention, and underestimates the 'messiness' of health service interventions. What, for example, is the 'best' treatment for depression? Open or log onto the current volume of 'Clinical Evidence' (subscription only, www.clinicalevidence.org) - a regularly updated summary of evidence from randomised controlled trials in medicine distributed to all GP's - and look it up. The answer? There isn't one. A wide range of treatments, pharmacological, herbal, behavioural, electrical and psychotherapeutic are discussed, so is exercise, be-friending and bibliotherapy. Depending on the severity of the condition, there is evidence for the effectiveness of all these approaches, compared to doing nothing. Some of the evidence is stronger, some is weaker, with some the jury is still at least partially out. Even at the cutting edge of evidence based medicine, the most that can usually be achieved is that a patient is fully appraised of the range of treatment options, their respective pros and cons, and is able to make an informed choice about what's best for them.

Secondly, there is a perception that evidence-based practice devalues the narratives of the powerless and privileges the good and the great. On the contrary, we would argue that what devalues the powerless is being subject to unsubstantiated claims of authority. These may be based on expert knowledge (the 'I have more letters after my name than you' approach), a long career (the 'I have nothing left to learn' approach), practice wisdom (the 'I have arrived at the right answers by a process which transcends analysis' approach), membership of an oppressed group (the 'our history of suffering renders us immune from criticism' approach) or personal experience (the 'I have walked through the valley of the shadow of death and you haven't' approach). All these sources of authority are legitimate and indispensable; however, they are also not enough. Those who believe that their chosen approach - whether based on 'knowledge', 'experience', 'intuition', 'practice wisdom', or simply an ideological conviction - is sufficient justification for their actions are adopting authoritarian positions (Chalmers, 1983), and these positions are no less authoritarian when they come dressed in anti-oppressive rhetoric. As well as individuals, organisations and special interest groups with territory to defend - and yes, Barnardo's falls into this category - may react fiercely to criticism if their well-intentioned actions are found to be unsupported by a robust evidence base. Recent examples of this are systematic reviews that have suggested that screening for breast cancer does not save women's lives (Olsen and Gotzsche, 2001), and that programmes run by the Driving Standards Agency in schools may result in more rather then fewer accidents (Achara *et al.*, 2001).

Evidence based practice is thus not, as is frequently alleged, a search for 'certainty' in either medicine or social work (Taylor and White, 2001). It is rather a genuine attempt to give vulnerable people a better chance of having good, rather than bad things happen to them, by a continuous process of improvement. As the physicist turned philosopher Piet Hein remarked:

> *The road to wisdom?*
> *Well, it's plain and simple to express*
> *Err and err and err again*
> *But less and less and less*

The Barnardo's approach

While the collision between empiricism and intuition is hardly new (William Blake was picking a fight with Newton two centuries ago), the dispute is more than a tedious argument between academics and their pet methodologies. Important issues concerning the welfare of vulnerable people are at stake. Will those who utilise empirical methods of investigation be inoculated against outrage at poverty and disadvantage? Can social justice really be promoted through randomised controlled trials? The subject matter of 'books that have changed my life' tends to feature spirituality, biography or fiction. No-one, to the best of our knowledge, has ever claimed that their life was changed by the Handbook of Empirical Social Work Practice (yes, it exists; in two volumes). However, a recent analysis of twelve months of queries to the 'Advice Shop' of the leading social work journal 'Community Care' by Katherine Curtis at City University revealed rather more prosaic concerns. The majority of practitioners wanted practical information on how to work more effectively with (in order of frequency) disabled people, looked after children and service users from ethnic minorities. Questions about epistemology were thin on the ground.

Promoting social change through appeals to both reason and emotion was well known to Thomas Barnardo. While basing much of his early success on photographic images of children's misery, it was also important for him to establish a reputation as a serious social scientist. Addressing a social science convention in 1879, he provided an early example of a cost benefit analysis. He suggested that we could choose between expenditure:

> ...in the shape of rates and taxes for the support of police, magistrates, justices, houses of detention, convict prisons ... or in the form of donations to institutions like ours ... every convict costs England upwards of £80 per head per annum. Every boy or girl taken from the streets costs but £16 per year (Night and Day, September 1879).

That early investment can reap handsome social rewards was reiterated over a century later. The longitudinal study of the Perry Pre-School programme noted that, 'over the lifetime of the participants, the pre-school program returns to the public an estimated $7.16 for every dollar spent.' (Schweinhart *et al.* 1993, p.xviii). Then, as now, the crucial factor driving public investment was hard data on social gains combined with narratives arising from personal encounters with disadvantaged children. There is little doubt, for example, that the initial £550M investment in the national

Sure Start programme would not have taken place without compelling evidence from US and UK early intervention programmes of the positive long term impacts on child well-being of pre-school support (Macdonald and Roberts, 1995; Zoritch and Roberts, 1997).

Introducing an evidence based model

Barnardo's has made a commitment to work towards basing all its child care practice on the best current evidence of effectiveness. Barnardo's is fortunate in having a well resourced research and development team with six permanent staff and a number of others employed on a temporary basis. This team has, with the support of policy and training officers, operational child care staff and colleagues in our Marketing and Communications divisions, led the evidence based practice strategy. This, in itself, is an important factor which the literature on organisational change stresses - the need for product champions of sufficient seniority with access to change levers.

Our primary concern has been to focus on the outcomes most wanted by children and families, and to make judgements about what information we need to assure ourselves that our efforts are making these outcomes happen. To this end, Barnardo's has commissioned a range of reports, the *What Works?* series, which address important areas of child care practice. Each report summarises the best current evidence in its particular field, highlighting, where possible, evidence from controlled trials and systematic reviews. Volumes published to date include reviews of early years interventions, services for families with disabled children, leaving care services, youth justice, inclusive education, child protection, parent education, stability in care, support for parents with learning disabilities, the education of looked after children and community development, among others. A programme of seminars designed for Barnardo's staff and led by the report authors has been delivered. To complement these volumes, a series of shorter 'key message' fact sheets have been prepared are available to Barnardo's staff through the organisation's intranet. Dissemination and implementation are crucial dimensions of any evidence based approach. Barnardo's R&D staff recently completed a commission for the Joseph Rowntree Foundation reviewing the most effective ways of making the leap from theoretical to applied knowledge, and have cascading the results to our national child care regions (Barnardo's R&D team, 2000). As members of Research in Practice, research officers are currently piloting the REAL (Reflection on Evidence for Action and Learning) team working pack with a number of Barnardo's projects, which helps staff identify key practice issues, research the literature, formulate a change strategy and implement the results.

Listening to the voices of children is a key element in our programme of research. A range of studies drawing directly on children's views have been completed, the most recent being a major review of children's participation for a London Health Action Zone (McNeish *et al.*, 2000). This process has been greatly assisted by Barnardo's R&D intern programme, which offers one and two year contracts to young graduates, and is financed by external commissions and awards. Barnardo's library provides a crucial support service to staff seeking specific information, either on the shelves, on CD-Roms or on-line. In collaboration with R&D staff, reviews of effective interventions are carried out in response to requests from services that are being set up or re-focused. Recent examples are reviews of sensory integration therapy for a pre-school service working with autistic children and a summary of what we know of the effectiveness of community based support services for bereaved children. It is our long term intention that all Barnardo's services are based on such reviews, and that new services will be designed around what is currently known to be the most effective service structure or intervention.

Examining and synthesising previously published material is cheaper and, in many cases, more productive than undertaking original research. In the near future, all Barnardo's staff will have access to on-line data bases and will know how to use them. A series of workshops designed to assist staff locate and download relevant evidence based material has been piloted. This will involve help staff discriminate between poor quality information and material that is more credible.

Conclusion

What evidence is there that Barnardo's child care practice, and more importantly, outcomes for children have changed as a result of these strategies? While it is early days yet, there are encouraging signs of change. Requests for evidence based reviews from services are increasing. The 'What Works?' series is widely consulted. The use of the Barnardo's library and information service by practitioners has improved. The proposition that *not* seeking to base one's work on best evidence of effectiveness is an ethically indefensible position has penetrated the powerful moral universe of social work. None of this yet constitutes any paradigm shift in service delivery and is certainly no indication of whether children have benefited. However, it has become clear that there is in Barnardo's - and undoubtedly in other child care organisations in both the voluntary and statutory sectors - a hunger for robust, well crafted evidence based research that has utility for day to day practice. We have moved through the phase of stimulating need, and now have to provide the product, which will undoubtedly be a more difficult but highly invigorating task.

References

Achara, S. and colleagues in the Cochrane Injuries Group Drivers Education Reviewers, Evidence based road safety: the Driving Standards Agency's schools programme. *Lancet*, 358, 230-2

Barnardo's Research and Development Team (2000) *Making Connections: Linking research and practice*. Ilford: Barnardo's

Chalmers, I. (1983) Scientific enquiry and authoritarianism in perinatal care and education. *Birth*, 10, 3, 151-66

Department of Health (1998) *Modernising Social Services*. London: The Stationery Office, Cm. 4169

Everitt, A. and Hardiker, P. (1996) *Evaluating for good practice*. Macmillan: Basingstoke

Fagan, T.J. (1975) Nomogram for Bayes's Theorem. *New England Journal of Medicine*, 293, 257

Lewis, J. (1998) Building an evidence-based approach to social interventions. *Children and Society*, 12. 136-40

Macdonald, G. and Roberts, H. (1995) *What Works in the Early Years?* Ilford: Barnardo's

McNeish, D; Downie, A; Webster, A., Newman, T. and Brading, J. (2000) *The Participation of Children and Young People: Report for Lambeth, Southwark and Lewisham Health Action Zone* (2000), Ilford: Barnardo's

Myers, L.L. and Thyer, B.A. (1997) Should social work clients have the right to effective treatment? *Social Work*, 42, 3, 288-98

Night and Day (1897). Cited in Rose, J. (1987) *For the Sake of the Children*. London: Hodder and Stoughton

Oakley, A. and Roberts, H. (1996) (Eds.) *Evaluating Social Interventions: A report of two workshops funded by the Economic and Social Research Council*. Ilford: Barnardo's

Olsen, O. and Gotzsche, P. (2001) Cochrane review on screening for breast cancer with mammography. *Lancet*, 358, 1340-2

Petrosino A., Boruch R.F., Rouding C., McDonald S. and Chalmers I. (2001) The Campbell Collaboration Social, Psychological, Educational and Criminological Trials Register (C2-SPECTR) to Facilitate the Preparation and Maintenance of Systematic Reviews of Social and Educational Interventions. *Evaluation and Research in Education*, 14, 3&4, 206-219

Rosen, A., Proctor, E.K. and Staudt, M.M. (1999) Social work research and the quest for effective practice. *Social Work Research*, 23, 4-14

Sackett, D.L., Rosenberg, W.M., Gray, J.H.M., Haynes, R.B. and Richardson, W.S. (1996) Evidence-based practice: What it is and what it isn't. *British Medical Journal*, 312, 71-2

Schweinhart, L., Barnes, H., and Weikart, D. (1993) *Significant Benefits: the High/Scope Perry pre-school study through age 27*. Ypsilanti, MI: High/Scope Press

Shaw, I. And Shaw, A. (1997) Keeping social work honest:

Evaluating as profession and practice. *British Journal of Social Work*, 27, 847-69

Sheldon, B. and Chilvers, R. (2000) *Evidence-Based Social Care: A Study of prospects and problems*. Lyme Regis: Russell House

Sheldon, B. and Macdonald, G. (1999) *Research and Practice in Social Care: Mind the gap*. Exeter: Exeter University, Centre for Evidence Based Social Services

Sinclair, R. (1998) Developing evidenced based policy and practice in social interventions with children and families. *International Journal of Social Research Methodology*, 1, 2, 169-86

Sure Start (April 1999) *A Guide to Evidence Based Practice: 'Trailblazer' edition*. London: Sure Start Unit

Taylor, C. and White, S. (2001) Knowledge, truth and reflexivity: the problem of judgement in social work. *Journal of Social Work*, 1, 1, 37-59

Trinder, L. (1996) Social work research: The state of the art (or science). *Child and Family Social Work*, 1, 233-42

Webb, S. (2001) Some considerations on the validity of evidence-based practice in social work. *British Journal of Social Work*, 31, 57-79

Witkin, S. (1999) Editorial. Constructing our future. *Social Work*, 44, 1, 5-8

Zoritch, B. and Roberts, I. (1997) The health and welfare effects of day care for pre-school children: A systematic review of randomized controlled trials, *The Cochrane Library, Issue 4*. Oxford: Update Software.

9
Towards a more reflexive research aware practice: The influence and potential of professional and team culture

John Lawler and Andy Bilson

Introduction

Evidence-based practice (EBP) is a fashionable idea in social work. Whether it develops into a more enduring aspect of social work will only become clear with the passage of time. Despite some of the reservations about the use of evidence in this and other contexts, it is important to highlight the benefits of building awareness of evidence into practice. Without this, it is unlikely that evidence-based practice will develop beyond the transience of fashion. This will involve considering some aspects of social work practice with fresh eyes, but will also utilise other more familiar processes of support, communication and development. This article reviews the current debates including those outlined in the recent special edition of this journal on the nature of evidence, as well as the possibilities for evidence-based practice in social work. We will consider how to encourage a more reflexive, research aware practice in social work. We conclude that the focus for attempted reforms needs to be widened from the current primary focus on individual professionals and their education to a broader perspective that can enable development of new practices in social work teams and organisations. Our focus is predominantly that of culture and knowledge in social work teams.

Evidence in Social Work

There are many different views on the causes of problems that result in social work intervention and therefore on appropriate ways of responding to them. To that extent, the issue of evidence-based practice in social work will always be problematic (see Newman and McNeish, 2002). A key challenge to the implementation of evidence-based practice is how to deal with the tacit and socio-politically based knowledge which informs social work practice (see Frost, 2002; Taylor and White, 2002; Smith, 2002). There is a continuing need to explore this knowledge base and the development of 'received wisdom' in social work. In many ways there is a clear parallel with the development of received wisdom in management, again in part a strongly, socially-orientated area of work with much tacit operational knowledge. Whilst some areas of management, e.g. production management, have powerful rationalist, explicit traditions, areas of management such as human resource management and organisational change are much less so and propose more emergent, more interpretive approaches. This similarity between the disciplines of management and social work, noted by Booth *et al.* (2003), is of particular relevance in an era of increasing managerialism in social work. They cite Stewart's definition of evidence-based practice, (itself a paraphrase of that by Sackett *et al.*, 1996), that it is the:

> *explicit and judicious use of current best evidence in making decisions [Stewart 2002, p.6] (Booth et al., 2003, p.192)*

and argue that the source of this definition is managerial:

> *The management origin of this pragmatic definition signals similarities between social care and management as disciplines where there is apparent under-utilization of research evidence (Booth et al., 2003, p.192).*

One interpretation of evidence-based practice in general, is that, in common with many management practices, it is an attempt to limit uncertainty in decision-making in individual cases and as such, is a characteristic of the growing rationalist focus within social work organisation and delivery of services (see Taylor and White, 2002). The rationalist approach to certain aspects of management is well documented in management texts (e.g. Mullins 2003; Darwin *et al.*, 2002) and can be seen today within the health and social care contexts as discussed by Moullin (2002, p.100). Writers such as Bilson and Ross (1999), Webb (2001), Harlow (2003) and Harris (2003) point to the development of techno-rationalist, managerial models pervading social work, which is manifest in a 'performance-driven' culture (see also Frost, 2002). The emphasis on the use of evidence to inform practice reinforces this, with its particular ontological position and its assumptions of near universal (and as yet undiscovered) answers to particular problems. Social work practice does not sit happily with this. It is an 'invisible trade' (Pithouse, 1987) and as such its processes present particular challenges for research and evaluation. Its practice is reconstituted through re-telling in different contexts. It is also open to different interpretations by professional and user and its 'outcomes' are complicated and often long term, if they can be regarded as outcomes at all. Additionally, but not exclusively to social work, its interventions are crucially dependent for (intended) effect (or effectiveness) on the collaboration and commitment of the user. The techno-rationalist approach relies on a 'scientific' basis of evidence in social work practice, which Webb (2001) questions. He highlights a fundamental point about social work defining or realising its position within an 'aporia', which is unrecognised by policy makers and, through emphasis on certain aspects of policy, is disregarded by managers.

An alternative view is that the use of evidence is an acknowledgement of the inherent uncertainty in social work and a means of highlighting this. Despite the potential problems, Gibbs and Gambrill (2002) argue the benefits of evidence-based practice in social work. According to them it

> is a process (not a collection of truths) in which the uncertainty in making decisions is highlighted, efforts to decrease it are made, and clients are involved as informed participants. (p.473)

The process in practice involves several fundamental elements, according to Bilsker and Goldner (2000)

> *questioning of unfounded beliefs, rigorous scrutiny of methodology, critical appraisal of proposed treatments. (p.665)*

The move towards evidence-based practice constitutes a shift in both form and content of knowledge, according to Newman and Nutley (2003), away from the current tacit knowledge base to the more explicit. This in turn implies a major, longer-term change in professional knowledge and therefore in training.

Culture and evidence-based practice

The potential barriers to the adoption of evidence-based practice are several, as noted by Sheldon and Chilvers (2002). Issues such as professional identity and status; established values and practice; and professional training can all be seen as aspects of 'professional culture'. If certain aspects of professional culture themselves present a barrier to EBP, other objections to the introduction of EBP might be reinforced by it. McKenna *et al.* (2004) point to the conflicting nature of research conclusions as being a barrier to the introduction of evidence-based practice in primary care. Any potential conflict in results, it is argued, causes confusion amongst practitioners. Furthermore, the conflict is likely to be emphasised as a means of resisting any change in practice. Bilsker and Goldner (2000) stress the need to convince both practitioners and users of the value and feasibility of evidence-based practice as a precursor to any plans to develop it. However, these views imply that social workers consider research conclusions as a matter of course, an issue challenged by the research carried out by Sheldon and Chilvers (2002). Similarly Gibbs and Gambrill note that

> *research suggests that few social workers draw on practice-related research findings. (p.452)*

The reasons for this may vary, but include professional practice and the time practitioners might or might not have to access research information. Gira *et al.* (2004) make a similar point:"

> The daily pressure to see more clients makes it extremely difficult for social workers to find time to read research literature even if they were inclined to do so. Social work as a profession has not found ways to help practitioners identify and use the latest research evidence in their practice. (p.69)

Professional culture may be challenged by the concept of EBP. Newman and Nutley (2003) argue that EBP, within the context of probation for their discussion, is perceived as a threat to professional practice, status and identity, as exemplified by a research participant:

> a shift in the definition of what constitutes professional knowledge was not easy to accomplish. The old status and identity of probation officers had been based on a tacit pool of knowledge.... This tacit, experiential knowledge was perceived to be being devalued in the search for more explicit, research- based knowledge. The autonomy of individual probation officers was also being curtailed .... (they) perceived themselves as 'ticking boxes' rather than using their judgement and discretion. (p.551)

Tacit knowledge forms an important part of such an operating culture and relies on experience and verbal transmission. Barratt notes that:

> [there] is an oral, rather than a knowledge-based, culture within social services which results in staff valuing direct practice experience over, and often to the exclusion of, other forms of learning [Sheldon & Chilvers, 1995] (2003, p.145).

Gira *et al.* (2004) point to the difficulty presented by a different culture of practice within social work as opposed to the medical culture, where the introduction of evidence-based practice has arguably been more successful. A further aspect of organisational culture is also highlighted by Barratt who notes the perception of social workers that they operate within a 'blame culture', with the attendant difficulties this presents for changing practice. The social work workforce is also seen as being relatively poorly qualified, unqualified to some extent, having little in its culture which promotes critical appraisal and little time to read and reflect. This is aptly summarised by Booth *et al.* (2003):

> *A literature review reveals a workforce, poorly equipped by professional education, relying heavily on personal communication and 'gut instinct' to deliver packages of care. A workplace culture of action, not reflection, and the absence of information, resources and skills, make social care practitioners less likely to consult research to improve their practice. (p.191)*

The current system of professional training needs revision if evidence-based practice is to be fundamental to the culture of professional practice in the future according to Howard *et al.* (2003). They argue that qualifying students, despite having access to a greater wealth of information than previous generations of students and practitioners, do not develop the skills through their training to be able to access and analyse critically the research which might inform practice.

The rationalist approach of reliance on disseminating published information alone is very unlikely to have any significant impact in the development of EBP. Combinations of approaches appear most likely to have an effect on changing practitioner behaviour (Gira *et al.*, 2004) and offer a greater likelihood of influencing professional culture. Gira *et al.* conclude that:

> *The literature from health care suggests that disseminating information alone is insufficient. Many interventions have been designed to improve practitioners' adherence to EBP guidance and are differentially effective. To date no intervention has demonstrated powerful effects. (2004, p.77)*

The majority of the approaches reviewed above, reflect a growing technocratic rationality. This presents a set of institutional reactions to the perceived need to change which are largely rationalist in their analysis and bureaucratic in their responses. Whilst this may be apt in the bio-medical context, in the socio-medical and social work contexts such responses have limitations. Such limitations are compounded when considering the intangibility of professional culture and the difficulties of trying to change it (Ormrod, 2003).

Developing an evidence informed social work culture

Whilst bearing these limitations in mind, we will argue the need to develop a way forward which, we believe, is more fitting to social work than the techno-rationalist approach evident in much of the implementation in medicine and which addresses the issue of professional culture. To reiterate: the aim of EBP is to develop practice so that the most convincing information is used fully to inform the delivery of social work interventions for the most positive outcomes, from the perspectives both of service deliverer and user.

The development of EBP constitutes a considerable change to the tradition of social work practice. It is important here to acknowledge the considerable and developing literature of organisational change, but it is not our intention to review that here. The change management literature in general has a concern with looking for universal solutions to the problems of 'change management' (Sturdy and Grey, 2003) and can be very prescriptive. Some of the more recent change literature, which offers most utility for developments in the social work context, is that which acknowledges the complications and unpredictabilities of professional service interventions and delivery and the role of discourse in studying change. The importance of culture in organisational change is a recurrent theme. It is important to note that the literature on organisational culture is itself characterised by debate. In simple terms this revolves around the issue of whether culture is something an organisation/profession *has* and which it can change relatively easily, or whether it is something the organisation/profession *is*, that is, a manifestation of the values, experiences and perspectives which inform its practice

(Ormrod, 2003). The former perspective implies a managerialist, rationalist approach to change, whilst the latter highlights the role of personal and professional values and implies the need for a reflective, discursive approach to change. It is this second approach that we feel has value in the development of evidence and evidence-based practice in social work.

Culture and tacit knowledge

The need to recognise and alter the particular culture within both health (Pettigrew *et al.*, 1992) and within social work (MacDonald, 1999) is acknowledged in the literature. Any focus on changing individual practice without taking due note of the operational culture is unlikely to lead to sustained change. MacDonald recognises the particular need to change 'culture and practices of (social work) organisations' (p.31) if effective EBP is to be introduced. Mullen (2002) similarly notes the culture of social work as paying little attention to research findings and argues the reasons for this:

> the place of systematic reviews of effectiveness research has grown in importance, such as seen in the Cochrane and Campbell Collaborations. Systematic reviews provide an important means to accumulate and assess the cumulative results of research pertaining to outcomes of health, education and social interventions. However, systematic reviews do not provide a direct linkage to practice prescriptions. This is because practice decisions need to be made on the basis of knowledge derived from not only scientific investigations, but also experience, values, preferences, and other considerations deliberated by providers, users, and carers within the constraints of available resources. (p.10)

The point on the nature of practice decisions is key here. It demonstrates the need to acknowledge the role of tacit knowledge - built up through experience and incorporating professional knowledge - to be used in delivering a service in a manner which is sensitive to the specific needs of the vulnerable individual, that is, caring for human sensibilities.

The literature on knowledge conversion (from tacit to explicit to tacit) is useful in relation to this. Nonaka and Takeuchi (1995) outline a 'knowledge spiral' within the context, for their purposes, of organisational innovation. This approach recognises that tacit knowledge is developed through practice and through socialisation with colleagues and that it is informed by aspects of explicit knowledge, internalised by practitioners. Similarly, aspects of tacit, practitioner knowledge are made explicit, externalised to others, through more formal rather than verbal means, a process which de-contextualises the knowledge to some extent. Explicit knowledge from various sources is then combined and adapted by individual practitioners to meet specific circumstances, which in time becomes integral to the tacit knowledge that informs their practice and thus the spiral continues. Elements of this process, which are crucial for practitioners, are reflection, both with colleagues and users, on effective practice; ready access to external explicit information; and the support for individual reflection in order to combine and apply evidence appropriately.

Professional teams

The role of teams in developing professional culture, in socialising new members and in developing tacit knowledge is important (Pithouse, 1987; Hall, 1997; White, 1998; Bilson and Barker, 1998). The change literature is too often concerned with the individual 'change agent' to the neglect of the role of the team itself as an instigator and supporter of change. This may be an important factor implied rather than explicit in some models of change. For example, Rogers' (1995) approach to the diffusion of innovations highlights the key role of the 'critical mass' in the adoption and sustenance of innovation. His model follows a process of dissemination, adoption, implementation and maintenance. The role of dissemination in the traditional sense has its limitations in the social work context, as already discussed. However at the team level dissemination can take a different turn, involving the sharing of learning, - dissemination of experience from research and practice - to other team members, the stage of combination in Nonaka and Takeuchi's spiral, noted above. Such a process model of change provides a more complete systematic approach than many other models, highlighting as it does, the maintenance or institutionalisation of new practice. Our view is that the team can be very influential at each stage of Rogers' model. Shared experience, shared values and tacit knowledge characterise the professional team. These teams have an important support function and themselves provide a forum for discussions which share information (e.g. on both evidence and on local context; tacit and explicit), share experience (e.g. on effective practice), and which provide the opportunity to develop evidence to share with and beyond the team.

The research into teams in social care (e.g., Pithouse, 1987; Hall, 1997; White, 1998), medicine (e.g., Bloor, 1976) and nursing (e.g., Latimer, 2000) show how cultures are locally accomplished and reproduced and can sustain the tacit practices of occupations, organizations and teams and indeed may be used to resist the sort of approaches to policy and practice change usually associated with rational approaches to implementing evidence-based practice. A key problem in cases where practice is framed in a strong local culture that supports the resisting behaviour, is recognising that this presents a problem at all. This is because these cultures and the practice that is supported by them are based on tacitly held assumptions that are difficult to challenge as they are taken for granted as truths.

Armstrong (1982), in a similar vein, states:

> *The rational approach is rational only for the change agent. For the changee, change seems irrational. Should we change important beliefs each time someone thrusts disconfirming evidence on us? It is not surprising that 'people are resistant to change.' The rational approach implies that the target of the change is irrational. (Armstrong, 1982, p.463)*

An example of how an attempt to implement an evidence-based approach can falter because it is unable to challenge strong team cultures, can be seen in social work practice regarding contact between parents and their children in care

(Bilson and Barker, 1994, 1995, 1998). This area of child care has a well developed research base that stresses the importance of regular contact for the well-being of children (Lawder *et al.*, 1986; Millham *et al.*, 1986; Bullock *et al.*, 1990). Following the 1989 Children Act in England, serious attempts were made to implement evidence-based practice in this area through extensive training programmes, regulations and rules, publishing research reviews and good practice guides. Research by one of the authors into how this evidenced informed practice was undertaken and demonstrated that levels of contact varied widely within and between local authorities. It was also found that large variations between teams within local authorities could not be explained by the factors usually linked to differing levels of contact. Evidence that team culture played a crucial part in these differences came from feedback from the teams. Some teams had a local culture of low levels of parental contact, acting on premises related to rescuing children from their parents whilst other teams had high levels of contact (dealing with similar problems in the same authority) from a culture of cooperation with parents. Following research seminars using the principles outlined below four from five authorities achieved high levels of contact in a follow up study.

Our point here is that human agents easily develop routinized patterns of thought, action and interaction in relation to their activities. These aspects are supported by, and become the local cultures of teams and organisations. They tend to be relatively invisible to those within the culture and thus are also extremely durable. They are vitally important in understanding reasoning and action, as Varela notes:

> ... *my main point is that most of our mental and active life is of the immediate coping variety, which is transparent, stable, and grounded in our personal histories. Because it is so immediate, not only do we not see it, we do not see that we do not see it, and this is why so few people have paid any intention to it ...* (Varela, 1992, p.19)

Varela goes on to question how we can apply this distinction between 'coping behaviours and abstract judgement' to making judgements which are moral and ethical. This point is central to the judgements of social workers. The evidence cited so far leads to the conclusion that many social work judgements are of the immediate coping variety. We will suggest that to develop a response to decision making in this context, it is important both to have an analytic approach to ordinary activity - a way of reflecting on what is taken for granted - and an emotional and ethical engagement with the moral nature of social work decision making.

This tacit dimension of practice often seems very difficult to extract and articulate. However, its nature is essentially social, and it cannot therefore be located entirely in the social worker's internal thinking. It must from time to time be visible, accessible and reportable – this will be particularly evident in the way that novices are inducted into team practices or 'deviant' behaviour is punished. We therefore argue that, if we are to develop the capacity of social workers to evaluate whether they want to make changes to tacit foundations of their practice and base decisions on available evidence, we need techniques to help them reflect on their tacit assumptions (Taylor and White, 2000; White and Stancombe, 2003).

The support function of the team can be crucial here. The team provides an important opportunity to reflect on and to discuss practice generally. Thus a forum is presented which permits members to discuss the emotional aspects of their work; a dimension recognised as important within social work, but one which receives less attention in the 'evidence' and change literatures. Bilson and White (2004), Gira *et al.* (2004) and Webb (2001) all note the potential impact on professional workers of emotional engagement in evidence, for example using case studies to exemplify practice rather than relying on the less engaging material from more traditional research summaries. The potential of team discussions that engage individuals using direct case information may be an important part of the development and dissemination of practice evidence. Allowing an emotional aspect in the development of evidence-based practice is important as is recognition that the relationship between new knowledge and change in professional practice is not a direct causal link. Changing professional practice might involve questioning basic practice assumptions and this can cause considerable concern, threat or discomfort for the individual. Certain models of change acknowledge this, such as the 'transition model' described, for example, in both Hayes (2002) and Hopson *et al.* (1992).

Two further aspects of social work culture are important for consideration here. The first is the historical collective culture of social work practice; generic social work is particularly team based and relies on team discussion and support. Whilst there may be significant individualization in many aspects of society, this collective aspect of social culture appears to continue and provides an opportunity as a facilitator to EBP. The second aspect of social work culture and practice is the holistic nature of the social work perspective. Mirroring the evidence-based approach in medicine would present social work practice as a fragmented set of activities, with each aspect subject to investigation of its own evidence base, but the need is to see it as a systemic whole. The change literature generally notes the need to acknowledge the factors which might promote or hinder particular change initiatives and to utilise the former in promoting change. Change such as implementing EBP involves challenging long held assumptions and altering established patterns of behaviour. As we have said, the professional team provides the forum for both these as it presents an opportunity to develop reflexive discussion and to support, encourage and reinforce changing practice, which might be more difficult as an unsupported individual initiative. Mullen (2002) notes this opportunity:

> supervisors, consultants, and teams [our emphasis] seem to be the most promising conduit for knowledge dissemination in organizations, ... regarding practice guides and other forms of evidence-based practice for social workers. (p.9).

The evidence of using groups as a means of implementing evidence-based practice is particularly light and we believe an under-regarded aspect of EBP, both in its possibilities to assist and to resist EBP. However, it is not totally disregarded. Gabbay *et al.* (2003) consider the potential of 'communities of practice' in implementing evidence-based policy. Whilst their study considered multi-disciplinary teams, the points they make in relation to groups of professionals using and considering evidence are important. They note the value of collective sense-making and the ways in which evidence can be explored and interrogated in the collective context. Whilst their study reveals the ways in which evidence might be mediated, and its translation to practice might be deferred as well as encouraged, they present important findings which highlight how such communities of practice can be supported to examine evidence and its implications in a useful manner.

> *The rationalist, linear model of evidence-based practice is not reflected by the experience of these communities of practice. Nevertheless, with a clearer understanding of the processes of collective sense making, it may still be possible to encourage the more systematic use of relevant knowledge in collective decision making (Gabbay et al., 2003, 328).*

In the rationalist, linear model 'evidence' is used to prescribe practice in a top-down manner. We would suggest the need for a different approach starting from the idea that actions to create a more reflexive practice should come from practitioners and managers in local teams and similar groups and should be realised through using research to reflect on their own understandings of what is good practice.

Implications for research and use of evidence

Our approach then, stresses the need to engage participants in reflecting on their assumptions. So what are the implications of this approach?

Research into the tacit

First, there is a need for data that falls outside the usual research approaches valued in traditional approaches to EBP. This requires us to find ways to collect data on the way that social workers create and maintain their culture and tacit knowledge and on its content. We have already outlined the way that data on patterns of practice, such as that found in parental contact, can give indicators of how culture affects practice. We would also suggest that there is a need to research local cultures themselves. This can be achieved, for example though studying inter-professional talk and interaction in everyday settings (Taylor and White, 2000; White and Stancombe, 2003). This is because cultures must necessarily reinforce themselves and this making and remaking of occupational or team cultures takes place most visibly in interaction and talk between professionals. Research into local culture may also differ in terms of data collection and analysis of artefacts such as written records, statistical data, transcripts of talk. These need to be read, not in order to evaluate or prescribe practice, but for what they can tell us about the tacit presuppositions which order professional activity. For example, it is recognised that files represent 'a potential resource for vindicating practice' (Pithouse, 1987, p. 34). However it is the very way in which professionals attempt to vindicate their practice, which gives important information about their view of the official definitions within which they operate. Thus the aim is not to find more about the 'reality' of the lives of users, or to evaluate the adequacy of recording against some normative template, but to consider what presuppositions or world-views inform the social work decisions being made.

The following case closure summary from an audit of older people's services (Bilson and Thorpe, 2004) illustrates the use of files in this way. The case concerned a bedfast woman whose husband was worried about his continuing ability to care for his spouse, exacerbated by living in a third floor apartment with restricted access:

> *Mrs. Y is a very poorly lady all of her needs are met by her husband (he will not accept help). ... issues raised were around housing issues. Mr. and Mrs. Y have been waiting for ground floor accommodation for a long time. I have liaised with housing re my concerns.*

The extract shows what the researchers saw as the tacit assumption of the worker and the manager who closed the case: that their role was to provide packages of physical care and that social aspects of the problem, such as inappropriate housing, were not part of the team's responsibility. Note the bold statement that 'he will not accept help' and that 'the issues raised were around housing'. Once data of this kind has been generated, the assumptions underpinning such statements and the process of professional 'sense-making' can be examined through professional reflection.

Reflexive conversations

A second issue relates to the use made of findings. In the scientific-bureaucratic model 'evidence' is used to prescribe practice in a top-down manner. Our approach is similar to a 'knowledge spiral' (Nonaka and Takeuchi, 1995) described above. It starts from the idea that any actions that need to follow data collection should come from social workers and managers themselves and should be realised through reflection on their own understandings of what is good practice. To achieve this is not simple and we suggest the need to develop what have been termed 'reflexive conversations' (Bilson, 1997; Bilson and White 2004). These seek to focus attention on the tacit assumptions that shape practice.

Atkinson and Heath's suggestion that a reflexive approach to research needs to encourage the consumers of research '*to be more open to the research process*' (Atkinson and Heath, 1987, p.15) stresses the need not only to give direct access to the research 'data', but also to demonstrate how the researcher constructed the results from them and the researcher's own premises. 'Consumers of research' in our context refers to practitioners. Thus this approach does not make truth claims about the findings or value the research 'evidence' above the wisdom of practitioners. Rather it accepts its own groundlessness and seeks to demonstrate how the distinctions made by the researchers lead to a particular moral view of the data. Rather than hiding the processing of the data into the 'findings' this process is exposed to share the possibility of constructing a view and the distinctions used to create it. The researcher thus demonstrates reflexivity and then encourages practitioners to reflect on their own assumptions.

Thus, for example, one of the authors had studied reports

for the children's hearing system (the Scottish equivalent of a juvenile court) and found them to be full of negative comments about the children and their parents, and yet the social workers and their team leaders believed that they acted only in the best interests of children. Rather than simply present the results to them in the hope that they would accept the researcher's 'more objective' position, a seminar was held for team leaders in the organisation. This involved: presentations of the theoretical model which informed seminar leaders' practice with young offenders; exploring participants' views about the causes of offending and the premises upon which reports were written; encouraging dialogue and critical and emotional review of these premises by practitioners through a reappraisal of actual cases and their outcomes. It quickly became clear that the staff used many different tacit models of the causes of crime, from the social through to the psychological. From further work and discussions amongst practitioners, the lack of information about the strengths of the children and the overwhelmingly negative focus of the descriptions of their lives (which stemmed from their premises about the causes of delinquency), became clear to those involved.

This reflexive conversation helped to make participants aware of the consequences of their views of delinquency for the lives of those they were supposed to help. Proposals for change were developed to include: a new structure for reports; a plan for repeating the seminar for the range of staff in the department who were responsible for children; and a proposal for quality assurance of reports. This approach led to significant drops in the numbers of children entering care and an increase in the provision of services in the community (for a more detailed account of this work and its theoretical background see Bilson and Ross, 1999).

Conclusion

In this article we started by reviewing the developments in evidence-based practice and stated our preference for a reflexive approach to the use of research. Above all we are concerned that if social work uncritically embraces the rhetoric of evidence-based practice there is a danger that, in the current political climate of increasing central control and managerialism, it may increasingly lead to a prescriptive, one-size fits all approach to interventions with a consequence for individual users of services. At the same time we are concerned that social workers need to reflect on the tacit assumptions on which they make decisions about their everyday practice. We argued that these tacit assumptions are principally created and maintained in the day-to-day interactions in the teams, practice groups and organizations within which social work practice is organized. Research can play an important part in creating 'News of Difference' to enable teams to create a more reflexive stance in which the hidden assumptions become more open to critical reflection by practitioners and their managers. This will require research to be presented in new ways and social workers and their teams to be given time and space to consider the outcomes of their practice.

In taking this approach we are aware that we are asking for major changes in the way research is usually seen and used. We are asking managers, social workers and researchers alike to develop ways to have reflexive conversations. We are proposing an alternative and complementary approach to the research process and its products, designed to encourage reflection. Cultures in teams and organisations have the capacity to sustain forms of reasoning which function as taken for granted truisms about what works. This reasoning has the tendency to close down debate. Our intention has been to outline ways in which social workers can participate in dissolving these forms of folk wisdom if they so choose. We are suggesting that research and other evidence can play a part to provide social workers themselves with a means to examine and reappraise what they have previously taken as 'common sense' truths and make any changes that they wish.

References

Armstrong, J.S. (1982) Strategies for implementing change: An experiential approach. *Group and Organization Studies*, 7, 4, 457-75

Atkinson, B.J. and Heath, A.W. (1987) Beyond objectivism and relativism: Implications for family therapy research. *Journal of Strategic and Systemic Therapies*, 1, 8-17

Barratt, M (2003) Organizational support for evidence-based practice within child and family social work a collaborative study. *Child and Family Social Work*, 8, 143 –150

Bilson, A. (1997) Guidelines for a constructivist approach: Steps towards the adaptation of ideas from family therapy for use in organizations. *Systems Practice*, 10, 2, 153-178

Bilson, A. and Barker, R. (1994) Siblings of children in care or accommodation: A neglected area of practice. *Practice*, 6, 4, 226-235

Bilson, A. and Barker, R. (1995) Parental contact in foster care and residential care after the Children Act. *British Journal of Social Work*, 25, 3, 367-381

Bilson, A. and Barker, R. (1998) Looked after Children and contact: Reassessing the social work task. *Research, Policy and Planning*, 16, 1, 20 – 27

Bilson, A. and Ross, S. (1999) *Social Work Management and Practice: Systems principles*. 2nd Edition, London: Jessica Kingsley

Bilson, A. and Thorpe, D. (2004) *Report on Study of Careers in Older People's Services*. unpublished research report. Preston: University of Central Lancashire

Bilson, A. and White, S. (2004) The limits of governance: Interrogating the tacit dimension. in A. Gray and S. Harrison (Eds.) *Governing Medicine*. Maidenhead: OUP

Bilsker, D. and Goldner, E.M. (2000) Teaching evidence-based practice in mental health. *Research on Social Work Practice,* 10, 5, 664-669

Bloor, M. (1976) Bishop Berkeley and the adeno-tonsillectomy enigma: An exploration of variation in the social construction of medical disposal. *Sociology*, 10, 43-61

Booth, S.A., Booth, B. and Falzon, L.J. (2003) The need for information and research skills training to support evidence-based social care: A literature review and survey. *Learning in Health and Social Care*, 2, 4, 191–201

Bullock, R., Hosie, K., Little, M. & Millham, S. (1990) The problems of managing the family contacts of children in residential care. *British Journal of Social Work*, 20, 591-610

Darwin, J., Johnson, P. and McAuley, J. (2002) *Developing Strategies for Change*. Harlow: Pearson Education

Frost, N. (2002) A problematic relationship? Evidence and practice in the workplace. *Social Work and Social Sciences Review*, 10, 1, 38-50

Gabbay, J., le May, A., Jefferson, H., Webb, D., Lovelock, R., Powell, J and Lathlean, J. (2003) A case study of knowledge management in multi-agency consumer-informed 'communities of practice': Implications for evidence-based policy development in health and social services. *Health*, 7, 3, 283–310

Gibbs, L. and Gambrill, E. (2002) Evidence-based practice: Counterarguments to objections. *Research on Social Work Practice*, 12, 3, 452-476

Gira, E.C., Kessler, M.L. and Poertner, J. (2004) Influencing social workers to use research evidence in practice: Lessons from medicine and the allied health professions, *Research on Social Work Practice*, 14, 2, 68-79

Hall, C. (1997) *Social Work as Narrative: Storytelling and persuasion in professional texts*. Aldershot: Ashgate

Harlow, E. (2003) New managerialism, Social Services Departments and social work practice today. *Practice* 15, 2, 29-44

Harris, J. (2003) *The Social Work Business*. London: Routledge

Hayes, J. (2002) *The Theory and Practice of Change Management*. Basingstoke: Palgrave

Hopson, B., Scally, M. and Stafford, K. (1992) *Transitions; The challenge of change*. London: Mercury Books

Howard, M.O., McMillen, C.J. and Pollio, D.E. (2003) Teaching evidence-based practice: Toward a new paradigm for social work education. *Research on Social Work Practice*, 13, 2, 234-259

Latimer, J. (2000) *The Conduct of Care: Understanding nursing practice*. Oxford: Blackwell

Lawder E.A., Poulin J.E. and Andrews R.G. (1986) A Study of 185 Foster Children 5 years after placement. *Child Welfare*, 65, 3, 241- 251

MacDonald, G. (1999) Evidence-based social care: Wheels off the runway? *Public Money and Management*, Jan-Mar, 25-31

McKenna , H.P., Ashton, S. and Keeney, S. (2004) Barriers to evidence-based practice in primary care. *Journal of Advanced Nursing*, 45, 2, 178–189

Millham, S., Bullock, R., Hosie, K., Haak, M. (1986) *Lost in Care: The Problems of maintaining links between children in care and their families*. Aldershot: Gower

Moullin, M. (2002) *Delivering Excellence in Health and Social Care*. Buckingham: Open University Press

Mullen, E. (2002) 'The impact of guides on practice and the quality of service'. Social Care Institute for Excellence Inaugural International Seminar. London: SCIE

Mullins, L.J. (2003) *Management and Organisational Behaviour*. 5th edition. London: Prentice Hall

Newman, J. and Nutley, S. (2003) Transforming the probation service: 'What works', organisational change and professional identity, *Policy & Politics*, 31, 4, 547–63.˝

Newman, T. and McNeish, D. (2002) Promoting evidence in a child care charity: The Barnardo's experience. *Social Work and Social Sciences Review* 10, 1, 51-62

Nonaka, I. and Takeuchi, H. (1995) *The Knowledge Creating Company: How Japanese companies create the dynamics of innovation,* New York: Oxford Press

Ormrod, S. (2003) Organisational culture in health service policy and research: A third way political fad or policy development. *Policy and Politics,* 31, 2, 227-237

Pettigrew, A., Ferlie, E. and McKee, L. (1992) *Shaping Strategic Change: The Case of the NHS*, London: Sage

Pithouse, A. (1987) *Social Work: The social organisation of an invisible trade*. Aldershot: Avebury

Rogers, E. M. (1995) *Diffusion of Innovations*. 4th edition. New York: Free Press

Sackett, D.L., Rosenberg, W.M., Gray, J.H.M., Haynes, R.B. and Richardson, W.S. (1996) Evidence-based practice: What it is and what it isn't. *British Medical Journal,* 312, 71-72

Sheldon, B. and Chilvers, R. (2002) An empirical study of the obstacles to evidence-based practice. *Social Work and Social Sciences Review* 10, 1, 6-26

Smith, D. (2002) The Limits of Positivism Revisited. *Social Work and Social Sciences Review* 10, 1, 27-37

Stewart, R. (2002) *Evidence-based Management: A practical guide for health professionals*. Oxford: Radcliffe Medical Press

Sturdy, A. and Grey, C. (2003) Beneath and beyond organizational change management: Exploring alternatives. *Organization,* 10, 4, 651–662

Taylor, C. and White, S. (2000) *Practising Reflexivity in Health and Welfare: Making knowledge.* Buckingham: Open University Press

Taylor, C. and White, S. (2002) What works about what works? Fashion, fad and EBP. *Social Work and Social Sciences Review* 10, 2, 63-81

Varela, F.J. (1992) *Ethical Know-How: Action, wisdom and cognition.* Stanford: Stanford University Press

Webb, S. (2001) Some considerations on the validity of evidence-based practice in social work. *British Journal of Social Work,* 31, 57-79

White, S. (2002) Accomplishing the case in paediatrics and child health: Medicine and morality in inter-professional talk. *Sociology of Health and Illness,* 24, 4, 409-435

White, S. and Stancombe, J. (2003) *Clinical Judgement in the Health and Welfare Professions: Extending the evidence base.* Maidenhead: Open University Press

Summaries

A pre-post empirical study of obstacles to, and opportunities for, evidence-based practice in social care

Brian Sheldon, Rupatharshini Chilvers, Annemarie Ellis,
Alice Moseley and Stephanie Tierney

This chapter reports a summary of results from the largest and arguably the most representative study (a) of the attitudes of professional-grade social care staff to the idea of evidence-based practice; (b) of the facilities to encourage this which are available to them (or not); and (c) of their reading habits and levels of knowledge of basic research matters. It makes suggestions for improvement but also raises some concerns regarding the current content of professional training in our field

Evidence based social work practice: A reachable goal?

Frank Ainsworth and Patricia Hansen

In New South Wales the heads of Departments of Social Work in Teaching Hospitals support evidence based practice. Likewise, in 2002 the Association of Children's Welfare Agencies bi-annual Sydney conference will have the theme 'What-works? Evidence based practice in child and family services'.

There are debates about what constitutes evidence and how evidence should shape practice interventions. Some community-focused services are able to prosper through advocacy of a cause, issue or social problem. This is not enough in health care and child and family service settings where other disciplines have developed evidence about their effectiveness. Social work must do the same.

Social workers need to put aside old maxims and favourite theories. They need to develop a readiness to examine research evidence and to modify direct practice. The challenge is how to build a stronger research orientation into professional education and social work practice.

Reframing an evidence-based approach to practice

Stephanie Tierney

The positive aspects of evidence-based practice have often been overlooked in arguments about the appropriateness of such an approach to social and personal problems. This chapter, by illustrating such aspects, hopes to further the debate and reframe understanding and (mis) perceptions of evidence-based practice, highlighting the essential component it has to play in contemporary social care.

What works about what works? Fashion, fad and EBP

Carolyn Taylor and Susan White

This chapter considers some key debates about evidence-based practice. It is intended to be a contribution to the process of appraisal of this key contemporary initiative. The paper begins by briefly outlining the key premises of EBP and its underlying assumptions, before considering what are its limits and how it may usefully be supplemented by other approaches. In particular, I argue for a more methodologically inclusive reframing of what is meant by EBP.

The limits of positivism revisited

David Smith

The title alludes to a paper (Smith, 1987) in the *British Journal of Social Work* called 'The limits of positivism in social work research'. At the time it was written, it was not unusual to hear academic colleagues argue that there was something inherently conservative about positivist approaches to social research, and that such approaches inevitably served the interests of the powerful and maintained the *status quo*. I was never clear about the stages involved in this argument and remained unpersuaded by it, and this was not the line followed in the article (though I might be more readily persuaded now, for reasons discussed in this chapter). Instead, the 1987 article was mainly taken up with a critique of the work of Brian Sheldon, as the leading advocate over the previous ten years – and, as it turned out, over the next fifteen - of what would now be called 'evidence-based practice'.

A problematic relationship? Evidence and practice in the workplace

Nick Frost

This chapter examines the emergence of the evidence-led school of thought in social work and related professions. The basic tenets and influence of this movement are explored. The author develops a critique of the movement which explores four fundamental challenges: the problem of evidence; the problem of applying evidence to practice; the relationship between evidence and values; and the relationship between providers and service users. I argue that the evidence school is vulnerable in these four areas. The chapter concludes by briefly exploring a possible alternative model of policy and practice development.

The Social Care Institute for Excellence: The role of a national institute in developing knowledge and practice in social care

Mike Fisher

The English Department of Health is instituting a new framework for regulating social care, and a key part of this is a new *Social Care Institute for Excellence* (SCIE). SCIE will have the job of developing the knowledge base for social care, extracting messages for practice from research reviews and from existing best practice, and developing knowledge resources that social care practitioners can freely access.

This chapter explores the epistemological implications of this development for social work and social care, and the role that national bodies can play in developing excellence.

The development of SCIE includes key assumptions about the nature of knowledge underpinning social work and social care. It implies that

- there is a coherent supply of knowledge of which SCIE can be an 'intelligent customer';
- existing sources and modes of production deliver knowledge relevant to practice;
- it is possible to identify relevant knowledge, particularly through reviews;
- the state of the knowledge base is sufficient to develop guidelines for practice;
- it possible to develop a common framework for rating the quality of different types of knowledge, including the experiential knowledge of service users, so that practitioners may have confidence in what is made available; and that
- the dissemination of knowledge can be linked to excellence in practice.

This chapter examines these assumptions in the light of existing research evidence, and in the light of the debate about the nature of evidence-based practice. I conclude that, while national institutes such as SCIE can significantly enhance the coherence of the social care knowledge base, it will be critical to avoid narrow definitions of the nature of knowledge and to avoid ossifying the relationship between knowledge and practice.

Promoting evidence based practice in a child care charity: The Barnardo's experience

Tony Newman and Di McNeish

Barnardo's, the UK's largest child care charity, has a long standing interest in, and commitment to evidence based practice

(EBP) in social care. This chapter discusses some of the dilemmas, both ideological and practical, that challenge social care organisations trying to implement EBP, defends EBP on grounds of both morality and utility, and describes how Barnardo's has sought to translate theory into practice.

Towards a more reflexive research aware practice: The influence and potential of professional and team culture

John Lawler and Andy Bilson

This chapter reflects on the debates about Evidence Based Practice and suggests a new approach to implementing a more reflexive and research aware social work practice in professional teams. We show that there has been a substantial focus on the responsibility of individual professionals for using best evidence to guide their practice and on the organisation to provide an environment and policies suited to EBP. We argue that there is a need to balance this by an increased focus on the professional and team culture in which social work takes place. We draw on the literature on organisational change and social work research to suggest a new direction for encouraging greater reflexivity and developing a more open participative approach to the use of evidence to shape new practices in social work at the local level.

The contributors

Andy Bilson Professor of Social Work, University of Central Lancashire

Brian Sheldon Professor Applied Social Research and Director, Centre for Evidence-Based Social Services, University of Exeter

Rupatharshini Chilvers NHS Research Project Leader, South West Action Team

Annemarie Ellis Centre for Evidence-Based Social Services, University of Exeter

Alice Moseley Department of Politics, University of Exeter

Frank Ainsworth Research Scholar), School of International, Cultural and Community Studies, Edith Cowan University

Patricia Hansen Head, Department of Social Work, Sydney Children's Hospital, Randwick

Stephanie Tierney Centre for Evidence-Based Social Services, University of Exeter

Carolyn Taylor Senior Lecturer in Social Work, University of Salford

Susan White Senior Lecturer in Social Work, University of Salford

David Smith Professor of Social Work, University of Lancaster

Nick Frost Senior Lecturer in Continuing Education, University of Leeds

Mike Fisher Professor and Director of Research and Reviews, Social Care Institute for Excellence

Tony Newman Principal Officer, Research and Development, Barnardo's

Di McNeish Head of Research, Barnardo's

John Lawler Lecturer, Nuffield Institute for Health, University of Leeds

Printed in the United Kingdom
by Lightning Source UK Ltd.
117592UKS00001B/40

The GEMSTONE IDENTIFIER

WALTER W. GREENBAUM, G.G.

ARCO PUBLISHING, INC.
NEW YORK

To the one gem I can identify
with . . . my wife Henrietta

Published by Arco Publishing, Inc.
215 Park Avenue South, New York, N.Y. 10003

Copyright © 1983 by Walter W. Greenbaum

Library of Congress Cataloging in Publication Data

Greenbaum, Walter W.
  The gemstone identifier.

  Bibliography: p.
  Includes index.
  1. Precious stones—Handbooks, manuals,.etc.
I. Title.
QE392.G74   553.8   82-4074
ISBN 0-668-05387-9 (Cloth Edition)   AACR2
ISBN 0-668-05391-7 (Paper Edition)

Printed in the United States of America

10 9 8 7 6 5 4 3 2 1

WITHDRAWN

Contents

Acknowledgments

I am grateful to the following publishers for permission to quote from previously published material: Gemological Institute of America, Santa Monica, California, (*Gems and Gemology* periodical); Lapidary Journal Inc., San Diego, California ("Practical Gem Knowledge" by Charles J. Parsons, G.G., F.G.A.); and Emerson Books Inc., Buchanan, New York (*Gem Testing* by B.W. Anderson, B.Sc., F.G.A.).

Further acknowledgment is made to the Gemological Institute of America's Gem Instrument Company for their black-and-white photographs of gem-testing instruments and their diamond weight estimators. Acknowledgment is also made to Charles Bloom and Company of New York City for their special oval-shaped diamond weight estimator.

A special thanks to the Institute of Geological Sciences of London for their color plates of assorted fine cut gemstones, the American Gemological Laboratories (Analytics Inc.) of New York City for their beautiful colored photographs showing internal structures of gemstones, and to John Looker, photographer of Basking Ridge, New Jersey, for his excellent cover picture.

I also wish to extend my thanks to Dr. Edward Gubelin, Ph.D., of Lucerne, Switzerland, leading gemologist and worldwide authority in the field of gemstone inclusions, for his vivid description of examining gemstones under magnification.

Finally, my personal thanks to my editor, Virginia Griffin, who gave so much of her time and guidance in the editing of the manuscript.

Preface

When it comes to colored stones, many people involved in the jewelry business, as well as Mr. John Q. Public, know very little about them. Some consumers and, unfortunately, some jewelers can easily be fooled by substitutes and synthetic stones through lack of knowledge.

Picture the following scene. A young man has a loose stone that he thinks might be a ruby. He takes the stone to a jewelry store and asks a salesperson to identify it. The salesperson is unable to tell him anything and asks the manager. The manager fondles the stone in his hand, looks at it quickly through a loupe and returns the stone, stating, "I'm sorry, but I really don't know what stone this is." The young man, who is quite puzzled by this answer, leaves. Can you imagine the thoughts running through his mind? This is what I believe he is thinking as he walks away. "I just can't understand it. I ask a jeweler to identify a stone and he can't do it. Who else does one go to? After all, he's a jeweler. He's supposed to know his business, but apparently he doesn't know much. He won't see me in his store again."

This is what is going on in the person's mind . . . perhaps not in exactly those words, but thoughts to that effect. This person, who could very well be a potential customer, will never return to that establishment because he has lost all confidence in the personnel working there.

When asked to identify an unknown stone, a competent jeweler should be able to classify it with some degree of accuracy. A little knowledge of gemstones will enable the jeweler to talk more intelligently, and the customer's interest will be greatly increased by such a discussion, immediately putting the jeweler in a more favorable light.

Another situation that arises time and time again, and which I have experienced on numerous occasions, should serve to amplify the importance of knowledge. At times I drop my role as a gemologist and act the part of an ordinary consumer interested in purchasing a diamond ring. One such occasion stands out vividly in my mind.

My interest in how personnel handle diamond sales led me to visit the jewelry department of a well-known department store noted for its fine quality merchandise. A young saleswoman approached me and asked if she could be of help. I told her that I was soon celebrating my twenty-fifth wedding anniversary and wanted to purchase a diamond ring for my wife. Looking in the showcase, I spotted two rings with diamonds. Both looked fairly similar in size and I asked her the price of each. Reaching into the showcase, the woman turned over the two tags and told me that both diamonds were a half carat but that one cost five thousand dollars and the other ten thousand dollars. When questioned on the vast difference, since both stones were equal in size, she hesitated for a moment and then said, "Well, because the price tickets say so." Trying to hold back a loud burst of laughter, I quickly composed myself and decided to do a little more probing by asking her to tell me something about the color and quality. She kept examining the price tags, looking for some clues. Finding none, and looking as though she'd been through the "third degree," she finally said in desperation, "All I can tell you is that they both have good color, but one is better than the other." In all sincerity, I explained that I could not purchase any expensive ring without knowing something about the stone. She shrugged her shoulders and told me that perhaps the manager might know, but he was off that night, which happened to be the only night the store was open late.

It was this incident that prompted me to think about the thousands of consumers who are confronted with similar predicaments, learn very little, and finally become fearful of entering a jewelry store.

From the above, it would appear that this book has been written solely for jewelers. This is not true.

It is only natural to expect the owner of a jewelry store, who is involved with gemstones every working day, to be interested in knowing all there is to know about precious stones. However, there are others who take as much interest in these glittering minerals, if not more. Seasoned retail salespeople, employees in the jewelry industry, rock hounds, gemstone collectors, hobbyists, precious stone investors, and just average interested people will find this book an educational beginning to unlocking the fascinating mysteries of the gemstone world.

These groups have their own particular interests. The knowledge gained from reading this book will steer them toward the goal they are seeking in the field of gemstones. Whatever the goal, being able to identify gemstones is a prerequisite for getting involved with gemstones in the first place.

The material in this book does not provide all the answers to identifying gemstones correctly, but is designed to aid the reader in detecting a phony gem with a reasonable amount of accuracy. He or she will be able, for example, to distinguish between a ruby and a spinel, an emerald and a green tourmaline, a genuine emerald and a doublet or triplet, or a blue sapphire and a blue piece of glass.

If this book opens the door slightly to some of the secrets of stone identification and the reader realizes that a stone is not an emerald, ruby, sapphire, or diamond, even though he or she may not be able to tell exactly what it is, the reader will still be in a better position. Remember, this is not a course in gemology.

Some eminent gemologists may claim that the methods of identification, as outlined here, are not sufficient to identify gemstones accurately. As a gemologist, I am fully aware of the important methods of gem identification. It is not my intent to present an extensive work on identifying stones, but rather to provide easy-to-use methods and quick references. However, it is interesting to note that gemologists take extraordinary measures to equip themselves with the appropriate scientific instruments in their laboratories as they perform the task of identifying precious stones.

At various places in the book I have endeavored to explain words or phrases as they are introduced, to add to the reader's understanding.

At the conclusion of the book, there is a glossary of terms with which the reader should become familiar. For those who desire additional information on the subject of gemstones, there is a list of recommended books which immediately follows the glossary.

I hope that, after the reader has digested the contents thoroughly and has used the various tests in determining the identity of many stones, he or she will have realized the potentials that are here for the asking. It is further hoped that some readers might give serious thought to continuing the study of gemstones by enrolling in gemological courses and becoming professional gemologists.

I

Visual Training

The following story was once told by an instructor of a course in gem identification. A loan officer had one of his employees watch to see the sort of car driven by people as they arrived to have their jewelry appraised for a loan. If the employee notified the appraiser that the car was an expensive one, such as a Cadillac or a Mercedes, it was assumed that the stone being brought in was a natural gem. This assumption would be taken into consideration during the appraisal. An old or less expensive vehicle was assumed to indicate that the stone was a synthetic. Unfortunately, today we find many people dealing in precious stones who follow the same line of reasoning. They will assume that a stone mounted in gold or platinum, is a natural one (a diamond if it is colorless). If the stone is set in silver, it is then thought to be an imitation. This is definitely not the case, and an examiner is foolish to be guided by such nonsense.

Let's consider what the term "synthetic" means. Basically, a synthetic is something that is not genuine or natural. With reference to gemstones, a synthetic stone is one that has been formed by combining various chemicals similar to those found in a natural stone, under certain pressure and heat conditions, to produce a stone possessing the same chemical and physical characteristics as the natural gemstone. Actually, the synthetic stone is "grown" in a laboratory from tiny specks by using the same chemical components of a natural gemstone under the same conditions of pressure and heat. Although some synthetic stones are difficult to detect, in many cases they can easily be identified by careful examination.

It is a known fact that a blind person develops the remainder of his senses to compensate for the loss of his sight. The person working with a limited amount of equipment should develop his sense of sight and utilize, to the fullest extent, whatever device he has.

Gemologists may or may not examine a stone with the naked eye, but more frequently they will start the identification process of an unknown stone by using certain instruments. However, since many people will not have this equipment, it will be necessary to train the eye to recognize certain characteristics in gemstones.

Upon receiving a stone for identification, carefully examine it under a strong direct light, paying attention to observe strong doubling of the back facets, fractures, surface luster, cleavage marks, and color. The following sections explain briefly each of these characteristics.

Doubling of Back Facets

Light passing through certain doubly refractive stones will break up into two distinct rays going in different directions and at different speeds. Zircons and tourmalines are stones that have this characteristic (*See*

Chapter 6). In observing these two stones under magnification, two images of the facet edges between the back facets (pavilion facets) are made visible by the two rays. This "doubling," as the effect is called (*See* Fig. 1a), is so evident in zircons and tourmalines that one can see this remarkable occurrence even in stones as small as one-third to one-half carat. Other gemstones that are doubly refractive like corundum, quartz, and beryl also exhibit this feature, but not as strongly. In examining a stone for doubling, observe it through the table to get a clear picture of the entire pavilion facets. This doubling characteristic distinguishes tourmalines and zircons from other stones which might be mistaken for them. It will be helpful for beginners to study these two types of stones which distinctly show this doubling effect so that it will be recognized in other stones that have weaker doubling.

Figure 1a. Doubling of back facets

Fractures

Fractures are characterized by a jagged or splintery line that always starts breaking at some point on the surface of a gemstone and works its way into the stone. Stones with a fibrous structure like jade will often exhibit this effect. Fractures can also appear shell-like (curved inward) or conchoidal, as it is called, which is very common in glass and quartz to a great extent and in other stones to a lesser degree.

Fractures are often a natural result of heavy pressure within a stone when it is being formed far beneath the earth. It also can be caused accidentally by a heavy blow. Fractures can appear almost anywhere in a gemstone.

Surface Luster

Three qualifications must be met in order for a mineral to be considered a gemstone: durability, beauty, and rarity. One of the properties that determines beauty in a stone is its surface luster. This property is a distinguished feature of reflected light shining off the surface of a gemstone. There are those who believe that luster is associated with the stone's hardness. That is not so. Luster is related to the stone's refraction and transparency,

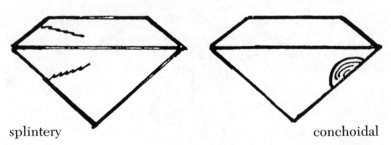

splintery   conchoidal

Figure 1b.   Fractures

such as in a diamond with a high refractive index. The higher the refractive index, the higher the luster. The following are kinds of luster frequently found in gemstones:

Dull luster—no brightness
Greasy luster—oily appearance
Vitreous luster—that which is found in glass
Adamantine—the high glitter and sparkle of diamonds

Cleavage

Cleavage has often been mistaken for fracture and vice versa. However, there is a difference. Whereas a fracture entails breakage, cleavage refers to a state of splitting. This separation occurs in definite directions which are parallel to the stone's crystal faces and can be seen as straight parallel lines.

A gemstone can be cleaved by hitting it with a hard blow in the direction of the cleavage plane. This procedure is usually performed by an experienced cutter who receives a large rough stone. He will study the natural arrangement of the crystal faces and then decide exactly where to make the first blow in order to split the stone along a line parallel to the crystal surface.

Cleavage can be better understood if one pictures a long piece of wooden two-by-four. If the wood is laid horizontally and shaven with a plane (woodworking tool), the shavings will come off easily. However, if one were to place the two-by-four on one end and then try to shave the top end, the wood would splinter off into many uneven pieces because the direction of shaving was against the grain. In gemstones, we must split the stone in its "grain" or cleavage direction, or else the stone will crack into a number of pieces.

Cleavage lines are helpful in separating diamonds from glass imitations because diamonds show this splitting effect, while glass, which has no definite crystal structure, shows only shell-like fractures.

Color

Color, in diamonds refers to the degree of whiteness within the stone's body. Shades of white vary from colorless to yellow with many degrees of white and yellow in between.

If ten diamonds were placed in a row and numbered from one to ten in graduating color shades, it would be difficult to separate numbers one and two by their color. Likewise, in examining numbers six and seven, it would be difficult to tell them apart by their color. However, there would be a considerable difference in color between numbers one and seven.

Although evaluating diamonds by color requires the use of a set of comparison stones previously graded for color, one can readily detect a light yellow tinge of body color, a fairly colorless diamond or one that is very yellow.

A yellow diamond that is vivid or intense in its shade of color belongs in a category all its own. Diamonds come in practically all colors of the rainbow and these special diamonds are classified as "Fancies."

When it comes to all the other colored gemstones, there was a belief among many that the color of a stone identified it. It was taken for granted that a red stone was a ruby, a blue stone was a sapphire, a green stone was an emerald and so on. Today it is known that many stones may have the same color. (*See* Table 7, p. 76). There are some instances when a gemologist with an experienced eye can recognize a stone by a certain characteristic shade of color. For example: a violetish-blue colored stone of low intensity might indicate a tanzanite. However, the identification process would probably not stop there. The gemologist would perform other tests before deciding the stone was actually tanzanite.

Thus, the characteristics of doubling, fractures, luster, cleavage, and color may enable the reader to identify certain stones without going any further. One would be surprised by how many stones can be identified this way. For example, synthetic rutile, zircon, peridot, and tourmaline show strong doubling of the back facets but not many stones fall into this group. In many cases, this doubling can be seen easily with a low-powered loupe and often with the naked eye. For example, if you were to see a greenish-blue, transparent, faceted stone that displayed doubling of the back facets, you might be reasonably sure it was a zircon. Or if the stone were pinkish, or dark green, it would probably be a tourmaline.

Another instance when visual perception is useful is in examining a stone that has a conchoidal fracture and a vitreous luster and is opaque or semi-opaque. This would indicate a glass imitation of such gems as turquoise or jade.

With a little practice, you should be able to differentiate between those stones that show a high luster and those that do not. Look at a rhinestone and then at a diamond and notice the vast difference. Examine the crown portion of a red stone—above the girdle—with that of the pavilion section—below the girdle. If there is a difference in luster, there's a good chance that the stone in question is a garnet doublet.

A word or two on facets would be appropriate at this point.

Facets are the small polished surface areas on a cut

gemstone. These surfaces are carefully and scientifically placed by the skilled cutter when fashioning one of the various gemstone shapes.

The faceting process is a two-fold procedure with the main facets (table, culet, bezel, and pavilion facets) being placed first in order to obtain the stone's proper proportion. The second stage is the placing of the remainder of the facets (stars and upper and lower girdle facets). (*See* Figure 2, p. 8.)

When examining a stone with the naked eye, it is necessary to notice the type of facets. If the facets are round instead of flat and do not meet at the proper junctions, the stone is not a natural mineral but rather a molded imitation.

A rather long period of time is needed to polish a facet so that the finished surface will produce the required brilliance of the stone. The polisher must be

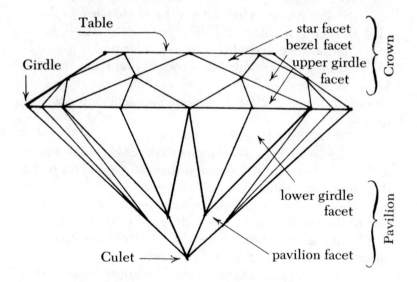

Figure 2.   Parts of a gemstone

especially careful not to polish a facet too far down, else he will ruin the meeting of the facet edges and the stone's symmetry.

Wheel marks, caused by a build-up of heat resulting from speedy polishing, are another factor which the polisher strives to keep at a minimum. These marks are visible on the facet surface as very tiny groove lines and result in a definite loss of brilliance.

In summation, if you do not have expensive instruments, then it becomes imperative that your eyes be employed to the fullest extent. Adding up the various factors that the human eye can determine, such as doubling of the back facets, luster, cleavage, color, and fractures, the unaided eye can accomplish much in the process of gem identification.

II

Hardness of Stones

There are some two thousand known types of minerals but only about seventy-five meet the requirements to be considered gemstones. **Beauty, rarity,** and **durability** are the three main qualifications necessary for a stone to be called a gemstone. For present purposes, beauty and rarity will not be discussed since these two factors do not enter the picture of identifying stones.

The most important single property which affects a gemstone's durability is its hardness. As the word is defined in mineralogy, hardness is the resistance which a mineral offers to abrasion. It further means the stone's ability to resist scratching by a still harder substance. This important property enables a gemstone to resist breakage and also to retain the high luster of its polished facets for an indefinitely long period of time. Determining the hardness of a stone as one means of identification can shorten, in many cases, the many other tests that would be needed.

Hardness depends upon the force between particles within a stone that acts to unite them. However, a stone's hardness must not be confused with a stone's brittleness. A stone can be hard and resist breakage from a hard blow, but if it shatters into a powder as a result of impact, the stone would be considered brittle. This brittleness is also known as a stone's tenacity or the resistance which it has to being broken or crushed. Thus the degree of tenacity that a gemstone possesses will indicate whether that stone is tough or brittle.

Many gemstones are harder than any substances they will come in contact with. One difference between gemstones and glass imitations is that glass imitations lose their luster very quickly because they are quite soft and their surfaces are easily scratched by dust particles which settle from the atmosphere. Dust contains particles of quartz, which is harder than glass. Thus when a glass imitation is rubbed against one's hand or clothing, the quartz begins to scratch the glass and in a short time the luster is diminished. Of course, a gemstone can collect grease and dirt, but these substances can easily be removed as there are no scratches where the grease and dirt can lodge.

The Mohs scale, named after F. Mohs, a German mineralogist who lived in the early nineteenth century, is usually employed as a measure of the hardness of minerals. It consists of ten minerals arranged in order of their increasing degrees of hardness:

1	Talc	6	Orthoclase (feldspar)
2	Gypsum	7	Quartz
3	Calcite	8	Topaz
4	Fluorite	9	Corundum
5	Apatite	10	Diamond

The numbers or values assigned to these minerals show relative hardness and not actual hardness. For example: diamond isn't just a little harder than corundum. It is many times harder than corundum is to topaz. Each of these minerals on the scale can be scratched by

TABLE 1 HARDNESS OF STONES

Stone	Hardness	Stone	Hardness
Diamond	10	Jade (Nephrite)	6.5
Corundum	9	Moonstone	6–6.5
Chrysoberyl	8.5	Rutile	6–6.5
Yag	8.5	Turquoise	6
Spinel	8	Hematite	5.5–6.5
Topaz	8	Opal	5.5–6.5
Beryl	7.5–8	Glass	5–6
Zircon	7.5	Lapis	5–5.5
Tourmaline	7–7.5	Titanite	5–5.5
Quartz	7	Coral	3.5
Garnet	6.5–7.5	Pearl	2.5–3.5
Jade (Jadeite)	6.5–7	Amber	2–2.5
Peridot	6.5–7	Jet	2–2.5

all of the minerals above it and will itself scratch all of those minerals below it. (*See* Table 1.) Topaz with a hardness of eight can scratch all the minerals from one to seven, but can be scratched itself by corundum and diamond. Of course, substances having the same hardness will scratch each other.

Scratching one mineral with another is not an easy procedure when testing below the hardness of five. Here one can extend the Mohs scale by adding the following supplementary scale of the hardness of common minerals*:

Fingernail .... about 2½

Copper coin .... about 3

Knife blade .... about 4½

Glass .... about 5½

Steel file .... about 6 to 7

Excerpted from "Practical Gem Knowledge for the Amateur" by Charles J. Parsons, copyrighted by Lapidary Journal, Inc., by express permission of the Lapidary Journal, Inc.

In determining a stone's hardness, one must locate the mineral on the Mohs scale that will just scratch it. For example, if a mineral is scratched by a piece of quartz with a hardness of seven, but the mineral cannot be scratched by orthoclase, with a hardness of six, the stone in question then is said to have a hardness of seven.

One must be aware of the difference between an actual scratch and a chalk mark. The chalk is left on the harder of the two minerals and is a powder of the softer mineral. This powder can easily be rubbed away with one's finger.

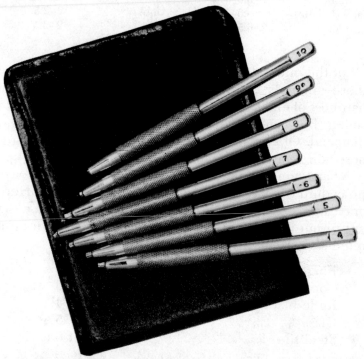

Set of hardness points   (courtesy of Gem Instrument Company, Subsidiary of Gemological Institute of America, Los Angeles, Calif.)

Although the hardness of rough or cut stones can best be determined by the use of a set of hardness points, as they are called, a simpler way is to employ a very fine steel file (available at most hardware stores) which has its own hardness of between six and seven on the Mohs scale. If this file "bites" the stone, its hardness is below seven. Stones that are harder than seven will not show this bite but will slide over the tested edge and usually leave a steel streak. Many imitations, especially those made of glass, have a hardness below seven, whereas the precious stones are much harder. This method of identification can generally be used to separate the imitations from the real stones. With quartz having a hardness of seven, one will soon discover that the precious stones (diamond, ruby, sapphire and emerald) all have decidedly higher hardnesses.

In using the hardness test, be sure that the scratch you make is as short as possible, no more than one thirty-second of an inch. On a faceted stone, the scratch should always be made on the girdle and never on the table or other prominently exposed areas. Discretion must be used in this method since careless use of this test has many times resulted in damaging stones.

When using a knife blade, hold it as though you were going to cut the mineral with the point. Do not pick at the mineral surface with the flat side of the blade towards yourself.

With the steel file, do not file as though smoothing down a piece of metal, but rather scratch with the sharp, angular end. It might be a good idea to first practice with some cheap or discarded stones so as to get the feel of the tool as it goes over the different hardnesses. When testing a mounted stone, use a broken file that has a sharp corner and apply it to one of the lower facets near the girdle, making a very short scratch and watching this through a ten-power loupe.

Once reaching feldspar, which is six on the Mohs scale, one must use minerals themselves as testing implements. To make it easier, pieces of minerals having a hardness of six to ten are mounted in metal holders (hardness points). These instruments can be purchased from a local supplier and are very inexpensive.

When testing a gemstone for hardness it is not necessary to start at either end of the Mohs scale. Scratch the gemstone with any one of the ten hardness minerals. If the stone is scratched, that would indicate that the gemstone is softer than the hardness mineral. Then it becomes just a matter of finding which hardness mineral scratches the gemstone and is scratched itself. This would indicate that the gemstone has the same hardness as the hardness mineral.

You can purchase very inexpensive stones in most hobby stores for practicing the hardness test. You can also check the *Lapidary Journal* (see list of periodicals) for the addresses of various rock shops that sell very inexpensive stones.

It is reasonably acceptable to use the hardness test when you have an immediate decision to make regarding the identification of a stone; that is, to determine whether a stone is real or a glass imitation. It is advisable to practice on very inexpensive stones where the danger of damage will not be costly.

I must emphasize that this method should be avoided in most cases on all transparent stones suspected of being valuable except as a last resort and should never be used at all on emeralds.

Use the hardness test only after having had plenty of experience with cheap stones and then proceed only with great caution.

III

Cleavage and Fracture

A discussion of cleavage and fracture can be very lengthy and technical. Although both have been touched upon in Chapter I, it is important to discuss these two properties a little further in so far as their relationship to identification of stones is concerned.

Cleavage, when referring to gemstones, is the ability to readily split or separate along definite planes and in definite directions. This property is characteristic of crystalline structured stones having a systematic molecular architecture (a definite arrangement of molecules). A cleavage can usually be seen when examining diamonds and topaz under high magnification, since both these stones split easily. Most times the cleavage will be recognized by cracks within the stone or by the irregular character of the stone's surface which might show up as small parallel planes (*see* Fig. 21). Amorphous stones (stones having no regular internal order of molecular arrangement or definite crystalline structure), like glass and opal, are easily distinguished.

The difference between glass and diamond is readily observed by examining the stone under high magnification along the girdle. If tiny portions have been broken off along the girdle, sometimes by the pressure of prongs, one will be able to see what type of breakage the stone has. A glass imitation will show a shell-like fracture.

The following example will help the reader to understand the difference between crystalline and amorphous stones. Picture a crowd of people gathered around someone giving a lecture in the street. These people take their positions in no particular formation. It can easily be seen here that there is no form or symmetry in their arrangement. If these people were molecules they would represent the structure within an amorphous stone. To get back to these people again, assume they were lined up in a marching order for a parade. They would be arranged in regular rows and they would march in regular files. Here again, if they were molecules, they would be displaying a crystalline stone (*see* Fig. 3).

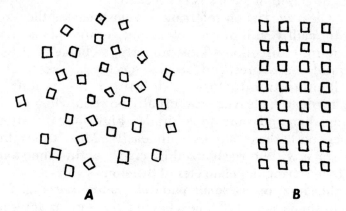

A   B

Figure 3.   Molecular arrangements   (A) Molecules arranged with no definite form or symmetry. (B) Molecules arranged in a definite pattern.

In the study of crystalline structures we find there are many patterns of molecular arrangements, but for our purpose, suffice to say, all crystalline stones are alike in that they have regular arrangements of their molecules. Amorphous stones do not.

Whereas the property of cleavage is characteristic only of crystalline stones, fracture is a property possessed by all minerals. A curved or shell-like fracture is known as a conchoidal fracture. This type is seen in many stones. Quartz, opals and glass are typical examples. Stones that are fibrous in structure break with a splintery type of fracture. Jadeite is a good example. In amorphous stones with no orderly structure there is no cleavage, and there is no telling in what direction such a stone will break. However, we can predict where a stone of crystalline structure, with good cleavage, will break.

It is important to distinguish between breakage and brittleness. Breakage is related to brittleness only when a break results in the shattering of a stone into a powder. When the breakage results in a piece chipped or broken off from a stone, it is a fracture.

The property of fracture can be seen with a powerful loupe in a stone that has been damaged. The stone's surface will be pitted where chips broke out. At times, this condition can also be seen near the prongs of a setting.

IV

Specific Gravity

Specific Gravity or S.G., as it is sometimes called in the jewelry business, is the relationship between the weight of a substance and the weight of an equal volume of water. To say it another way, it is a measure of how many times heavier a substance is than an equal volume of water.

Everyone knows that a pound of feathers is larger in size than a pound of metal. It is obvious, then, that there is an internal difference in the two substances. Without becoming too technical, the atoms of the metal are packed closer together and therefore take up less room than those of the feathers. Thus when we refer to substances and their weight, we actually mean their density. This ratio is known as the specific gravity of the substance.

At this point you are probably asking yourself, "What does all this have to do with identifying gemstones?" Determining the specific gravity of a stone is valuable evidence in its identification. All gemstones have this property (*see* Table 2), and since gemstones vary in their specific gravity, determining a stone's S.G., then comparing it to a list of common gems and finding the one

TABLE 2 MINERALS AND THEIR SPECIFIC GRAVITY

Stone	S.G.	Stone	S.G
Zircon	4.0–4.8	Tourmaline	3.1
Rutile	4.2	Nephrite	3.0
Corundum	4.0	Beryl	2.75
Chrysoberyl	3.7	Lapis	2.75
Spinel	3.6	Turquoise	2.72
Topaz	3.53	Coral	2.7
Diamond	3.52	Quartz	2.66
Titanite	3.5	Pearl	2.6
Jadeite	3.34	Opal	2.15
Peridot	3.3	Jet	1.32
Apatite	3.18	Amber	1.08

with the same value will put you one step closer to identifying an unknown gem.

It is important to note that this test can be used only with loose stones.

Although there are many methods used in determining the specific gravity of gemstones such as the ordinary diamond balance, the chemical balance, the pycnometer, heavy liquids, the jolly balance, and the direct reading balance, for our purposes, the easiest and most economical method is the use of heavy liquids. A set of standard S.G. liquids with fixed intervals can easily be made by obtaining the following liquids purchased from any chemical company:

Bromoform .... S.G. 2.89
Potassium Mercuric Iodide .... S.G. 3.19
Cadmium Borotungstate .... S.G. 3.28
Methylene Iodide .... S.G. 3.31
Baruim Mercuric Iodide .... S.G. 3.58
Thallium Formate .... S.G. 4.65

Two prepared sets can be purchased from the

Specific gravity liquids   (courtesy of Gem Instrument
Company, Subsidiary of Gemological Institute of
America, Los Angeles, Calif.)

Gemological Institute at their Gem Instrument Division, 1660 Stewart Street, Santa Monica, California, 90406. One set contains S.G. liquids numbers 2.57, 2.67 and 3.10. The second set contains S.G. liquids numbers 3.32, 2.85 and 2.62.

All of the above-mentioned chemicals are toxic and must be handled carefully. Do not breathe in their fumes. When through using these chemicals, wash your hands thoroughly with soap and hot water to remove the smell, which has a tendency to linger. These chemicals will not damage stones in the small amount of time that is required to perform specific gravity testing; these liquids can be used to test all stones.

All of the above solutions with their maximum S.G. given can be weakened (lowering the specific gravity value) if one wishes to obtain a more graduated scale. This can be accomplished by diluting the methylene iodide with benzol, and others with water. However, from my own personal experience, I feel that the above liquids are sufficient to distinguish the various stones that frequently appear without diluting any of them.

As you place a stone (using a clean tweezer) into one of the solutions, you can determine the stone's specific gravity by watching whether it sinks or floats. If it sinks, the stone's S.G. is higher than that of the liquid. If the stone floats, its specific gravity is lower than the liquid's. If the density of the liquid is the same as that of the stone, then the stone will remain stationary in the liquid wherever it was placed (*see* Figure 4).

All stones, and the tweezer, should be washed after immersion in these liquids. Wash first in water and then in benzene. If this is not done the liquids will become contaminated and their density will change.

Example of Stone Being Tested: You wish to know the identity of a green stone. Holding it with a tweezer,

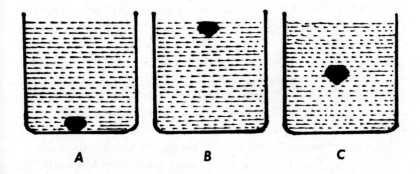

Figure 4. Specific gravity testing (A) Stone sinks to bottom of container, indicating that the stone has a higher S.G. than the liquid does. (B) Stone floats on top of liquid, indicating that the stone's S.G. is lower than the liquid's. (C) Stone remains where it is placed, indicating that the stone's S.G. is equal to the liquid's.

drop it into liquid 2.89. If the stone sinks, place it into the next higher liquid and continue to place it into other higher liquids until you find the liquid that the stone will float in. This would indicate that the stone's S.G. is between that of the last liquid in which it sank and the present one in which it floated. If the stone floats in S.G. 2.89, the S.G. of the stone is lower than 2.89 and that would immediately eliminate all green stones above the 2.89 S.G., such as zircon, garnet, corundum, spinel, jade and peridot. The stone could be either beryl (emerald) or quartz. (*See* Table 2.)

In later chapters other identifying tests will be discussed that will provide additional proof as to whether the green stone is an emerald.

The **heavy liquid** test should not be used on

such stones as opal, pearl or turquoise if possible. The liquids are too strong for these stones and long immersions can result in damage to the stones. If the test must be used, do it quickly and wash the liquids off the stones immediately.

For those who would like to use another method besides the **heavy liquid** test, there is a device manufactured by the Four Cover Mine, P.O. Box 1552, San Leandro, California, 94577. The "Specific Gravity Balance," as it is called, is an inexpensive, do-it-yourself kit which comes complete with instructions.

Up to this point, I have discussed four methods of identifying colored gemstones, all of them with inexpensive equipment. The reader should begin to realize by this time there are ways of determining a stone's identity without getting too involved with technical procedures. This is not to lose sight of the fact that with the proper gemological training and special scientific instruments, the gemologist will make test after test until a gemstone is correctly identified.

V

Refraction Testing

In his book, *Gem Testing*, B.A. Anderson, a well-known gemologist, states, "Man is a profound lazy creature and it has been said that most of his inventions have been born of the urge to save himself trouble. Apart from a few enthusiastic amateurs, what people seem to ask of scientific or mechanical devices is that they should be so simple to operate and so foolproof that they can be used without any technical knowledge whatsoever."*

Mr. Anderson couldn't have said it any better, for this is precisely what this book is all about. Although not exactly foolproof, what is being persented here are some simple devices and techniques to verify the identity of a gemstone or at least to narrow down the possibilities of what type of stone is being evaluated. The main purpose here is to welcome any apparatus or procedure that will aid in making this determination.

Using refraction liquids as a means of identifying stones can provide helpful information. Significant discoveries such as various inclusions, doublets and color distribution will also be detected.

Gem Testing by B.W. Anderson, (chapter 2), published by Emerson Books, Inc., Box 158, Buchanan, N.Y. 10511

Believe it or not, the word "inclusion," when used for gemstones, is practically unknown to most people. Most jewelers, rock hounds, gem collectors, and other interested individuals, when examining or discussing the internal structure of a stone, refer to whatever they see within the stone as flaws or carbon spots. These two characteristics have been used to describe every type of internal blemish. The term "flaw" seems to me to be indicative of a damage. The word itself sounds too severe, and therefore I never use it. As for the word "carbon," it has been used so frequently that people tend to describe everything within a gemstone as carbon.

Inclusion is the proper word to use. The dictionary defines inclusion as "something that is included," and in the case of gemstones, it refers to anything solid, gaseous, or liquid that is present within the mass of a mineral. Inclusions will be discussed in more detail in later chapters.

To get back to the subject of refraction, try this simple experiment. Place a pencil or drinking straw into a glass of water. You will notice that the pencil or straw appears to be bent. That is, the part which is out of the water is not in a continuous straight line with the portion in the water (*See* Fig. 5). To bring this phenomenon closer to home, when light passes from one medium to another as from air into water, the light ray is bent or **Refracted**. Those who have studied physics in school will recall this interesting occurrence. The amount that a ray is bent as it passes through various mediums, in our case gemstones, is called the **Index of Refraction**, sometimes known as the R.I. of a stone. This index is expressed in a ratio indicating the speed of light in one medium to that of another.

Every stone has been found to have its own refractive index, and therefore determining the R.I. of a given stone will provide further evidence of its identity. The

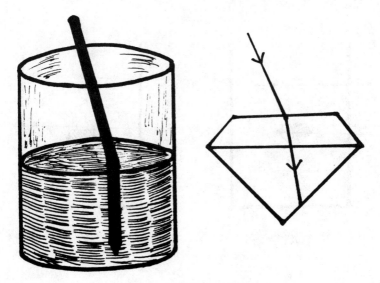

Figure 5.   Bending of light rays

refractometer, an expensive instrument, is the most accurate device for determining the R.I. of any stone. However, to keep expenses at a minimum, you can use a much less costly method, the **Liquid Immersion Test**, which will, in most cases, identify an unknown stone by providing a close enough reading to eliminate other possibilities.

The principle behind this method is that a transparent solid becomes practically invisible when placed in a liquid that has the same index of refraction. (*See* Fig. 6). The solid (gemstone) and the liquid form a continuous medium for the passage of light so that the boundaries of the stone tend to disappear. By using a series of liquids with different indices of refraction, the approximate index of most stones can be found. The stone is immersed in one liquid after another until the liquid is found in which the stone most completely disappears.

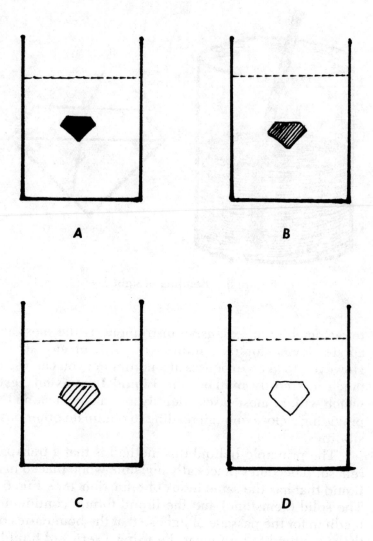

Figure 6. Refractive index immersion test The stone becomes lighter and lighter until it is placed in the last beaker, where it seems to disappear. The stone's R.I. is equal to that of the liquid in *D*.

TABLE 3 IMMERSION LIQUIDS EMPLOYED IN TESTING FOR REFRACTIVE INDEX

Liquid	R.I.
Water	1.33
Ethyl Alcohol	1.36
Glycerine	1.47
Mineral Oil	1.48
Clove Oil	1.54
Anise Oil	1.55
Bromoform	1.59
Cinnamon Oil	1.60
Monochlornaphthaline	1.63
Monobromnaphaline	1.65
Methylene Iodide	1.74
Sulphur in Methylene Iodide	1.79

TABLE 4 INDEX REFRACTION TABLE

Stone	R.I.	Stone	R.I.
Rutile	2.61–2.5	Spinel	1.71
Diamond	2.41	Zoisite	
Titanite	2.40	(Tanzanite)	1.69–1.70
Zircon (high)	1.93–1.98	Peridot	1.65–1.69
Garnet (Andradite)	1.87	Jadeite	1.65–1.66
Garnet		Tourmaline	1.62–1.64
(Spessartite)	1.81	Turquoise	1.61–1.65
Zircon (low)	1.81	Nephrite	1.60–1.63
Garnet (Almandite)	1.80	Topaz	1.60–1.62
Corundum (Ruby,		Beryl (Emerald	
Sapphire)	1.76	and Aquamarine)	1.57–1.58
Garnet (Rhodolite)	1.76	Quartz	1.54–1.55
Chrysoberyl		Amber	1.54
(Alexandrite)	1.74–1.75	Lapis	1.50
Garnet (Pyrope)	1.74	Coral	1.48–1.65
Garnet		Opal	1.45
(Grossularite)	1.73	Glass	1.44–1.81

The stone then has approximately the same index as that of liquid (*see* Tables 3 and 4).

In examining the table of immersion liquids on page 31, it is important to note that Bromoform, Monochlornaphthaline, Monobromnaphaline, Methylene Iodide, and Sulphur in Methylene Iodide are very toxic. One should be careful not to breathe in their fumes. Methylene Iodide and Sulphur in Methylene Iodide have a tendency to stain the hands. However, they can be removed by washing first with benzene or alcohol and then with hot soapy water. None of these five liquids will burn the skin if contact is made with them.

When testing a mounted gemstone in an immersion liquid, you should wash the mounted stone immediately in water and dry it before immersing it in another liquid. If this is not done, the liquids will eventually become impure and therefore unsuitable to provide correct refractive index determinations.

The immersion liquid test is very useful when handling mounted stones, where their shape, size and location make it difficult to use a refractometer.

Although there are no liquids having an index as high as the zircon (1.92), diamond (2.42), and rutile (2.61), once having proved an unknown stone's R.I. to be over 1.79 you have eliminated many gemstones; other tests will allow you to complete the identification.

VI

Polariscope Testing

Light rays that pass from one medium to another do not always exit as one distinct ray. In such stones as glass, amber, opals, diamonds, spinels, and garnets, light rays do pass through as one ray. However, in many of the minerals, like corundum, quartz, beryl, and zircon, light will pass through as more than one ray. The stones split light rays. These stones are known as **Double Refractive Stones**. Those that allow light to pass through as one ray are called **Single Refractive** (*see* Table 5).

The polariscope is an instrument that indicates to the viewer whether a transparent or translucent (semi-transparent) gemstone is single or double refractive. This test is another valuable aid in identifying stones. The polariscope cannot be used with opaque stones (stones which do not allow light to pass through).

The polariscope employs two Polaroid film plates. These plates are actually linear plastic plates, that is, small, thin, round pieces of plastic coated with microscopic crystals. When two Polaroid film plates are lined up in the same way, light will pass through them. When one plate is turned one hundred and eighty degrees or at right angles to the other, the light will be completely

33

TABLE 5
POLARISCOPE TESTED STONES

Synthetic Rutile	D
Strontium Titanite	S
Diamond	S
Zircon	D
Garnet	S
Corundum	D
Synthetic Corundum	D
Chrysoberyl	D
Synthetic Spinel	S
Spinel	S
Peridot	D
Tourmaline	D
Topaz	D
Beryl	D
Synthetic Emerald	D
Amethyst	D
Amber	S
Moonstone	D
Opal	S
Glass	S
Plastics	S

D—double refractive
S—single refractive

blocked out. These plates also contain a diffusing element that allows light from a light source to pass through the entire film plate evenly.

Sample pieces, enough for use in the construction of an inexpensive polariscope, can be obtained by writing to the Polaroid Corporation in Norwood, Massachusetts. Companies in Japan also produce Polaroid film plates, but the Polaroid Corporation is the foremost manufacturer.

A sturdy polariscope can be constructed using a cardboard cylindrical shell about eight inches long and two inches in diameter, with a Polariod film plate at each end. The top plate should be rotatable. (*see* Fig. 7).

With a bright light source at the opposite end of the rotatable Polaroid film plate, look through the rotatable plate to the bottom plate. If you see light coming through the bottom plate, rotate the top plate until the bottom plate becomes dark. When the bottom plate is dark,

Polariscope (courtesy of Gem Instrument Company, Subsidiary of Gemological Institute of America, Los Angeles, Calif.)

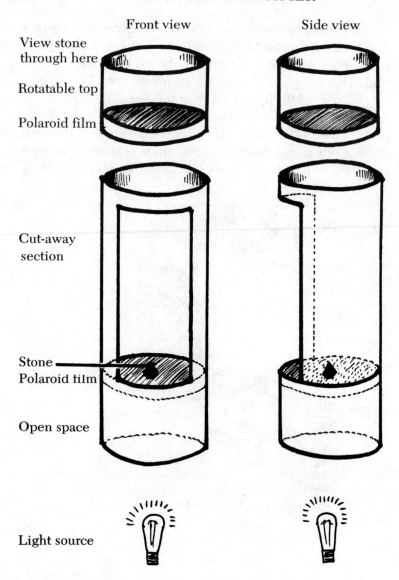

Figure 7.   Homemade polariscope

place the transparent or translucent stone that you are examining on the bottom plate, face down.

With a tweezer or any other pointed instrument, move the stone around slowly in a clockwise direction. If the stone becomes light and dark as you are moving it, then it is doubly refractive. If, on the other hand, the stone remains dark, it is singly refractive. When the stone remains light, the stone is known as an aggregate (a mineral made up of a cluster or group of tiny particles). Some of the better-known aggregates are coral, jadeite, lapis, and nephrite.

A much more simplified instrument can be put together by taking two pieces of Polaroid film and attaching them to a thin rod on which the front film plate is movable. The two film plates should be set so that, when looking through the bottom or back piece towards a light source, you cannot see any light come through. Use this position to examine a stone. Practice for a few minutes as you change the position of the front film plate. When you cannot see light coming through the back plate, use two fingers to hold a stone between the two plates. Rotate the stone to obtain the refraction (*see* Fig. 8).

In examining a stone under the polariscope it will be helpful to study the effect when the stone is placed with the culet down (stone laid on its pavilion facets), as well as with the table down, since many gemstones with high refractive indexes transmit light only through the culet.

Another factor to be considered in using the polariscope is that most gemstones are not flawless internally, due to various types of inclusions, and are often poorly polished. This results in some stones' having a noticeably odd appearance under the Polaroid plates. Some singly refractive stones may appear somewhat similiar to doubly refractive stones. This condition is known as

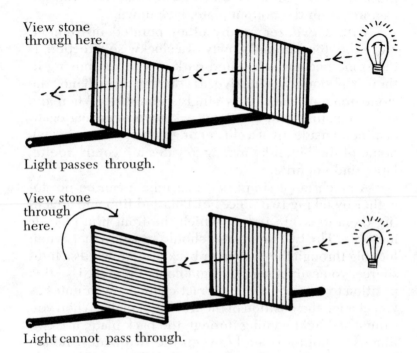

View stone through here.

Light passes through.

View stone through here.

Light cannot pass through.

Figure 8.   Simplified polariscope

anomalous double refraction, a situation in which single refractive stone will not produce the distinctive dark appearance and will not exhibit the light and dark effect of double refraction. Black streaks or shadows will appear as the Polaroid film plate is rotated.

The rule that is usually adhered to, that a dark appearance in a stone under examination indicates a single refractive stone, and a light and dark appearance indicates a double refractive stone, cannot always be applied. You should be aware that not all single refractive stones react in the same way.

VII

Use of the Dichroscope

Another factor related to refraction is the strength of a stone, or how strong or weak the two shades of color in a doubly refractive stone appear. This is known as the stone's birefringence. This strength usually reveals itself in two shades of color when a doubly refracted stone is viewed through a small instrument called a dichroscope, which is a lens system built into a small tube. This instrument cannot be made easily by the reader. However, it is very inexpensive and definitely worth having. It can be purchased through your local supply house or the G.I.A.

Ruby is a good example of a gemstone showing two shades of color (dichroism). As you look through the instrument, while holding it close to the eye and near a good light source, you will see two square apertures side by side at the opposite end of the tube. In the case of the ruby, as the dichroscope is rotated in one direction, both openings will display the same color. In the other direction, the two apertures will show a maximum difference in color (red and purple). Such a stone is said to be dichroic or possessing dichroism (*see* Fig. 9).

It is also important to move the stone around as you

Dichroscope (courtesy of Gem Instrument Company, Subsidiary of Gemological Institute of America, Los Angeles, Calif.)

view it, so as to see it from all angles in order to be certain of catching the two colors if the stone is doubly refractive. Hold the stone being examined between two fingers so that you can rotate it easily. In some stones the color change will not be seen if the stones are held in one position only.

Sometimes you may see a third color in a gemstone while viewing it in a particular direction. When this occurs the stone is said to have pleochroism. Topaz and spodumene are two examples of pleochroic stones. Three colors are very seldom seen, if ever, by the unaided eye. However, three colors may become very apparent when a stone is viewed through the dichroscope, thus providing another aid in the identification of gemstones.

It is interesting to note that red garnet and red spinel are constantly used to imitate the ruby, but because they do not show the dichroic colors under examination, these stones are easily distinguished from rubies, which are very dichroic.

Thus we have another method of separating singly refractive stones from the doubly refractive; singly refractive not showing any color differences, and doubly refractive showing color changes.

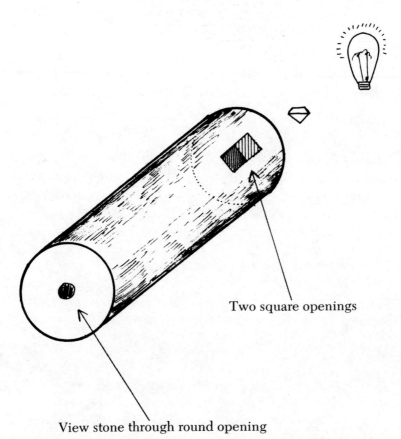

Light   source

Two square openings

View stone through round opening

Figure 9. Viewing a stone through the dichroscope

VIII

Magnification

Examining a stone under high-power magnification will prove to be one of your most important means of identifying gemstones.

Dr. Edward Gubelin, leading gemologist and worldwide authority in the field of gemstone inclusions, had this to say in one of his early publications on inclusions in gemstones:

"Very few people realize that in these jewels, they have the revelation of natural monuments of a past that reaches back beyond the excavations of archaeologists in Mexico, Egypt and Mesopotamia to many many thousands of years. To those who are able to explore their secrets, precious stones relate to a story as interesting as that of the huge pyramids by the pharaohs of Luxor.

"The microscope alone is able to probe their innermost secrets and it is recognized as one of the most important instruments for revealing the internal features of gems. Through the eyes of this remarkable assistant, we are able to see those peculiar characteristics and formations of the minerals, liquids, gas bubbles, and feathers which we term inclusions."

Up to this point in the text, I've kept close to my promise of discussing and promoting the most inexpensive methods to use in identifying gemstones. However, in all fairness, I must introduce one instrument that, although expensive, would be very advantageous and constantly used. Therefore, I feel it worthwhile to spend a few minutes discussing this valuable "right arm." There are much less costly ways to magnify gemstones and still obtain acceptable results, these methods will be pointed out soon.

I firmly believe that of all the gem testing instruments, a ten-power, dark field binocular microscope,

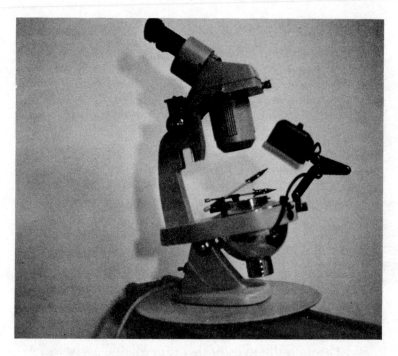

Gemoscope (courtesy of Gem Instrument Company, Subsidiary of Gemological Institute of America, Los Angeles, Calif.)

known as a gemoscope, is the best investment for examining and identifying stones that anyone interested in gemstones could make.

If you are a jeweler, picture potential customers' reactions at seeing such a sophisticated instrument near your diamond and colored stone showcase. Your customers will have tremendous confidence in you as a professional when you allow them to view the stones of their choice in a manner they have never used before.

The gemoscope, also known as a gemolite, gem detector or diamondscope, is a microscope with high and low magnification. The instrument is binocular (having an optical device for use with both eyes) and has a specially designed substage in which a stone is held in an easily movable and rotatable prong. A light installed at the base produces a dark field illumination; that is, the bulb is shielded by a dark plate so that the light bends around the sides of the shield before reaching the stone. The stone can thus be viewed through its interior. Without the dark shield, the light would pass directly through the stone, making it very bright and glaring, so that the examiner would not be able to study its internal structure. Accordingly, dark field illumination enables the viewer to recognize inclusions, cracks and other internal and external imperfections, as well as the cutting.

A gemstone should always be examined from all directions when it is under magnification. Under low power, the examiner can see color, luster, girdle surface (the widest portion of the stone), quality of the polish, amount of fire, cleavage, fracture, and doubling of back facets. This last quality is a positive identification for doubly refractive stones.

Under high magnification, for example, one will be able to separate many synthetics from natural stones. Although synthetic ruby and natural ruby are very much alike in most properties, under high magnification, curved growth lines and spherical gas bubbles will indicate synthetics. Angular inclusions and straight line banding will indicate naturals. Many other characteristic growths identifying gemstones can be seen easily under such magnification. This instrument can be purchased from the G.I.A.

Enough! I believe the point has been made. I am not insisting that you run out and buy this gemoscope, but I feel it was necessary to explain its importance. The intention of this book is to keep the costs down, but I hope that you will give some serious thought to purchasing this valuable microscope (even a used one).

A middle-of-the-road approach can be followed by doing a little improvising with an inexpensive ten-power monocular (one eyepiece) microscope used by some amateurs and mineral collectors. It is easy to build a small attachment consisting of a light bulb with a movable dark shield in front of the bulb. The microscope can then be placed upon this device so that the stone being viewed is not only magnified, but also illuminated. I had the occasion to examine one such innovation made by a gem enthusiast. I decided to make one to see whether it really was as simple a matter as he claimed. He was right. You have only to apply a little ingenuity and the rest is easy.

Of course, the least expensive type of magnification is the ever-popular loupe. If this is what you expect to use, purchase a good one. It is not advisable and will only be a waste of money to use a plain five-power loupe, one that is usually found on a watch repairman's bench. This type of loupe distorts the image and color of a gemstone.

A loupe of ten-power magnification is highly recommended. It should be composed of three lenses so that it corrects distortion and focuses all parts of the stone

Ten-power loupe   (courtesy of Gem Instrument Company, Subsidiary of Gemological Institute of America, Los Angeles, Calif.)

being viewed. The loupe should also be corrected for spherical and chromatic aberration (color correction). The Bausch and Lomb Hastings loupe is very highly recommended and meets F.T.C. regulations. It can be purchased from your supply house or the G.I.A.

Whether you expect to use the gemoscope or the eye loupe, one of the most important things to remember is to clean the stone before examining it under magnification. It is very easy to mistake lint, dust, and other minute particles for internal substances. In fact, your fingerprints on a stone will fool you into believing the marks to be inclusions. Make certain the stone is thoroughly cleaned before your examination.

One of the best ways to clean a gemstone is to employ an ultrasonic cleaner. There are many models of ultrasonic cleaners, some deluxe and some very inexpensive. However, one of the least expensive models will do a satisfactory job.

The process of ultrasonic cleaning consists of placing a gemstone into a container with special cleaning fluid. Then when the electric current is turned on, the gemstone is "cold boiled." This means that the solution appears to be boiling but is actually vibrating while not getting hot. After a few minutes, rinse the stone in cold water and wipe dry with a soft, lint-free cloth. Ultrasonic cleaners can be purchased from jewelry supply houses.

In the event that no ultrasonic cleaner is available, a jar of jewelry cleaning fluid (there are many brands on the market which can be purchased in a local jewelry store) will be sufficient. Using a tiny eyebrow brush, clean the stone all around, while dipping it into the solution. Rinse under cold water and dry with a soft, lint-free cloth.

Loose stones should not be held with the fingers as the oil from the fingers will leave marks on the stone. Grasping the stone with a tweezer will prevent this from happening.

If the loupe is to be your examining instrument it would be advisable to construct a dark shield and place it between the light source and the stone (*see* Figs. 10 and 11). In this way you will be simulating the principle of the gemoscope by having the light come around the shield before it reaches the stone. Hold the stone with a pair of tweezers. Moving the loupe up and down as you view the stone will enable you to see within the stone at all levels.

As with the gemoscope, when using a loupe you should examine a gemstone from all directions, starting first by looking through the table so that the complete inside is in view. Then, slowly turning the stone, look for characteristics that you might not have been able to see through the table. Let me stress this point again: When examining a gemstone under magnification, do not view the stone in one direction only. That is the biggest mistake you can make. Often a stone that appears to be clean when seen through the table will show inclusions when viewed either through the underside or from the side through the girdle. The difference will surprise you. This applies to diamonds as well as colored stones.

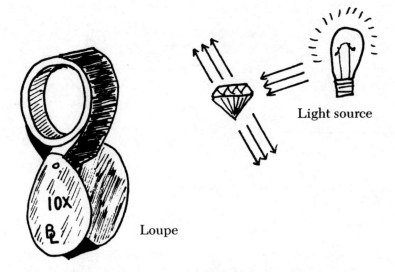

Light source

Loupe

Figure 10. Wrong way to examine a gemstone

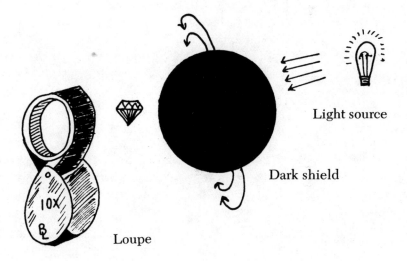

Light source

Dark shield

Loupe

Figure 11. Correct way to examine a gemstone

IX

Identifying Natural Colored Stones by Inclusions

Unfortunately, most amateurs and many people in the jewelry trade are of the opinion that each prismatic color represents one or two gemstones. However, many stones have similar colors, as Table 6 indicates. The cardinal rule to keep in mind is: **Do Not Identify a Stone by Color Alone.** There are many who believe that every violet stone is an amethyst, every red stone a ruby and every green stone an emerald. Only by a series of tests can one determine the identity of a gemstone.

Whether the gemoscope or loupe is employed, looking for characteristic inclusions and recognizing them could be the first and only necessary step in identifying an unknown stone (*see* Figs. 13 to 16). Then, depending upon the particular situation, you can perform a specific gravity test and, if necessary, continue with a refraction test or even a polariscope test. However, after becoming familiar with certain inclusions that are characteristic of various gemstones, it will not always be necessary to

TABLE 6
COLORS OF GEMSTONES

Red: Zircon, spessartite, garnet, spinel, jade, glass, spodumene, tourmaline, quartz, amber, chalcedony, opal, and plastics.

Green: Zircon, garnet, corundum, chrysoberyl, spinel, jade, peridot, malachite, tourmaline, turquoise, beryl, labradorite, quartz, chalcedony, glass, opal, and orthoclase

Blue: Diamond, zircon, corundum, spinel, jade, topaz, tourmaline, beryl, quartz, labradorite, glass, opal, chalcedony, lapis, and plastics

Yellow: Synthetic rutile, diamond, zircon, spessartite, corundum, chrysoberyl, tourmaline, topaz, beryl, labradorite, quartz, opal, glass, and plastics

Brown: Diamond, zircon, spessartite, corundum, chrysoberyl, garnet, jade, topaz, beryl, quartz, amber, opal, glass, and plastics

Pink: Garnet, corundum, spinel, spodumene, tourmaline, beryl, glass, quartz, and plastics

White: Corundum, spinel, jade, coral, tourmaline, quartz, chalcedony, opal, glass, and plastics

Colorless: Strontium titanite, diamond, zircon, corundum, synthetic spinel, topaz, beryl, opal, glass, and plastics

Violet: Corundum, garnet, spinel, amethyst, jade, spodumene, topaz, tourmaline, opal, glass, and plastics

Black: Hematite, jade, quartz, chalcedony, opal, glass, and plastics

carry out all the tests in order to identify the stone, or at least to know what it is not.

Let me inject another reminder here. The gemologist, who is capable of identifying almost all gemstones because of his vast knowledge of the subject and his ability to use the necessary instruments in testing a stone, very seldom fails to come up with the correct stone. However, if a situation arises in which he cannot determine a stone's identity, he will consult someone in a better position to know. This is no different from a general practice medical doctor who consults a specialist. Therefore, if you find yourself in a similar situation where it becomes necessary to determine a difficult stone's identity, consult a gemologist.

The following list of popular gemstones shows various inclusions most often visible under ten-power magnification. With a little practice, the reader will be able to spot most of these internal imperfections.

Corundum: needle-like rutile crystals (a common mineral usually reddish brown in color) .... rubies show short needles crossing at approximately sixty degree angles, whereas sapphires (blue) show long needles not densely packed .... zircon crystals surrounded by a halo of black fractures .... fingerprint patterns of liquid inclusions .... six-sided opaque inclusions .... straight parallel lines (striae) .... angular inclusions .... doubling of facets when viewed through crown facets.

Tourmaline: pink and red variety usually reveal parallel internal fractures .... green stones showing irregular elongated and thread-like liquid and gas inclusions evenly distributed .... doubling of back facets.

"Horsetail" inclusion in green garnet (demantoid).

Three sets of parallel "silk" rutile needles crossing at 60-degree angles in natural ruby and almandite garnet. Lines are usually coarser in garnets.

Three-phase inclusion seen in the emerald. This is a liquid-filled inclusion with gas bubble and solid.

Curved "striae" (lines) parallel to each other in synthetic ruby.

Figure 12.   Colored gemstone inclusions

Long, straight, parallel striae as seen in the natural sapphire; these are also found in the ruby, but with shorter lines.

Fine, needle-like lines crossing each other in two directions. Usually found in almandite garnet.

"Fingerprint" inclusion, found many times in corundum and occasionally in spinel.

Two-phase inclusion, showing gas bubble in a liquid. Often found in quartz (amethyst) and in topaz.

Figure 13.   Colored gemstone inclusions

Synthetic stone will often show spherical gas bubbles.

Inclusion of zircon with an appearance of a dark border, as seen in natural corundum.

This garnet and glass doublet shows a red ring around the girdle when viewed with stone face-down.

Eight-sided spinel crystal (two pyramids back to back). This is usually seen in rubies and natural spinels.

Figure 14.   Colored gemstone inclusions

Agate quartz shows a green, moss-like inclusion.

"Natural" exposed rough girdle surface of diamond.

Bubbles found in glass are round and elongated; they are often seen in rows.

Short, worm-like inclusions (gaseous) are often seen in synthetic spinel.

Figure 15.   Colored gemstone inclusions

Spinel: Inclusions of tiny enclosed eight-sided crystals, usually very dark . . . . clouds of hair-like inclusions (tangled).

Garnet: **Rhodalite**—deep rose color with slight tinge of purple.
Almandite—"silk" (white, radiant, silky thin needles) . . . . two sets of long needles intersecting at approximately 70 and 110 degrees . . . . the "silk" is coarse and shorter than that found sometimes in ruby . . . . evenly distributed colorless grains in abundance.
Grossularite—short, stubby, rounded, hollow, or liquid-filled prisms in quantity . . . . reddish to yellow-orange in color.
Andradite—(Demantoid, green in color) . . . . showing brown inclusions similar to fine "silk" in curved arrangements like a "horse tail" . . . . this stone is easily identified as no other stone shows this characteristic.
Pyrope—internally like Almandite, but often with large round crystal grains and liquid inclusions.

Emerald: (beryl family) . . . . shows many inclusions of the three-phase type (irregular spaces filled with solid, gas, and liquid matter) . . . . tiny square crystals . . . . flat, diamond-shaped inclusions . . . . brassy—yellow cubic crystals of pyrite often seen . . . . a badly fractured appearance is very common . . . . wispy and feathery inclusions . . . . usually shows doubling of back facets when viewed through crown facets.

Exceptionally fine cats' eye chrysoberyl, approximately 23 carats (courtesy of American Gemological Laboratories, Inc.)

Burma star ruby (courtesy of American Gemological Laboratories, Inc.)

Exceptionally fine Australian opal, approximately 7 carats. (courtesy of American Gemological Laboratories, Inc.)

First Row (vertical): Topaz, Beryl (Emerald), Topaz Tourmaline, Spinel, Sinhalite, Topaz
Second Row: Brazilianite, Fire Opal, Corundum (Purple Sapphire), Beryl (Morganite), Garnet (Pyrope), Spinel, Beryl   **Third Row:** Opal, Beryl, Topaz, Black Opal, Danburite   **Fourth Row:** Scheelite, Garnet (Almandine), Labradorite, Quartz (Citrine), Fluorite, Tourmaline, Tourmaline   **Fifth Row:** Danburite, Cordierite (Iolite), Apatite, Moonstone, Garnet (Hessonite), Diopside, Orthoclase

First Row (vertical): Fluorite, Garnet (Demantoid), Garnet (Spessartine), Spodumene (Kunzite), Zircon, Amblygonite, Fluorite   **Second Row:** Zircon, Phenakite, Corundum (Yellow Sapphire), Beryl (Aquamarine), Sphalerite, Spinel, Chrysoberyl   **Third Row:** Tourmaline, Olivine (Peridot), Quartz (Rock Crystal), Scapolite, Sillimanite (Fibrolite)   **Fourth Row:** Tourmaline, Zircon, Quartz (Amethyst), Chrysoberyl, Tourmaline, Andalusite, Tourmaline   **Fifth Row:** Garnet (Hessonite), Sphene, Beryl (Heliodor), Zircon, Apatite, Zircon, Zircon

Natural sapphire,
approximately 5 carats
(courtesy of American
Gemological Laboratories,
Inc.)

Fine intersecting silk in
natural sapphire with
fingerprints (courtesy of
American Gemological
Laboratories, Inc.)

Two Colombian emeralds,
approximately 2½ carats each
(courtesy of American
Gemological Laboratories,
Inc.)

Aquamarine: (blue variety of beryl family) .... often free of inclusions .... may show some brownish inclusions and tiny, parallel, liquid-filled spaces .... occassionally very small, fine crystals like snowflakes.

Topaz: Usually free of inclusions .... characteristic inclusions are irregular, often large liquid and gas-filled spaces .... sometimes cracks are visible .... doubling of back facets .... often cleavage is visible.

Lapis: (lapis-lazuli)—easily recognized as a bluish-opaque stone with tiny, bright-yellowish metallic particles, which, although present within the stone, are usually visible on the polished surface.

Amber: a resinous tree product .... often exhibits flies, gnats and other insects that become embedded as the sticky amber sap solidifies.

Moonstone: when examining a cabochon-cut moonstone with the naked eye, a milky iridescence coming from within the stone will be evident. It resembles the brightness of moonlight.

Moss Agate: a variety of quartz, exhibiting inclusions that resemble branches of trees.

Tiger Eye: This brownish-yellowish cabochon-cut stone displays a single line that is the center of the stone and that is composed of minute particles within the stone, causing it to resemble a tiger's eye.

Jadeite: Semi-transparent .... intense color (green) .... bright luster when polished .... feels slippery.

Nephrite: Often exhibits small flecks of graphite in the stone . . . . bland look when polished (wax-like or soapy appearance) . . . . less intense . . . . translucent to opaque.

Zircon: very strong doubling of back facets (can best be seen when viewed through the table) . . . . almost all inclusions will appear double . . . . white zircons have tiny inclusions that produce a "cottony" effect . . . . green zircon does not show doubling of inclusions . . . . a very brittle stone, and upon close inspection of the girdle, many chipped edges will be present . . . . zircons appear at times to be very cloudy . . . . often fingerprint inclusions that are flat and worm-like in contrast to the angular fingerprints found in corundum.

Quartz: Two-phase inclusions are often seen as liquid-filled crystals with bubbles . . . . needles of rutile that cross each other are often seen in the amethyst variety . . . . hair-like and milky inclusions often visible . . . . at times quartz can be very clean . . . . the citrine variety is usually a brownish-yellow color.

Peridot: strong doubling of back facets . . . . tiny, black, metallic inclusions surrounded by small fingerprint patterns of liquid inclusions . . . . will sometimes display fissures and cracks . . . . often the stone is clean internally.

X

Synthetics and Their Characteristic Inclusions

Although synthetic stones are manmade in the laboratory and natural stones are the product of nature and found in the ground, both are alike in all important essentials.

Synthetic stones have the same chemical, physical and crystal make-up as their natural counterparts. Since these properties are the same, it becomes necessary at times to depend upon recognizing the distinctive inclusions of synthetics rather than using the various testing methods described in earlier chapters.

In the last few years, diamonds and natural colored gemstones have risen in value at a rapid pace. Couple this with the fact that since synthetic stones can be controlled in their length of growth time, and naturals have to be expensively mined from the ground, the synthetics are a great deal lower in price. Thus we have a situation where the demand for synthetic stones has become greater than ever. As a result, those dealing in gemstones will be confronted more and more with these laboratory-grown stones (also referred to as "created" stones). It is, therefore, important to be able to distinguish between these synthetics and the natural stones.

The following are some of the more common synthetics you are likely to encounter. The inclusions should not be difficult to locate when using a good magnifier while slowly rotating the stone near a good light source.

Synthetic Rutile: shows spherical gas bubbles (natural gemstones, as a rule, do not exhibit spherical inclusions but rather irregular ones) and tremendous doubling of the back facets and of any inclusions that may appear.

Synthetic Turquoise: developed in 1970 ... the substance displays a milky color of blue .... no evidence of any matrix (the material in which natural turquoise is embedded) .... under magnification, fine grains will be visible, a sort of regular, fine pattern that is not seen in natural turquoise .... the color, at times, is too blue and cracks continue to show up on these specimens.

Yag: (a combination of yitrium, aluminum and garnet) .... although this stone has no inclusions other than some bubbles, it is important to mention yag at this time since it is manmade. Gemologists and other specialists in the field can immediately detect this synthetic when viewing it under magnification. The sharpness of facet edges and the overall brilliance is lacking. Yag can also be separated from the diamond by a simple test using mineral water. When you immerse a diamond and a yag into the solution, the yag immediately becomes transparent. The diamond does not.

Strontium Titanite: a fairly good diamond substitute only in the way it appears to the naked eye. Upon close examination under the loupe, the high dispersion (sparkling flashes of scattered light rays) tells you that it is not a diamond . . . . many spherical bubbles are also often seen.

Synthetic Corundum: many tiny spherical bubbles that are elongated . . . these bubbles are frequently found in groups with one or two large bubbles in addition, or a rough line of bubbles on a curve . . . . striae or growth lines often seen under high magnification.

Synthetic Spinel: usually shows very small spherical bubbles, widely separated and rarely grouped . . . . the bubbles are slightly irregular in shape . . . . sometimes there are small inclusions that have the appearance of white bread crumbs under dark-field illumination . . . . as the stone is rotated, curved growth lines will be seen as compared with the straight lines of natural stones.

Synthetic Emeralds: show no spherical bubbles, nor do they exhibit curved growth lines . . . . three-phase inclusions are visible (solid, gas, and liquid) . . . . there are no tiny square crystals, diamond-shaped crystals or pyrite crystals which are usually visible in natural emeralds . . . . very characteristic inclusions are the wisp-like (hair-like) groups of liquid inclusions, found in the Gilson, Chatham, and Linde emeralds (three manufacturers of created emeralds) since all of them are similarly made.

Synthetic Diamond: made by General Electric . . . . found to be too expensive to produce especially because the stones produced are small and of very poor quality. You can be fairly certain that these stones will not appear on the gemstone market.

With the continuous outpouring of manmade diamond substitutes such as the yag, GGG (a combination of gadolinium, gallium and garnet), and most recently, the slightly better rendition of cubic zirconia, stories are constantly heard of purchasers being fooled with losses running into the thousands. In the field of colored stones the situation is much more complex. Besides the synthetics, we also have the doublets, triplets, and imitations made of glass and plastic. To add more confusion to the problem, there are the colorless natural stones like the sapphires, spinels and quartz which are tested for better colors in the entire spectrum.

With so many inexpensive stones floating around the market, it is wise to heed the well-known Latin warning, "Caveat Emptor" (buyer beware).

XI

Doublets and Triplets

Not many know what a doublet is and how it differs from a triplet. So that we make no mistake between these two types of stones (also known as assembled stones), let me quickly define each. A doublet consists of two pieces, top and bottom, that are usually held together by colored cement. A triplet, as the word suggests, is a three-part stone (top, bottom, and a third center part made up of a colored layer of cement that resembles the color of the stone intended. (*See* Figs. 16 and 17.)

There is nothing wrong with producing these stones so long as the seller lets the buyer know that the stone is an assembled one and charges accordingly.

Since the prices of natural colored gemstones have skyrocketed over the past few years, there is a definite market for these stones and the prices are more in line with what the consumer can spend. Unfortunately, he is prey for the unscrupulous seller who passes these stones off as the real thing, either mounted or unmounted. It is important, therefore, to become familiar with doublets and triplets, since they are bound to appear sooner or later.

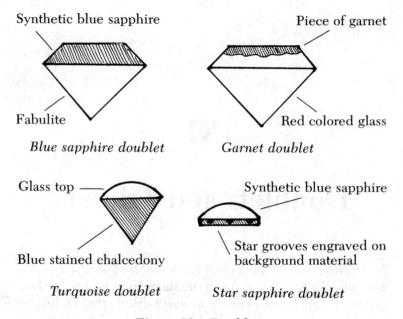

Synthetic blue sapphire

Fabulite

Blue sapphire doublet

Piece of garnet

Red colored glass

Garnet doublet

Glass top

Blue stained chalcedony

Turquoise doublet

Synthetic blue sapphire

Star grooves engraved on background material

Star sapphire doublet

Figure 16. Doublets

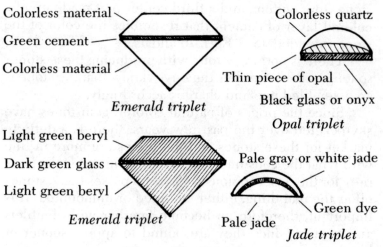

Colorless material
Green cement
Colorless material

Emerald triplet

Colorless quartz

Thin piece of opal

Black glass or onyx

Opal triplet

Light green beryl
Dark green glass
Light green beryl

Emerald triplet

Pale gray or white jade

Green dye

Pale jade

Jade triplet

Figure 17. Triplets

As stated above, there is nothing unethical or illegal in making these stones so long as they are sold as doublets or triplets. They are beautiful and inexpensive; a ready market exists for these stones. Selling these stones does not constitute fraud so long as the person who is selling them knows what they are and notifies his customer. The fraud is in having someone try to pass a doublet or triplet off as something else.

A very popular doublet is the garnet and glass combination, in which a piece of red garnet is used as the top and red colored glass is cemented to the bottom, thus giving the impression that the entire stone is garnet.

Another widely used combination is a synthetic blue sapphire top and a strontium titanite (fabulite) bottom. This duo can fool many because the synthetic holds down the well-known glitter of the strontium titanite. Since the synthetic sapphire is a hard stone, it also resists scratching, thereby giving the effect of a natural blue sapphire.

Turquoise has been found in a doublet combination with cabochon glass as the top piece and a chalcedony bottom that has been stained blue (chalcedony is a variety of quartz, sometimes translucent and milky).

There are numerous doublets and triplets of emerald. The most common emerald triplet uses two colorless materials with a green-colored cement in between. Another kind of emerald triplet is composed of two pieces of light green beryl with dark green glass cemented in between. An emerald doublet often seen is a pale yellow beryl top fused with a green member of the quartz family, aventurine (a transparent to opaque variety of quartz containing tiny particles of other minerals).

For a long time there was a stigma attached to the beautifully iridescent opal. To own one, unless it was one's birthstone, was to have bad luck. With the superstition recently put to rest, we find a number of doublets and triplets entering the market with black onyx or black glass cemented between two thin slices of pale opal, or, in the case of the triplet, a cabochon top of colorless quartz is added to give strength to the opal beneath it (cabochon is a convex hemispherical form, polished but not faceted).

Star sapphires are known to be found in assembled stones. A piece of synthetic sapphire can be mounted on a star-engraved background, thus giving the viewer a picture of a star sapphire.

Even among diamonds we are apt to find doublets consisting of two diamonds cut and assembled back to back to resemble a large diamond. Sometimes the top half is a diamond and the bottom a piece of quartz (rock crystal), or perhaps some other substitute like spinel, sapphire, or glass.

Last, but by far not least, I would like to mention the jade triplet. The popularity of jade has increased greatly during the past few years, and a large number of people have been fooled by jade triplets. A jade triplet consists of a rounded top of pale gray or sometimes white jade that has been ground out so that another piece of jade fits into the hollow part. Between the two pieces is a green dye that gives the stone its fine color that many people mistake for Imperial jade.

As you can readily observe, it is a simple matter to create doublets and triplets. The trick is to be able to spot them. With a little practice the problem, in the main, can be overcome.

One of the best methods of detecting an assembled stone is to immerse it in a refractive liquid like methylene iodide. This test will immediately reveal any foreign matter that indicates another substance.

A ten-power loupe examination at the girdle of a

stone will detect an assembled stone when the viewer notices the separation of top and bottom parts where cement was placed. Usually, a number of bubbles will be visible as the stone is held at different angles. The seam of the layer of garnet is usually seen as it rests on top of another stone if you move the stone slowly under a powerful light.

A third method employs the ultra-violet lamp. Whenever two or more different substances have been used in a stone, there will be a difference in the fluorescence. (*See* Chapter 14.)

One other means of spotting these doublets and triplets should be mentioned. This method involves the use of the Chelsea filter (a small but specially-treated green plastic film encased in a frame). This device is especially useful in the detection of an emerald doublet. When

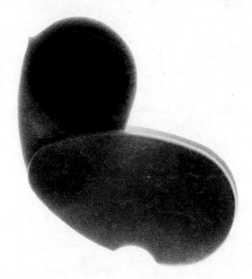

Chelsea filter   (courtesy of Gem Instrument Company, Subsidiary of Gemological Institute of America, Los Angeles, Calif.)

viewed through this filter with the aid of a strong light, the doublet will indicate the foreign material to be greenish in color, whereas natural emerald will appear red. The Chelsea filter is also used to distinguish emeralds, other natural gemstones, and synthetic emeralds (which appear red under the filter) from most glass imitations and other green gemstones (which show up green under the filter). The Chelsea filter is not a sure test but an additional aid in gemstone identification.

XII

Identifying Diamonds by Inclusions and Other Means

Many jewelers, gem collectors, and gemstone investors claim they can easily separate, by visual inspection, a diamond from all the other substitutes that have descended upon today's gemstone market. Some make this claim based on their association with the business and on their many years of experience. Most of the others say they "can tell just from handling them." These judgments are as illogical as agreeing with the following third statement after reading the first two:

1. Ruby stones have a red color.
2. This stone has a red color.
3. Therefore, this stone is a ruby.

Unfortunately, some people do make judgments about diamonds based on reasoning similar to that presented above; later they often regret their decisions.

Anyone who has dealt with gemstones has, at one time or another, heard or read of someone fooled by one of the diamond fakes or one of the natural colorless stones imitating a diamond.

For those not actually working in the jewelry industry, the problem is as acute, if not worse. Since most of this group is involved with gemstones on a very limited basis, they have not allotted much time to learning the rudiments of precious stones. What is more alarming is that those who spend thousands of dollars on diamonds and colored stones for investment purposes exclusively, often possess little or no knowledge about gemstones.

The necessity of arming yourself with a few important facts that will prevent your falling prey to embarrassment and costly mistakes cannot be over-emphasized.

One of the first things to do when examining a colorless stone is to look at its surface with the unaided eye. A diamond will reveal a fairly high luster (the reflection of light from its surfaces). Most other stones will look dull by comparison.

Examine the stone carefully, keeping a watchful eye out for a play of rainbow colors. If this display is quite strong and an unusual, dazzling array of colors is apparent, you can be certain the stone is not a diamond. Such a phenomenon indicates, in all probability, strontium titanite, commercially known as fabulite.

It is important to acquaint yourself with certain inclusions prevalent in diamonds (*See* Figs. 18 and 19).

Colorless crystals that are irregular or rectangular in shape are characteristic in diamonds as compared to the round shapes prevalent in synthetic and imitation stones. Look for the "natural," a very common feature on diamonds. This external blemish is found on the girdle edge. It usually covers a tiny area on the girdle where the diamond exhibits the original texture of the stone. Refer back to Figure 16. You will not find a "natural" on any other colorless stone.

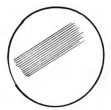

Grain lines (usually seen near where facets meet)

Inclusions of 8-sided diamond crystals within a diamond

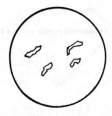

Irregular colorless inclusions

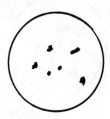

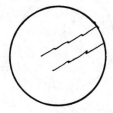

Dark carbon spots (usually irregularly shaped)

Line fractures

Figure 18. Diamond inclusions

Feathery inclusions
(irregularly shaped with
sharp edges)

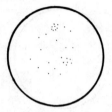

Pinpoint inclusions
(very tiny)

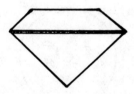

Bearded girdle (rough
girdle with numerous tiny
fractures entering the stone)

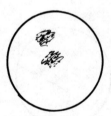

Cloudy inclusions
(described sometimes as
"cottony" areas)

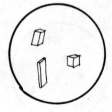

Colorless rectangular crystals
(often zircon crystals)

Figure 19.   Diamond inclusions

Many times a cutter, in his determination to retain as much weight as possible from the rough diamond, will leave this small portion on the girdle in its original form (unpolished) as an indication of his craftsmanship. This incomparable characteristic "natural" is one of the important features in identifying a diamond and usually does not affect its value in any way.

A "natural" is not to be mistaken for a fracture or break which is a characteristic appearance of a broken or cracked surface on a mineral, which occurs in a direction other than across a cleavage plane. (*See* Chapter 3.)

Since few gemstones show evidence of cleavage lines, you can be certain you are on the diamond track when you see a crack or cracks within a colorless stone. These cracks are often caused by strain.

These cleavage lines will be seen either as thin lines running across within the stone or at times as slightly parted lines. Cleavage runs parallel to the surfaces of the octahedral diamond, which is one of the frequently occurring forms. An octahedral stone is one which is found in nature having eight sides. (*See* Fig. 20).

Other inclusions that are associated with diamonds are: perfectly formed tiny diamond crystals within the main stone; black carbon inclusions; feathery inclusions; an occasional red garnet or green olivine; knots that are most often seen on surfaces but are actually included crystals protruding from the surfaces as irregular crystals; and a satin-like finish on the girdle, except for a few diamonds having a multi-faceted, highly polished girdle.

It is essential to notice the precision faceted edges that only a diamond possesses. The exact meeting points of the facets have been carefully calculated (*see* Figs. 21 and 22), their clarity and sharpness, due to the diamond's hardness, cannot be matched by any other colorless stone, including strontium titanite and synthetic rutile.

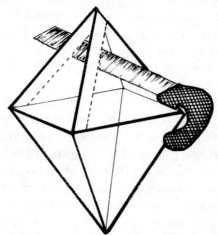

Fig. 20.   Cleavage lines
The frequently-occurring eight-sided diamond crystal is shown here. Since cleavage occurs parallel to the faces of a diamond crystal, there are eight planes where cleavage can occur. Here we see the saw cutting through a diamond parallel to one of its faces.

These two stones, when examined under magnification, are dull and milky in appearance when compared with diamonds. See Table 7 for a comparison of the characteristics of diamonds and their substitutes.

Mention should also be made of recognizing a diamond whose color has been altered. Although this has nothing to do with diamond inclusions, we are discussing the diamond's internal structure, and altering the color involves directing high energy particles of radiation into a diamond in order to intensify the attractiveness of its color.

In the early nineteenth century, poor color white diamonds were painted with a chemical to improve their whiteness. This method proved to be a failure as the painting washed off when alcohol was applied. Soon more sophisticated methods were to appear on the market such as spraying diamonds with a substance that could be removed only with sulphuric acid. The radium-treated diamond was the next step in altering

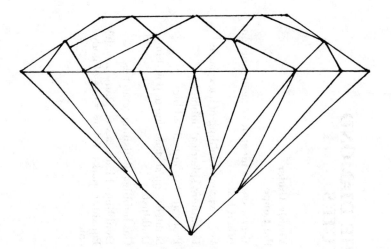

Figure 21. Poor faceting of a gemstone Note that a few of the facet edges do not meet at the proper points.

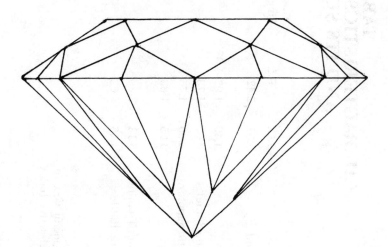

Figure 22. Good faceting of a gemstone Note that all facet edges meet at the proper points.

TABLE 7
CHARACTERISTICS OF THE DIAMOND
AND ITS SUBSTITUTES

Stone	S.G.	R.I.	Double or Single Ref.	Visible Under the Loupe
Diamond	3.52	2.42	S	Very accurate meeting of facet junctions. Bright luster.
Zircon	4.40	1.92–1.98	D	Very evident doubling of back facets.
Synthetic Spinel	3.65	1.73	S	Prominent spherical bubbles.
Synthetic Sapphire	4.00	1.76	D	Prominent spherical bubbles.
Yag	4.65	1.83	S	Scratches on surface due to polishing. Dull luster.
Strontium Titanite	5.13	2.40	S	Gas bubbles. Polishing scratches.
Synthetic Rutile	4.26	2.62	S	Doubling of back facets. Many bubbles. Polishing marks. Yellow tinge of body color.

S.G.: Specific Gravity
R.I.: Refractive Index

color, but this was soon discarded because the method was too expensive. Later it was found that particles of energy could be shot into the diamond, which improved the stone's color but left no undesirable effects.

There is currently a great rush to treat diamonds and other colored stones for finer color because of the dwindling supplies of better grade stones, combined with the fact that demand has further increased the necessity to offer the public better quality stones.

A chart published in the February 1979 issue of *Jewelers-Circular Keystone* showed that in today's gemstone market, most stones are treated for color enhancement. The public is slowly but continuously being made aware by gemologists and other authorities in the field of the improved color treatment available that will increase gemstones' value, as well as give them a more attractive appearance.

It is interesting to note that, among the trade rules passed by the Federal Trade Commission, rule number 36 (which deals with coloring of diamonds) states, "it is an unfair practice to advertise or offer for sale any diamond or other precious or semi-precious stone which has been artificially colored or tinted by coating, irradiation, or heating, or by any other means, without disclosing the fact that the natural stone is colored, and telling how permanent the coloring is."

Under high magnification, improvement in color can be viewed through the table. Induced color will become apparent around the culet when the stone is treated through the pavilion facets. When treated through the crown facets, the diamond will usually show a ring around the table, if the diamond is viewed when placed face down on a sheet of white paper.

Within the jewelry industry, there is currently a hot debate on one aspect of color treatment of gemstones. A clear-cut decision has not been made as to whether the consumer should be told of a stone's treatment at the point of sale, despite the fact that the Federal Trade Commission has stipulated that such information should be given.

On one side of the argument is the reasoning that those who purchased stones several years ago will be uncertain as to whether their stones are natural and this will destroy consumer confidence in the jeweler. The other side reasons that to inform the purchaser that a stone has been treated is an obligation on the part of the jeweler, and to do otherwise is to diminish the consumer's reliability and trust in the jeweler.

The author most certainly approves of improving the color of a poor "off-white" diamond. However, I must emphasize that this not be kept a secret. Not only should the process be revealed, but the price should be considerably lower because the stone was originally purchased as a poor quality stone.

Furthermore, I suspect a purchaser will be very excited after being informed of this process, so long as it is properly explained that nothing has been done to harm the stone, but rather that the diamond's inner structure was changed to one that is more desirable.

One last item deserves some comment before concluding this chapter.

The laser beam, which in recent years has become well known for its application to medicine, has also been employed in the improvement of a diamond's internal structure. The laser beam can remove dark inclusions found in diamonds. This procedure, in essence, involves the penetration of a powerful laser light beam into the stone in the direction of a dark inclusion. Upon reaching the dark spot, the beam burns it out, leaving a microscopic tunnel in the stone along the path where the

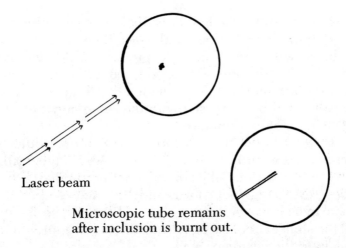

Laser beam

Microscopic tube remains
after inclusion is burnt out.

Figure 23.   Laser beam used to remove inclusions

penetration took place. This can be seen in the form of
two tiny lines visible only under high-power magnification (see Fig. 23).

This use of the laser beam has caused quite a stir in
the jewelry industry, the question being similar to that of
color treatment in gemstones. Should the consumer be
told that a certain diamond being considered for purchase has been subjected to a laser beam treatment?

To answer that question, another question must be
posed. Does the process of altering the internal structure
of a stone with the laser beam cause the stone to look
worse than before, decrease its capacity to endure, and
lessen its value?

The author is of the opinion that none of these
changes occur. As a matter of fact, most gemologists
agree that any procedure that increases the appearance
of a gemstone and therefore adds more value is to be
praised.

The removal of a few dark spots will not alter the stone's durability or its strength since the penetration of the beam will leave a microscopic tube which will be difficult to locate even with a gemoscope. Certainly, the value of the stone will not be lessened. On the contrary, the value will be increased with the stone now exhibiting a clean internal picture.

However, the most important point to consider is whether the would-be buyer is to be told. Emphatically yes! One must remember that the seller purchased the stone possessing inclusions, and he paid accordingly less than had the stone been clean. Therefore, he should sell the stone, after having it treated, at a lower price and explain to the customer why.

In most cases that have come to my attention where the laser beam process was carefully explained, it did not deter the customer from making the purchase. In fact, it actually increased his interest. An explanation of the process, coupled with a lower price for a stone that now resembled a fine-quality grade diamond, was all that was needed to complete the sale.

XIII

Shapes Versus Cutting

There are six shapes in fashioning stones that are familiar to both jeweler and layman. These are the round, (known as the brilliant); the marquise; the oval; the emerald; the pear; and the heart. (*See* Figs. 24 and 25.)

Do not become confused with the style or shape of a stone and the cut (often called "make" of a stone). The cut refers to how well the stone was proportioned when fashioned in one of the six shapes.

For example, if a diamond was cut in the brilliant style, several questions arise about its cut. Did the cutter slice off too much of the table, making it a "wide spread" cut? Did he cut the pavilion facets too shallow or too deep? Was the culet made too large and the girdle made too thick? These deviations will result in a stone with little brilliance and not much value (*see* Fig. 26).

The importance of cut is often not explained to many gemstone buyers. The only reference to this word (and it is so misused) is in the shape rather than how well it was shaped. Of course, the purchaser is happy to have obtained a "good buy," only to discover at some later date that his stone is not as valuable as he had hoped for because of its poor proportioning.

The diagrams on the following pages (*see* Figs. 27–31) illustrate many of the lesser-known styles of gemstone fashioning. A number of these types were used years ago in jewelry pieces. Some are still used today when certain designs are employed that necessitate special shapes for particular areas.

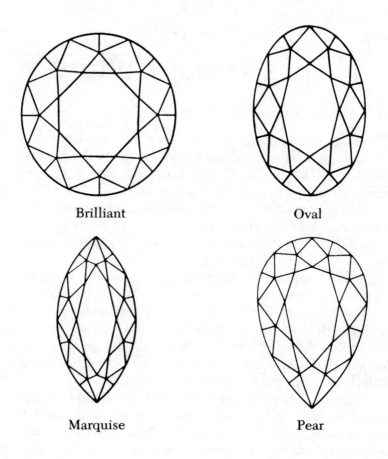

Brilliant   Oval

Marquise   Pear

Figure 24. Shapes of popular gemstone cuts

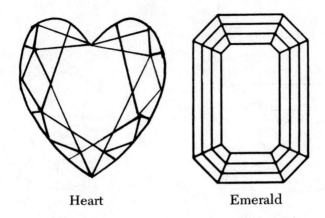

Heart   Emerald

Figure 25. Shapes of popular gemstone cuts

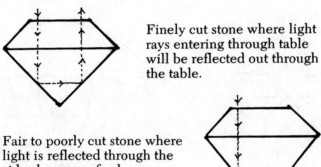

Finely cut stone where light rays entering through table will be reflected out through the table.

Fair to poorly cut stone where light is reflected through the sides because of a deep pavilion.

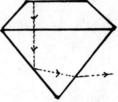

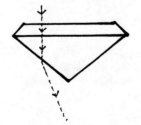

Poorly cut stone where light is reflected through bottom because stone is shallow.

Figure 26. Reflection of light in diamond cuts

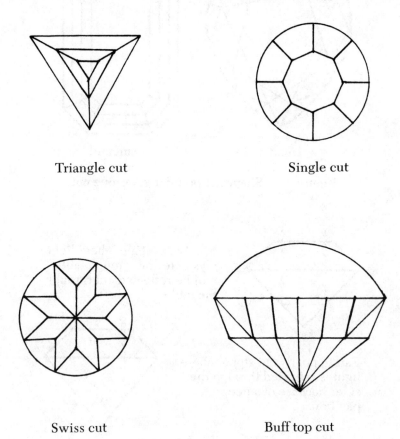

Triangle cut

Single cut

Swiss cut

Buff top cut

Figure 27. Lesser known gemstone shapes

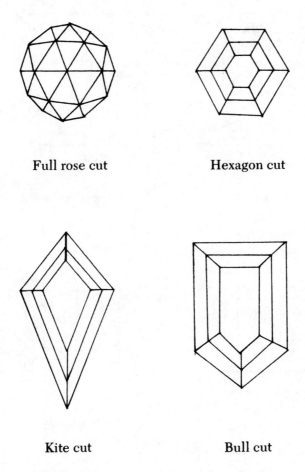

Full rose cut　　　　　　　Hexagon cut

Kite cut　　　　　　　Bull cut

Figure 28.　Lesser known gemstone shapes

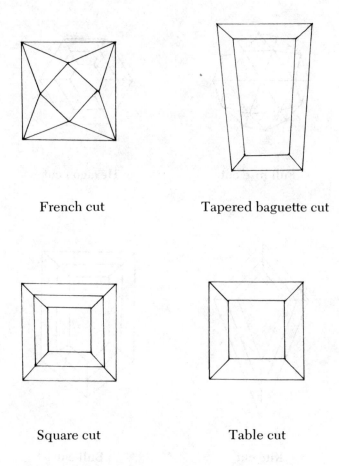

French cut   Tapered baguette cut

Square cut   Table cut

Figure 29.   Lesser known gemstone shapes

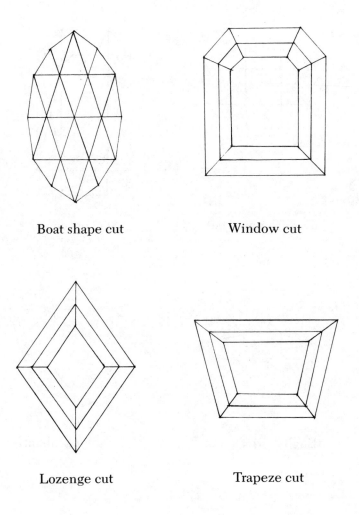

Boat shape cut

Window cut

Lozenge cut

Trapeze cut

Figure 30. Lesser known gemstone shapes

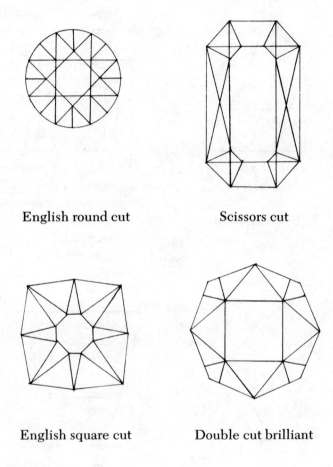

English round cut   Scissors cut

English square cut   Double cut brilliant

Figure 31.   Lesser known gemstone shapes

XIV

Fluorescence

Although most textbooks on gemstones make very little mention of the use of fluorescence as an aid to gem identification, there is still a need for this knowledge and a definite place exists for the fluorescent testing procedure. Any means that can help identify gemstones should be utilized by all persons working with valuable minerals.

There will be times when you run across difficult stones that may require all the methods you can muster. The ultraviolet lamp serves an important function by indicating whether a stone will fluoresce, and if it does, what color it will produce.

Let me caution, however, that this is not proof positive in identifying a stone, but in many cases with other tests previously made, the fluorescence of a stone will aid the examiner in arriving at a more conclusive decision.

Fluorescence or ultraviolet irradiation has long been known to mineral collectors. The striking reaction that some gemstones give when placed under an ultraviolet lamp is an impressive experience that must be seen to be appreciated.

Ultraviolet lamp   (courtesy of Gem Instrument Company, Subsidiary of Gemological Institute of America, Los Angeles, Calif.)

Let's examine what fluorescence is. The phenomenon is actually light from a substance (for our purposes, gemstones) that is being stimulated by radiating energy. As the lamp directs its ray (short wave or long wave) on a given stone, the internal structure of the stone reacts by causing various colors to appear within the stone.

Whether a mineral that fluoresces will do so, depends upon how agitated the particles of its fundamental matter become. Without going into lengthy detail, fluorescent minerals react to different wave lengths, some to short waves and others to long waves. The fluorescent color is characteristic of the particular mineral and depends on its physical and chemical structure. At various times a stone will continue to give off the fluorescent reaction for a period of time after the lamp has been shut off. This condition is known as phosphorescence.

Not everyone is aware that a high percentage of

diamonds give some sort of response to ultraviolet irradiation if the stone is placed on a piece of black velvet in a dark room. For example, a "Premier" diamond (extracted from the Premier Mines in Africa) will glow a brilliant blue under the ultraviolet lamp.

As a rule, fluorescence depends a great deal on the presence of foreign matter in the gemstone; you cannot expect consistent responses. Nevertheless, there are enough results to claim ultraviolet observations as significant in testing for identification.

Fluorescence also plays an important role in identifying synthetic stones. For example, synthetic emeralds produce an intense red fluorescent glow under the ultraviolet lamp, whereas natural emeralds show a weak red color. (There are ultraviolet lamps that emit only short wave rays and others that emit only long wave rays. These lamps range in price from $75 to $100. However, if you plan to invest in this instrument, it would be best to purchase a lamp that provides both short and long wave rays, which is in the same price range. Or try a hobby shop, where you may find much less expensive lamps.)

The following is a list of gemstones and their response to fluorescence under long wave (LW) or short wave (SW):

Alexandrite: Weak red under LW and SW.

Synthetic Alexandrite: Bright red, sometimes orange under LW and SW.

Amber: Usually an orange or yellow green under LW.

Emerald: Orange or red, usually weak under LW. Many do not fluoresce at all.

Synthetic Emerald *(Beryl)*: Red under SW . . . . an excellent test to separate the synthetic from the natural.

Aquamarine *(Beryl)*:   No fluorescence. Very blue aqua may show green under SW.

Pink Morganite *(Beryl)*:   Light violet red under LW and SW.

Diamond: The "Premier" shows a brilliant blue under LW. Diamonds can fluoresce many colors such as light green, yellow-green, red and orange under LW. Don't be surprised if you find that some diamonds do not fluoresce at all.

Garnet: Not too often will you find fluorescence here. This test is helpful in separating the garnet from the ruby or red spinel.

Ruby: Red or orangy-red under LW.

Synthetic Ruby: Strong red . . . . will phosphoresce after the lamp is shut off . . . . LW and SW.

Spinel: Weak red and orange under SW.

Synthetic Red Spinel: Strong red under LW.

Blue Sapphire: Medium red under LW and SW . . . . sometimes none at all.

Synthetic Blue Sapphire: Light blue and sometimes yellow-green under SW.

Malachite: None.

Peridot: None.

Jadeite Jade: Light green jade will show pale white colors under LW. Sometimes a weak green or yellow color will appear.

Nephrite: Does not fluoresce, which is one way to distinguish this jade from the jadeite jade.

Lapis Lazuli: Most often will not fluoresce . . . . some will respond with a weak to bright blue . . . . SW.

Pearls (cultured):   Often a strong blue or yellow-green . . . . at times a pinkish-red has been seen . . . . under LW and SW.

Rose Quartz: Red . . . . sometimes a weak purple . . . . LW and SW.

Green Aventurine (quartz):   Pale green under SW and LW.

Amethyst (quartz):   None.

Citrine: None.

Colorless Topaz: None at all or a weak yellow under LW.

Orange-Red Topaz: Weak yellow-orange color under LW.

Blue Topaz: Light yellow under LW. . . .at times none.

Brown Topaz: Pale yellowish-orange under LW.

Yellow Topaz: Light orange under LW.

Pink Topaz: Pale green under SW.

Tourmaline (green variety): None.

Tourmaline (pink variety):   Very weak red under LW and SW.

Colorless Zircon: Pale yellow under SW and LW. . . .sometimes an orangy-yellow under SW and LW.

Blue Zircon: Very light blue under LW. . . .sometimes none.

Green Zircon: Pale green under SW. . . .at times none.

Yag (colorless):   Medium to weak orange under SW and LW.

Yag (blue):   None.

Yag (green):   Intense red under LW.

Doublets and Triplets: Where more than one material is used, there is usually a noticeable difference in the fluorescence. Even the cement that is used will fluoresce if the two stones do not.

The popular garnet and glass doublet can easily be identified under the lamp. The top piece of garnet will most often not fluoresce, whereas the bottom glass portion will show a strong light green color, and the cement will show another reaction.

Celluloid and bakelite materials are used in many of the imitation stones besides glass. And whereas bakelite is not fluorescent, the celluloid will respond with a yellowish color under LW and SW.

XV

Turquoise

So little is known about turquoise stones and their treatment that it is important to explain a few facts in order to assist you in separating those stones that are treated from those that are not. I will also touch upon the imitations as well.

One of the first things that should be said is that a treated turquoise is not a poor stone or an imitation that should be avoided. A treated stone is not an imitation. The imitation stone is exactly what the word implies. It is a substance used to imitate the appearance of an authentic stone. It does not have the same chemical and physical properties as the genuine stone.

Naturals and synthetics can both be considered "real" stones since both have the same chemical and physical properties, except that the naturals are genuine, coming out of mother earth, while the synthetics are born in the laboratory.

Returning to the treated turquoise, one finds this stone to be soft, chalky, and greenish and found in most jewelry stores today. The rarity of the natural sky-blue turquoise makes it necessary to treat the green stones in order to make them more saleable.

These greenish stones, being so soft, will absorb all kinds of oil, grease, and perspiration, thus giving the stone a dull and ugly appearance not conducive to purchasing. To make matters worse, the stones are porous and difficult to cut.

As a result, in most cases, a treatment with wax or plastic is applied to overcome the problem of strength. A color dye is added to enhance its beauty, thus making the stone desirable.

Turquoise will often be found to have a backing. This is done primarily to protect the stone as it is being cut and also to help set the stone in a mounting.

It is important to remember that most often you will not be handling excellent quality blue turquoise. This quality turquoise is as rare as hen's teeth. What will be plentiful is either the treated turquoise or a good imitation made from either plastic, enamel, or glass.

The common imitation turquoise is the molded blue glass. When examined under magnification, if a fracture is visible on the stone its fragments will be conchoidal (shell-like) rather than splinter-like. Bubbles are usually visible on the surface and the stone will not have the waxy luster of the genuine. Sometimes the imitation is made with a mixture of very poor grade turquoise and plastics that have been colored. One will often find an added facsimile of the dark, vein-like matrix (that portion of the rock from which the turquoise was extracted) to give the appearance of true turquoise. It is actually easier to separate the imitation from the real stone than it is to distinguish between the various imitations.

A good test in determining whether a turquoise stone is genuine is to place a hot needle close to the stone somewhere where it will not be noticeable. The heat of the needle will expose oil on the surface. In the case of plastics, you will immediately smell a very sweet odor.

Another test is to apply a drop of acid to the stone. If it is a true turquoise the acid will dissolve without a bubbling effect (effervescence). This reaction is best viewed under magnification.

Imitating turquoise and trying to pass it off to the public as natural turquoise is criminal, and the supplier should be prosecuted to the fullest extent of the law. However, coating a poor quality natural stone so as to make it more appealing is acceptable, provided that the person selling it knows what has been done, informs the prospective customer of treatment, and prices the stone accordingly.

XVI

Pearls and Their Imitations

Natural pearls are found in several types of mollusks that live in salt or fresh water. (A mollusk is an invertebrate which has a hard shell.) What is this organic gemstone that has been called the queen of gems and has graced the bodies of women from biblical days?

The pearl is formed from a substance that is secreted from within the shell of certain mollusks. It usually forms in order to cover an irritant that worked its way naturally into the mollusk's shell. The animal secretes layer after layer of the substance to protect itself from the irritant, which becomes iridescent and is called nacre. It is this nacre covering that gives the pearl its fine luster or what is known as "orient."

Pearls are soft and, after years of wear, become discolored from contact with perspiration or any type of acid. Over a period of many years the organic substance within the pearl dries out and, as a result, cracks will appear on the surface.

Pearls are found in many colors, including white,

silvery-white, yellow, greenish-white, pink, blue and black.

Cultured pearls are different from naturals in that they are induced to grow. Rather than having an irritant find its way accidentally into the shell, an irritant is deliberately inserted into the animal's shell.

This substance, which usually starts out as a tiny grain of sand, is removed after a period of three to four years, having been fully coated with the nacre produced within the shell.

The Japanese discovered that, by inserting a tiny fragment of mother-of-pearl (the iridescent lining of a shell from any pearl-bearing mollusk), a much better pearl was produced.

There are three general shapes of pearls you are apt to encounter:

1. The round pearl, which is found loose between the soft parts of the shell.
2. The baroque pearl, which is unsymmetrical or irregular.
3. The half pearl, one which is half a sphere. This pearl has a broken surface when removed from the shell. This surface is later ground away and a flat mother-of-pearl piece is cemented to that portion.

Just as we have found in our discussion of diamonds, there are those who claim they can visually tell the difference between a cultured and a natural pearl. However, it is not advisable to depend upon one's unaided eyes, since it could mean a vast difference in dollar value.

For many years it was a difficult task to separate the cultured from the natural pearl by examining the outer surfaces only. Today we have such sophisticated instruments as the Endoscope and x-rays which will reveal the internal structure of a pearl and thus distinguish one from the other.

One of the quickest, easiest, and least expensive methods is the specific gravity test. Place a piece of calcite into a solution of bromoform and dilute it with grain alcohol until the calcite remains halfway suspended in the solution. This will give the mixture a 2.74 specific gravity. When testing pearls with this solution, you will find that cultured pearls show a higher S.G. and sink, whereas the natural pearls, with a lower S.G., float. Although this test is not proof positive, it will be effective more than 75 percent of the time. It is advisable to practice this procedure with a few loose pearls, both cultured and natural, in order to observe the results.

An old method, but interesting and very easy to perform, is readily accomplished with little or no cost at all. In the jewelry trade it is commonly known as pearl candling. The process involves covering an intense light source with an opaque shield that has tiny openings in the center. A strand of pearls is examined by viewing the individual pearls through these openings. Cultured pearls will appear to have straight parallel lines running across the internal structure. Natural pearls will show circular lines.

A third test that can be tried is the examination of the pearl's drill hole with a loupe and a good light source. With the light directed at the hole, look for the brownish mother-of-pearl core separated by the various layers of nacre, which in many cases is evidence that the pearl has been cultured.

None of the above three methods is proof as to whether a pearl is cultured or not. However, if all of these tests indicate the presence of a cultured pearl, you can be fairly certain that it is indeed cultured.

In considering imitation pearls, we are dealing with two types. One is the hollow glass bead containing wax. The other imitation is a solid glass bead or sometimes a mother-of-pearl. Both of these types are coated with many layers of a fish scale mixture to give the appearance of a genuine pearl.

It is not difficult to separate the imitation from the natural and cultured pearl. Under magnification, those that are wax filled will immediately be identified when a hot needle is applied somewhere near the pearl holes, so that the mark will not be visible. If it is the solid type, the luster of broken glass at the hole edges will be revealed.

A very quick test, but often not too accurate, is to run your teeth over the surface of the bead. If it feels smooth, seven or eight out of ten times, it is an imitation. Cultured and natural pearls always feel gritty. The other two or three times the bead could very well be one of the better quality imitations which may also have this gritty feeling, created by applying a special coating.

One other test which has proven helpful is the use of fluorescence. The imitation pearl will not fluoresce. The natural pearl and cultured pearl will often fluoresce blue.

Black pearls are often imitated by substituting the mineral hematite and giving it a high polish. If you are testing a single bead, the specific gravity test will reveal that hematite has a very high S.G. (around 5.20). Pearls show a reading of 2.60 to 2.78.

Pink pearls have been copied with plastics. Again, the S.G. of plastics are very low at 1.30 and pink pearls average 2.80 to 2.85.

Coral, which has also been used as an imitation, has a S.G. of 2.70.

Although imitations have been given various coatings to make them appear genuine, a few simple tests can often bring out their true identity.

Not to take any of the popularity away from the standard round pearl, recently the freshwater pearl, which is also cultured, has become a favorite among modern fashion-minded women. These pearls, which are easily recognized by their irregular shapes and wrinkled surfaces, are cultivated mostly in Japan at Lake Biwa and have become known as Biwa pearls.

Besides having an affordable price when compared with the traditional round pearl, exciting pastel colors that vary from white, grayish-violet, brownish-yellow, orange and pink, and which occur naturally, can be found in these pearls. It is to be noted that there are times when an off-color pearl can be enhanced by using a dye.

Although, as with the round pearl, size, color, luster, and surface cleanliness are important in determining value, in the freshwater pearl other obvious factors have to be considered—the various colors and the degree of irregularity in the shapes. Odd shapes and scarce colors would definitely influence price.

XVII

Understanding Value Determination

Although not directly involved in the actual identification of gemstones, value determination is an important aspect of gemstones. You should be familiar with those factors that establish a gemstone's value.

The following criteria, commonly known in the jewelry industry as the four "C's," are the basic factors in determining gemstone value: **Carat, Color, Clarity** and **Cut**.

When comparing stones whose color, clarity and cut are of equal quality, the stone whose weight is greatest will be the most expensive. The carat is the standard unit measure of weight for all gemstones, both natural and synthetic, and is accepted as such in all principal countries of the world. Just as the pound is a measure of weight that is broken down into sixteen ounces, the carat is also divided into one hundred points. Thus a hundred points equals one carat, twenty-five points equals a quarter of a carat, and fifty points is a half carat. It is interesting to note that there are 142 carats in one ounce.

The carat is often called the metric carat (a decimal system of weight), so that a three-point stone would be termed 0.03 carat and a forty-five-point stone can be expressed as 0.45 carat.

When referring to a carat term such as ¾ carat, ½ carat, or ¼ carat, there is usually a small spread in the number of points involved. For example, if we are talking about a half carat, it could possibly mean a stone within the range of 47 to 53 points. However, when a value is to be placed upon a half carat stone, the exact number of points would then be considered. See figures 32–34 for approximate weight in carats for diamonds of various sizes and shapes.

Generally, the less color a diamond has, the less value it has (we refer to color as whiteness or off-whiteness). Nature has provided diamonds that come in every color of the rainbow. However, for the sake of brevity, we will confine ourselves to the colorless diamond. Although gemologists use a set of comparison stones that have been pre-graded for their color, for the nonprofessional's purposes, one's eyes can be trained to recognize a fairly clean diamond, one that reveals a slight yellowish tinge, and one that is quite yellow.

The following scale of symbols, as prepared by the Gemological Institute of America, provides the basis for grading color in diamonds and is widely accepted by the jewelry industry and most gemologists:

D,E,F—Colorless
G,H,I,J—Nearly colorless
K,L,M—Faint yellow
N,O,P,Q,R—Very light yellow
S to Z—Light yellow
Above Z—Fancy yellow

In discussing a yellow color in diamonds, a distinc-

Oval Shaped Diamonds

Approximate weights based on size and average brilliance

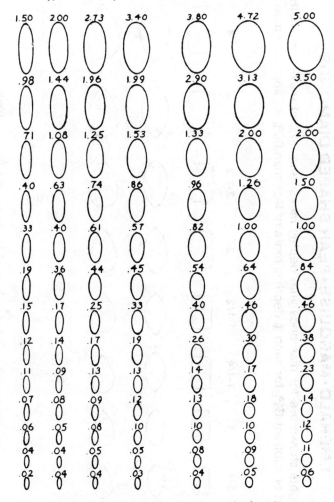

Created by Dr. A. Posamentier & Charles Bloom
formula upon request

Figure 32.   (courtesy of Charles Bloom & Company,
580 Fifth Ave., New York, N.Y. 10036)

DIAMOND WEIGHT ESTIMATOR –
EMERALD · MARQUISE · PEAR SHAPED DIAMONDS

Weights shown are for diamonds with depths measuring 60% of maximum width.
(Add or subtract 1⅔% for each % depth is more or less than 60% for approximation.)

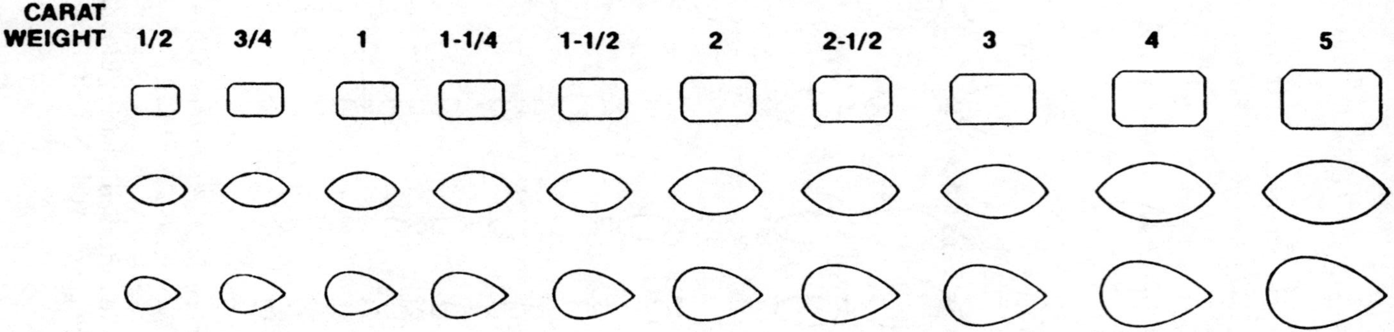

Figure 33. © Gemological Institute of America, 1981

DIAMOND WEIGHT ESTIMATOR – ROUNDS AND SINGLE CUTS

Weights given are for diamonds with depth equal to 60% of girdle diameter. Add or subtract 1-2/3% for each % depth is above or below 60%.

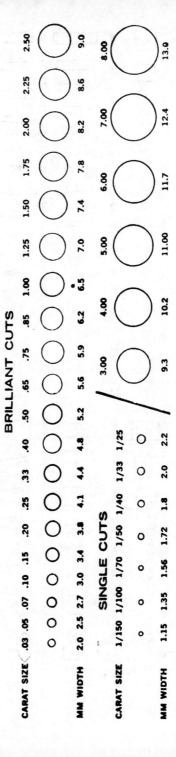

BRILLIANT CUTS

CARAT SIZE	.03	.05	.07	.10	.15	.20	.25	.33	.40	.50	.65	.75	.85	1.00	1.25	1.50	1.75	2.00	2.25	2.50
MM WIDTH	2.0	2.5	2.7	3.0	3.4	3.8	4.1	4.4	4.8	5.2	5.6	5.9	6.2	6.5	7.0	7.4	7.8	8.2	8.6	9.0

CARAT SIZE	3.00	4.00	5.00	6.00	7.00	8.00
MM WIDTH	9.3	10.2	11.00	11.7	12.4	13.0

SINGLE CUTS

CARAT SIZE	1/150	1/100	1/70	1/50	1/40	1/33	1/25
MM WIDTH	1.15	1.35	1.56	1.72	1.8	2.0	2.2

Figure 34. © Gemological Institute of America, 1981

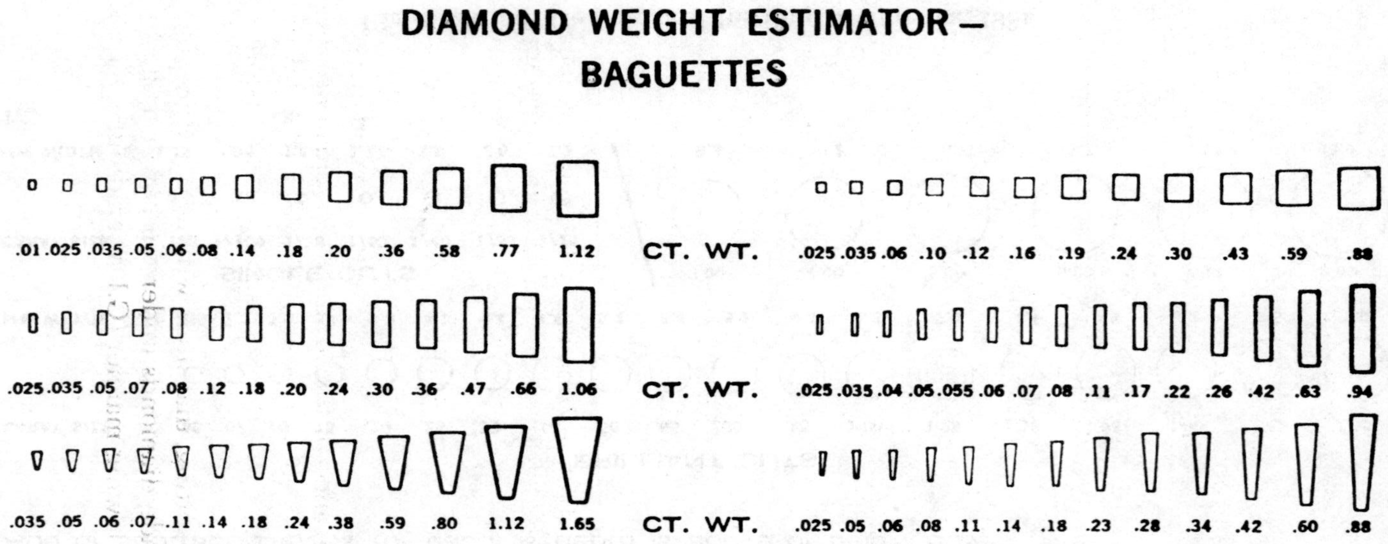

DIAMOND WEIGHT ESTIMATOR – BAGUETTES

CT. WT. .025 .035 .06 .10 .12 .16 .19 .24 .30 .43 .59 .88

CT. WT. .025 .035 .04 .05 .055 .06 .07 .08 .11 .17 .22 .26 .42 .63 .94

CT. WT. .025 .05 .06 .08 .11 .14 .18 .23 .28 .34 .42 .60 .88

CT. WT. .01 .025 .035 .05 .06 .08 .14 .18 .20 .36 .58 .77 1.12

CT. WT. .025 .035 .05 .07 .08 .12 .18 .20 .24 .30 .36 .47 .66 1.06

CT. WT. .035 .05 .06 .07 .11 .14 .18 .24 .38 .59 .80 1.12 1.65

Figure 35. © Gemological Institute of America, 1981

tion must be made between a poor color in diamonds that exhibit various degrees of yellow on the G.I.A. color scale and diamonds with a very intense yellow color. Here we have arrived at a different category of diamonds, namely, the "Fancies." These particular diamonds, with their vivid yellow hue, are known as Canary diamonds.

There is quite a difference between the accepted fine white diamond that is graded colorless or near colorless, when employing the comparison set of diamonds pre-graded in the G.I.A. laboratory, and a diamond that is graded the unattractive light yellow to yellow, resulting in a tremendous difference in value. Naturally, other factors of grading (size, cut and clarity) would further affect the stone's value.

In the case of two diamonds, each weighing one carat and having the same proportions in cut and similar clarity grades but with different color grades, the diamond that exhibits more yellow will have a lower value.

The Canary diamond, being in the class of fancy colored diamonds, will command a high price to a smaller market, which is usually confined to collectors or investors.

The chapter on inclusions emphasized the importance of recognizing the various characteristic features as a means of identification. It is of equal importance to grasp the significance of the location of inclusions, the number of them, their sizes, and their color. The fewer inclusions visible, the better the stone. If an inclusion is under the crown facets and can be hidden by one of the prongs in a ring setting, that stone will have more value. Gemologists grade diamonds under ten-power magnification in the following manner (G.I.A. grading):

F—Flawless, no visible inclusions.

VVS—Very, very slightly included.
VVS$\frac{1}{2}$—Very, very slightly included.
VS$_1$—Very slightly included.
VS$_2$—Very slightly included.
SI$_{1,2}$—Slightly imperfect.
IMP$_{1,2,3}$—Imperfect.

The fourth factor in value determination of diamonds is the cut. As you will recall from its earlier discussion, this element of value concerns the proper angle arrangement of a diamond's appearance. Barring the presence of an inclusion whose location would cause its removal to alter the stone's proper cut, most cutters strive to attain the ideal proportions. (*See* Fig. 36.)

The proportions in Figure 36, as calculated by Marcel Tolkowsky, are considered to be ideal because with these facet angles a diamond will exhibit the greatest amount of brilliance and fire attainable.

Diamonds that fail to meet these angle specifications will either lack brilliance or possess an appearance

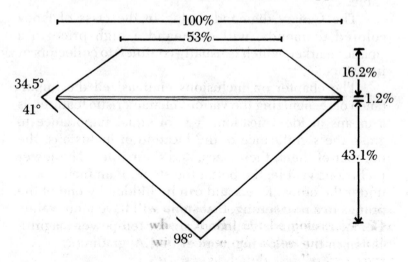

Figure 36. Ideally proportioned diamond

that is absolutely flat-looking. Other poorly cut diamonds will show a dark center if the pavilion area is cut too deep. Still others, with a shallow pavilion, will exhibit a glassy appearance.

These poorly cut stones will not be entirely desirable and therefore, will have a lower value.

In the determination of value in colored stones, the same basic factors are involved except that more emphasis is placed on the purity of its primary color, the strength of the color, and the tone or variations of light and dark shades. Although taken into consideration, cutting and inclusions take on a lesser importance. Because of many technical reasons, there is a diversity of opinions regarding proper cutting of colored stones. However, all cutters agree that the main goal is to retain as much weight as possible from the newly-mined stone.

XVIII

Additional Clues in Gem Identification

Besides the usual identifying characteristics that have been described in previous chapters, there are other clues that can be of help when you encounter difficulties in identifying certain gemstones.

1. Natural amber floats in salt water. When amber is rubbed, electricity develops and attracts bits of material.

2. Hematite is a grayish black, opaque mineral with a high luster. It is easily distinguished from substitutes by its splintery fractures (like that which appears on wood) instead of the conchoidal fractures found on jet, quartz, or glass.

3. Glass is a very poor conductor of heat and will feel warm to the touch. Glass is also attacked by acids that eat away its surface. Most major stones will resist acids except turquoise and opals. Another indication of glass is the spreading of a drop of water on its surface.

4. Synthetic rutile, often substituted for diamonds, has a pronounced yellowish tinge, contains many bub-

bles, and exhibits doubling of the back facets. It is never colorless.

5. Jade can be tested to determine whether it has been treated for color by using a tensor lamp and examining the stone under a chelsea filter (emerald filter). Natural jade remains green, whereas the treated jade will appear purple. Other stones resembling jade will not show up green under the filter.

6. Quartz in its many colors floats in bromoform and methyl iodide. Being a good conductor of heat, quartz will feel cold to the touch.

7. Topaz sinks in bromoform and methyl iodide. Smoky quartz, commonly called "smoky topaz," which is often mistaken for natural brown topaz, floats in the two solutions. Natural topaz is electrified when rubbed with a cloth; the friction developed will attract fragments of paper.

8. Tourmaline is electrified when rubbed with cloth. It will float in methyl iodide, whereas other stones that resemble it (corundum, zircon, and garnet) will sink. In a green tourmaline which is elongated and rectangular in shape, the long sides of the stone can be seen as clear, deep green in color, and the two short sides will appear olive-green. The red variety of tourmaline will display a pale rose and dark rose color under the dichroscope. Other precious stones in red will not show this color effect.

9. Natural alexandrite will appear green in sunlight or fluorescent light, while under an incandescent bulb it will appear raspberry red. The alexandrite type of sapphire, which is a synthetic, appears blue in natural light and purple in artificial light.

10. Aquamarine shows up greenish-black under the chelsea filter. Synthetic blue spinel, a good substitute, produces a red color under the filter.

11. Garnet becomes electrified when rubbed.

12. Linde star sapphires, (synthetics), aim at sharp and perfect stars. These stars descend to the girdle. All Linde stones have flat backs.

13. Synthetic emeralds will show a more intense red color under the chelsea filter than will natural emeralds.

14. Natural and synthetic emeralds can be identified by placing a piece of yellow glass over a piece of blue glass. Then examine the stone through the two glasses near a strong light. The genuine and synthetic stones will appear violet in color. Other green imitations will not change their color under the glasses.

15. Diamonds are good conductors of heat and will feel cool to the touch. They also become electrified upon rubbing. Examine the sharpness of facet edges. No other colorless stone is cut that way.

XIX

Deceptive Names of Gemstones

Knowing the correct names of gemstones and being able to recognize deceptive ones will be of great help in determining what a stone actually is.

If you are purchasing a red stone and are told it is a "Montana Ruby," do not be deceived by its name. If you are familiar with the proper nomenclature of gemstones and their corresponding deceptive names, Montana Ruby would immediately signal an incorrect term for what is actually nothing more than the red variety of garnet.

I recall a few years ago being shown a stone that the owner believed was a terrific buy for an emerald. Upon examining the stone with a ten-power loupe, I could tell his prize possession was not the stone he thought it was. On hearing this, the man produced his sales slip from the store where he had made the purchase while on vacation. The sales slip read "Brazilian Emerald." Knowing that anyone who called such a stone a Brazilian Emerald knew it to be a green tourmaline, I explained this to the man, but he was not fully convinced. So I tested the stone to prove that it was not an emerald. The tests proved the stone to be a tourmaline, much to the man's frustration.

Unfortunately, the deception is not always the fault of the person selling the stone, as he may have been told the misleading name from his source. The problem goes back many years and stems from the lack of an organized system of naming gemstones within the jewelry industry. As a result, misleading names were used over and over again and the public became more and more confused.

It is to your advantage to learn the deceptive names as well as their corresponding true names as another means of identifying gemstones.

The list following confines itself to those less expensive but popular stones with names that may mislead a prospective buyer.

GEMSTONES AND THEIR DECEPTIVE NAMES

Mineral Gemstone	Deceptive or Misleading
Fine grain transluscent calcite	Mexican jade
Colorless quartz	Herkimer diamond, Mexican diamond, Cape May diamond
Colorless zircon	Matara diamond
Pinkish-red spinel	Balas ruby
Red spinel	Spinel ruby
Blue spinel	Spinel sapphire
Pink topaz	Brazilian ruby
Rose quartz	Bohemian ruby
Red variety of garnet	Montana ruby or Arizona ruby
Pink tourmaline	Rubellite
Green tourmaline	Brazilian emerald
Green corundum (green sapphire)	Oriental emerald
Yellow quartz or citrine	Spanish topaz
Green grossularite (garnet)	Transvaal jade
Yellow sapphire	Oriental topaz
Smoky quartz	Smoky topaz

XX

Misconceptions

One of the least understood terms when applied to gemstones is the widely used expression "flawless stone." For those who are familiar with the evolution of gemstones within the earth, it should not be too difficult to perceive the fallacy of calling a gemstone flawless.

Nevertheless, a brief explanation is in order for those who are not aware of precious stones' geologic formation.

Gemstones, whether diamonds or colored stones, are produced alike. Volcanic eruptions, caused by tremendous heat and pressure deep within the earth's crust, result in the ejection of hot gases followed by molten rock containing gemstones. Some of these stones are washed down mountain sides, settling near the shores and sinking into the sand. Other precious stones remain within the earth, never reaching the top of the volcano. These stones have to be drilled out of rock thousands of feet below ground.

Materializing from the hot molten lava and rocks, gemstones reflect within their structures the effects of such tremendous pressure and extreme temperatures. These effects are revealed in such inclusions as fractures, stress lines, included bubbles and minerals, and other internal blemishes that are visible under magnification. Ninety-nine out of a hundred times, gemstones will have some inclusions, no matter how minute. The question is where do we draw the line?

The Federal Trade Commission, in a series of trade rules set down for the jewelry industry, emphasizes the fact that a diamond can only be called flawless if it shows no inclusions under ten-power magnification. Any other representation is considered to be misleading and in violation of the rule.

The fact that you do not see inclusions at ten-power magnification does not imply that a stone is absolutely clean. It simply means that the stone is considered clean for purposes of grading for value. It also means that if the stone were magnified to twenty- or thirty-power, some form of inclusion could possibly be observed.

Therefore it becomes evident that when one wishes to use the term "flawless," it must be qualified. That is to say, a stone showing no inclusions under ten-power should not be called a flawless stone alone, but expressed as "flawless under ten-power."

The "blue-white" diamond is another misconception. To begin with, there is a blue-white diamond. However, this stone will make an appearance in approximately one out of a thousand diamonds. It is, as the expression goes, "as rare as hen's teeth."

Over the years, many jewelers took it upon themselves to refer to their finest white diamond as a blue-white stone because it sounded good, and created added prestige to the establishment. They would go so far, when showing a diamond to a prospective buyer, as to place the stone under a bluish white light in order to bring out blue flashes of color.

Recently, it has become a practice, with the advice

of the Federal Trade Commission, not to use the term "blue white" diamonds because of its past misleading usage.

The phrase "a perfect stone" is another example of improper use when applied to a diamond. To be considered perfect, a diamond of a certain size would have to measure up to the top grading in three determining factors, namely, color, internal quality, and cut.

There are those who will call a stone perfect if the color of a diamond is D, E, or F on the G.I.A. scale and the cleanliness shows it to be flawless under ten-power. However, without the cut showing ideal proportions (which is almost impossible) that diamond is not perfect in every sense of the word. Perfection is only a goal which one endeavors to reach in producing a finely cut and polished diamond of the best color and quality available.

Surely you have heard the expression, "you can always tell when a stone is a diamond. It cuts glass." This is definitely not so. If you will refer back to Table 1, you will note that glass has a hardness of 5-6. This means that any colorless stone with a higher hardness number can and will cut glass and that includes white sapphire, spinel, quartz, zircon, rutile, and yag. Remember that glass is a very soft stone.

By the same token, there are many who are of the belief that since diamonds are the hardest mineral, they cannot be cracked.

I was approached once by a woman in tears who sobbingly told me that after being married for ten years, her husband did not really love her. When I inquired as to why, she replied, "Well, the stone in my engagement ring is not a diamond because it is cracked." When I probed further, she admitted hitting the stone while working in the kitchen. I explained that a diamond can and will crack if hit hard enough, especially if the impact is against the cleavage of the stone.

There is one term that is frequently used to describe certain gemstones that is worth mentioning here. The term "precious" is often used in reference to gems such as diamonds, rubies, emeralds, and sapphires. This term was applied to characterize these gemstones many years ago, and many jewelers and consumers alike describe these gems as being precious because of their high dollar value. Actually, the title "precious" is a misnomer. Let's consider an aquamarine and a diamond, each weighing one carat. The aquamarine, in this case, has a very fine dark blue color and is free from any inclusions. On the other hand, the diamond exhibits a visible yellowish color and shows numerous inclusions. You can be sure that the aquamarine will be more expensive. With all other factors being equal (size, cut, and shape), the quality, which includes clarity and color, will determine the value of a particular gemstone.

XXI

Interesting Characteristics of Popular Stones

In the realm of beautiful gemstones, a small number stand out as exceptional. Their uniqueness lies in their appearance which, when compared to the ordinary faceted gemstone, lend an excitement which only a lover of precious stones can appreciate.

The alexandrite, a mysterious but outstanding gemstone, was named after Alexander II, Tzar of Russia during the middle of the nineteenth century. This beautiful gem was discovered in one of the mines of the Ural mountains.

Alexandrite is one of two important varieties of the mineral chrysoberyl. It is translucent; when faceted and viewed through the table, finer quality alexandrite stones change their color from a dull green in daylight to a raspberry-red in artificial light. Alexandrite is also found in Sri Lanka (Ceylon); stones from this part of the world reveal an olive-green color in daylight and a less pronounced red color under artificial light.

The rarity of top quality alexandrite, together with the fact that it displays an exciting color change, places this stone in a class of very expensive gemstones.

Therefore, it is important not to mistake the synthetics for the natural. Alexandrite-like sapphires, which are actually synthetic corundum, show a bluish color in daylight and a reddish to purplish color at night.

Another relatively uncommon stone, the alexandrite spinel, reveals a grayish-blue color in daylight and an amethyst-violet color under artificial light. Both the alexandrite sapphire and alexandrite spinel show considerably weaker color changes than the true alexandrite.

The second variety of chrysoberyl is a yellowish-green stone; when cut in cabochon, this stone's attractiveness and fascination is revealed in very thin rods of parallel hollow tubes which resemble vertical bands of light appearing in the stone's center and reflecting off the stone's surface. Gemologically, this effect is called "chatoyancy," but is better known as "cat's eye" because of its resemblance to the eye of a cat.

It is important not to mistake the quartz eye, also known as "tiger eye," for the cat's eye stone. The quartz stone, upon close examination, will not exhibit the sharpness of the eye band that is found in the cat's eye. This is because the tiger eye contains coarser fibrous bands, and its color tends toward a brownish-yellow. It is not difficult to recognize the fineness of the tubes in a cat's eye which produces an opalascent appearance that easily distinguishes the cat's eye, from the much tamer tiger eye. The very sharp band lines and their central location in the stone make the cat's eye a rarity with a very high price tag.

The star sapphire and star ruby, two varieties of the mineral corundum, are very exciting stones. When occurring with a milky appearance in either the red ruby or blue sapphire, they are cut in cabochon, which produces an effect known as asterism (a six-sided star effect), caused by the reflection of light from inclusions in the stones that are arranged in certain crystal directions.

A stone that displays a well-balanced star, that is, one whose six rays are equally separated and centered, is rarely found. Because of numerous inclusions and an abundance of cloudiness, most corundum-occurring stars are either poorly defined or unsymmetrical.

The finest star sapphire will exhibit a fairly sharply defined six-sided star with a rich cornflower-blue color. The finest star ruby will also have a very pronounced star and will have a deep red color resembling that of blood. These fine quality stones are also quite rare and bring high prices.

You should be aware of the synthetic stars. Although beautiful in themselves, they can often fool the prospective buyer. Synthetic stones are usually distinguished from naturals because their stars are too even, too visible and overly sharp. Their bottoms are flat as compared to the unevenness of naturals; the synthetic stars do not extend all the way to the stone's outer edges. The lower portion of the synthetic cabochon is usually transparent. The natural's star points do extend to the stone's outer edges.

The imitation star, although easily detected upon close examination, is often mistaken by the public. When the underside of the stone is examined, you will readily see that the star has been artificially cut out of the back of the stone. This image is reflected through a cabochon-cut colored piece of glass or some other inexpensive transparent mineral.

One of the most amazing stones is the opal. This stone is considered by gemologists and others in the jewelry field to stand out among gemstones because of its extraordinary beauty.

The opal is not a crystalline mineral; instead, it resembles a jelly-like mass that formed numerous cracks in the hardening process. It is the light reflected from these tiny cracks which gives the opal its multi-colored appearance, which is different from other gemstones whose colors emanate from within.

Its many cracks make the opal not only a fragile stone but a very brittle one as well. Because of this structural arrangement, it has been very difficult to imitate natural opal. Lately, however, there has been some success in this endeavor as a few synthetic opals have filtered down into the market. However, it does not take an expert to recognize the difference. Anyone who has been handling opals for any length of time will always be able to pick out an unnatural opal.

There are four types of opal which you should know about if you are contemplating a purchase.

The white opal is a white opaque material, very common and widely used. It displays tiny flashes here and there as the stone is moved about.

Fire opals are so named because of the bright red and orangy colors that these transparent to translucent stones exhibit.

The third type is a colorless opal known as the water opal, which generally appears to have some color moving around within the stone.

Lastly, we have the black opal, which can be either black or very dark gray internally. This rare stone, which produces a play of colors emanating from a dark background, is highly prized for its iridescence, thus making it extremely expensive.

Do not get so carried away by a fine display of colors that you forget to examine stones to see whether they are doublets or triplets. Many assembled stones are made to look like opals.

One last point to remember is that good quality opals do not, as a rule, reveal their tiny cracks when viewed with the naked eye.

Jade has been called the mysterious healer of many ailments and the immortality stone, among many other names. This gemstone has two varieties, namely, jadeite and nephrite. Although both are found in jewelry, nephrite is also often used for ornaments and carved figures.

Even though jadeite and nephrite are different from each other, it has often been difficult to tell them apart. However, the differences become apparent if you take the time to scrutinize jade stones carefully. Whenever possible, a specific gravity test will aid in easily distinguishing the two stones, since jadeite reveals a 3.32 S.G. and nephrite shows a 3.00 S.G.

Pure jade is white, but the many colors found in this gemstone come from the presence of other minerals within the stone. In fact, the colors cover practically the entire spectrum, with some jadeite containing more than one color.

Jadeite, the more expensive of the two, is a granular stone with grains that seem to fit into each other; it is somewhat harder (resistant to abrasion) than nephrite.

Upon close examination you can readily distinguish jadeite, with its brightness and clarity as a polished stone, from nephrite, characterized by dull shades of color and an often oily and wax-like appearance. Whereas jadeite has its rich, vivid greens, nephrite lacks this intensity of color, exhibiting dark greens, brownish-greens and grayish-greens.

Nephrite is a tougher stone than jadeite because of its many interlocking crystals and fibrous texture. This means that nephrite will not break up easily when struck with a moderate blow. Nephrite colors have often been described as going from a deep spinach green to a mutton-fat white, lacking in life or spirit.

The most valuable jadeite is the kind exhibiting the emerald green color which is often referred to as "Imperial Jade." Although this stone is quite rare, any green jadeite approaching this specific tone would be considered an extra fine jade specimen.

A previous chapter was devoted to deceptive names of gemstones. Since many different stones have been labeled as jade, I thought it best to list these stones separately.

Deceptive Name	Actual Mineral
Transvaal jade	Green grossular garnet
Indian jade	Aventurine
Mexican jade	Green-dyed calcite
Australian jade	Chrysoprase
Amazon jade	Green feldspar
Jasper jade	Green jasper
Oregon jade	Very dark green jasper
American jade	Idocrase
Silver peak jade	Malachite

Examination for glass imitations is recommended if there is any doubt as to whether you are looking at jade or not. Under high magnification glass can easily be recognized by the presence of bubbles. Look for conchoidal fractures, which also indicate glass.

Natural daylight is best for examining jade as it brings out the true color, whereas artificial light only makes the specimen's color appear more intense.

Many would-be purchasers of jade are often uncertain about whether they are buying the real stone. It is, therefore, imperative to know your seller. Make certain you are dealing with a reputable person and that he stipulates in writing exactly what he is selling.

XXII

Encountering Some Unusual Stones

Although there are approximately 2000 known minerals, less than 100 have the requisites to be classified as gemstones, and of these only a handful are found in jewelry stores. With the recent soaring prices of many popular stones, more mineral specimens that meet some of the requirements to be considered gemstones have slowly but surely crept into the market place at much lower prices. Many of these stones are finding their way into exceptional pieces of jewelry.

Since anyone engaged in the pastime or occupation of obtaining gemstones is, at one time or another, bound to meet up with odd stones, the following partial list of mineral specimens should whet your appetite to search out more of these unusual stones.

Speaking of appetite, the first stone in this group is apatite. Both words sound alike, but watch out for the spelling. Apatite is one of a number of common minerals that occur in many colors but mostly in green and brown and can be transparent, translucent, or opaque. Apatite is a very soft stone, measuring five on the hardness scale.

The green variety has a vitreous luster and, like beryl, which it resembles, is a brittle stone. However, the specific gravity of apatite is 3.2, which distinguishes it from beryl, which has a 2.75 S.G.

Serpentine is translucent to opaque stone occurring in dull green and yellow colors. When translucent, due to its fibrous nature, serpentine often reveals a bright, silky luster. Being a soft stone, care must be taken to prevent scratching. Magnification will reveal splintery fractures. Serpentine is a poor conductor of heat and will feel warm to the touch. Although the stone is found in some jewelry, it is not recommended for rings.

Amber is a fossil resulting from the solidification of thick resin sap that was slowly secreted from ancient trees thousands of years ago. When transparent, amber has a deep yellowish-brown, honey-like color. Sometimes it appears as a brownish-red specimen exhibiting a waxy luster. Amber will often show conchoidal fractures and can be electrified by friction so that it attracts tiny bits of paper. One of its visible characteristics is the presence of insects or vegetable matter within the stone that was caught in the resin during the petrifying stage.

Sodalite, an opaque, soft, blue stone, resembles and is often mistaken for lapis-lazuli. In fact, it is often used as a substitute for lapis because of its color. However, sodalite does not display particles of yellow pyrite that are often seen in lapis, but rather exhibits numerous white spots. Its color, although blue, leans to the violet side. The blue color, with its many white areas, does not compare with that of the intense blue of lapis, which has been a sought-after stone since ancient times. As an often used substitute for lapis, sodalite has never been able to stand out as a beautiful gemstone and therefore, is a much less expensive stone. Under the long wave of the ultraviolet lamp, sodalite fluoresces bright yellow, orange, or orangy red. Although sodalite occurs in white, gray, colorless, pink, and green, blue is its most characteristic color. A good test for sodalite is to heat a specimen. If the stone decolorizes (turns white), you probably have sodalite.

A stone that has become very popular of late, is the mineral malachite. A soft, opaque, colorful stone with a vitreous luster, malachite usually exhibits bright green color bands alternately mixed with bands of black. The bands are characteristically curved and show fibrous texture from its inner make up. Malachite will effervesce and dissolve in acid; this is a good test for the mineral. Malachite is a brittle stone and often shows splintery fractures. Because of its fine colors and complex patterns, the stone brings a handsome price.

Spodumene is a transparent stone. When it occurs in reddish-purple colors, spodumene is called kunzite after the discoverer, George F. Kunz, a well-known gemologist. Spodumene also occurs in colors of yellow and green, this variety being known as hiddenite. Spodumene often exhibits a woody appearance and can easily be identified by a red color that is produced when the stone is heated in a flame. The stone will often show fractures that are uneven and conchoidal. Gem varieties are usually flawless and can display two colors.

Andalusite, although occurring most often as a stone one would not consider using for jewelry, produces a fine gemstone when occurring in a transparent, reddish-brown color. A green variety will resemble tourmaline but a specific gravity test will show andalusite to have a 3.2 S.G. and tourmaline a 3.06 S.G. Some specimens, depending on how they are viewed, will appear to change their colors.

A very unusual variety of garnet is andradite, better known as demantoid. This transparent, yellow-green to intense green stone resembles the vivid green of emerald. The stone contains very tiny fibrous inclusions that give the impression of a "horsetail" shape. Demantoid is a brittle stone showing conchoidal fractures. A specific gravity test and refraction test will easily separate demantoid from emerald.

Bloodstone is a dark grayish-green, opaque variety of the cryptocrystalline group of quartz minerals (those quartz stones having very tiny crystals that cannot be seen under ordinary magnification). Bloodstone is easily recognized by its numerous small red blotches resembling blood spots that appear throughout the stone and inspired its name. Other stones in the same family are the dark red brownish-opaque jasper; the translucent red to orangy red carnelian stone containing hematite; the translucent yellowish-brown sardonyx and the well-known moss agate, which displays wispy moss-like branches resembling trees.

Obsidian is a volcanic rock that was cooled quickly, thus causing it to have a glassy luster. Conchoidal fractures are very characteristic of this mineral, which often appears as a black stone and at times in combination bands of brown, red, and greenish-black, varying from opaque to translucent.

Aventurine quartz is a translucent, granular mineral occurring in brown and green colors and containing particles of mica or hematite that produce a spangled effect. This effect distinguishes the stone from aventurine glass, which exhibits a brilliant copper color under magnification and is often called "goldstone."

Lapis-lazuli, not a very common stone, occurs in a bright azure blue color, often with a violet tinge. It is translucent to opaque and brittle. It is distinguished by its pyrite particles that are quite noticeable. Sodalite, which resembles lapis, loses its color when heated, which is a good test to separate the two stones. Lapis is soluable in acid and will give off a terrible odor of rotten eggs when treated with acid. However, treating lapis with acid will cause the stone to dissolve.

Labradorite will often show a brilliant play of iridescent blue and green colors which is caused by the reflection of light from tiny plate-like inclusions. It is a fine-grained mineral with a vitreous luster. When labradorite contains hematite it will give off a golden sparkle and is referred to as "sunstone."

Finally, mention should be made of the moonstone with its silvery blue, considerably intense color. This milky, opalescent play of color, which is known as adularescence, is produced by light coming from numerous inclusions. The stone is brittle and shows uneven fractures. Moonstone is a transparent to translucent mineral with a vitreous luster and is not soluble in acid.

XXIII

Investing in Gemstones

Although this book has dealt primarily with the identification of gemstones, both colored stones and diamonds; it is appropriate to mention briefly the question of investment in gemstones.

There is sufficient material on the subject to fill an entire book, but I will present in this chapter some brief background information about gemstone investment.

One of the most important problems facing the investor, in dealing with gemstones as a means of financial gain, is to develop an understanding of the method of profit making. It is an entirely different concept from that which governs the various commodities on Wall Street.

In the Wall Street concept, most participants will purchase a stock either on a hunch, on the advice of a friend, or when a broker feels a certain stock is showing signs of "growing pains."

In purchasing a diamond for investment, one has to develop a new attitude when considering the profit angle. Although the establishment of a standard grading system (*see* Chapter XVII) assists the buyer in determining quite easily which qualities to consider for investment, he must get any notions of making a quick profit out of his mind and exercise restraint. He must be prepared to wait a period of at least three to five years for the diamond to appreciate. In other words, the buyer cannot expect a short term profit, but must be content to wait patiently and allow the diamond to move up in value as history has proven this to be the case.

Statistics on the growth of diamonds indicates that for the past forty years the king of gemstones has continuously increased in value, even during periods of recession. This has been chiefly due to the control of the market by the Central Selling Organization, the marketing arm of the De Beers Syndicate, through whose hands 85 percent of all mined diamonds pass. The secret of this organization's successful operation lies in the fact that it does not allow the supply to become greater than the demand. When the demand for diamonds at the retail level is at a low, De Beers will stockpile the stones and wait for conditions to change. As things get better and the demand for diamonds steadily increases, the syndicate will slowly release the stones and raise their prices.

In 1974 when the world economy was going through a recession, De Beers reduced its supply of fine quality diamonds at the "sights." (The "sights" is the term applied to the entire process of diamond trading at De Beers. Approximately 250 specially-chosen major diamond buyers, who are, in most cases, cutters of undisputed reputation, meet in London's Central Selling Organization ten times a year. Here each buyer is presented with a parcel of diamonds, sight unseen (that's how the term "sights" was coined), and a list of the parcel's contents with full descriptions of the enclosed diamonds (size, color and quality). This is a "take it or leave it" situation at De Beers' prices.) When in the early part of 1975 the economic conditions began to look better and the demand for diamonds rose, prices started to move upwards again.

Near the end of 1980 there was another decline in consumer demand, this time coupled with runaway speculation. Once again De Beers had to put the lid on releasing diamonds. As of this writing, retailers are slowly but surely reducing their diamond inventory and will soon have to replenish their stock to meet consumer demand. Thus prices will once more rise. With inflation certain to keep going up, diamond prices have no other direction to go but up.

There are those who feel that De Beers is a monopoly since most of the diamonds that are sold are channeled through their offices. However, if one reflects on the operation of De Beers, he will immediately recognize that stability in the industry is their main purpose. Coupled with that is their desire and intent to protect those within the diamond business from the top echelons down to the consumer. Such a monopoly, if one wishes to call it that, is very different from other monopolies in that De Beers has more than just a profit motive.

Those who were fortunate to have purchased diamonds ten to fifteen years ago, whether the stones were of top quality or were commercial grades (those often found in jewelry stores), have been happily shocked when they discovered, after having their jewelry appraised or re-appraised for insurance, that the values jumped 20 to 30 percent annually over the years. A one-carat diamond of medium grade investment quality, retailing for approximately $1,750 in 1970, was valued at $8,700 in 1979 and $11,000 in early 1981.

Turning to colored gemstones, a little background history will be helpful in understanding the subject of investing in these stones.

Before World War II many people were not aware of colored stones in general, nor were too many stones available. The fault has been laid mostly on the jeweler who, unfortunately, knew very little about these stones.

Industry records indicate that the desire for colored gemstones appears to have slowly developed after the war when the military need for minerals decreased. Interest in colored stones increased as the nation settled back into normal living and those in the colored stone market realized that the supply was at that time fairly plentiful and prices were low.

Some jewelers took time out to learn about the beauty and value of these saleable stones by taking courses. Armed with their new range of information, they began talking more and more to customers about colored stones.

It wasn't too long before shortages of colored stones began to occur because large quantities of gemstones were being bought by foreign countries. This, together with the devaluation of the dollar, forced prices up. Social, economic and internal political crises, coupled with sporadic wars with neighboring countries where important precious stones were mined, such as Zambia, Rhodesia, Brazil, Tanzania, and Cambodia, aggravated the shortages more and more with the result that scarcity of fine quality gemstones was felt everywhere and prices meanwhile kept spiraling upwards.

Whereas with diamonds there is a controlled market and a standard of quality grading to establish a price configuration, with colored stones the fact that the sources of stones are often located in areas of unrest results in a difference in the production and pricing of colored stones.

Competition flourishes and prices fluctuate in many countries that produce colored stones. Government leaders are constantly changing in these countries. Often a country's ruler and his ruling party force themselves into partnership with the small mining company so that the government has control of the stones leaving the country and also has a share in the profits. The lack of price stability causes a lowering of prices for colored stones because of the fierce competition among neighboring countries. The stones are quickly sold because the prices are vastly reduced; this results in faster mining, which adds to the already serious threat of depleting the mines' supply of stones.

Since such fine quality stones as rubies, sapphires, aquamarines, alexandrites, tourmalines, and tanzanites are hard to find, these gemstones are fast becoming great investment commodities.

Diamonds depend upon a lack of color as one of their value parameters. In colored stones the emphasis is on the purity and tone of color. Cut and inclusions are secondary.

Although there are a number of colored stone grading methods that have cropped up from time to time, none really had any widespread acceptance until a few years ago when one of the gem labs in New York developed a color grading system. This system is constantly upgraded and is being recognized by many stone dealers from coast to coast. I am happy to report that I find the system very acceptable in my appraisal work in that it employs a numerical color, tonal, and proportion grading scale so that the quality of a colored gemstone can be pinpointed very easily.

Living during a period where the dollar is worth less and less, where inflation is running at all-time highs, and where threats of war entanglements are frequent, people are searching for tangibles such as diamonds and colored stones as one way to realize considerable appreciation of investments over a period of time.

To be a smart shopper for gemstones, you would be wise to first educate yourself in precious stones by reading a few books (*see* book references) and then talking to those who are knowledgeable in the field of gemstones and their market.

Visiting a gemologist can be a most enlightening experience in that you will learn exactly what procedure to follow when purchasing a fine quality gemstone, whether it be a diamond or colored gemstone. A gemologist will also emphasize the various factors to look for and will explain the importance of protection both before and after the purchase.

When purchasing a stone, you should make certain that you obtain a written statement on your sales receipt saying that the stone is fully refundable within a period of time agreeable both to you and the seller (usually a week to ten days) if you learn that the gemstone is not of the quality stated or that the price you paid is not what the stone is worth. Next, take the gemstone to a gemological laboratory, where a trained gemologist can examine and evaluate the stone. This information will be documented on a certificate of appraisal, which you can then present to the seller in the event that the stone you purchased did not meet the standards of the original sale. The seller of the stone will not take the word of anyone except a qualified person (the gemologist), who must be from an independent laboratory, one that has no ties with any retailers, wholesalers, or manufacturers.

The gemologist from an independent laboratory will provide an unbiased opinion.

With a basic understanding of gemstones and the necessary precautions that must be taken, the risk of being "ripped-off" becomes practically nil.

It is important to recognize the fact that mother earth can only produce just so many gemstones and her supply keeps dwindling all the time, especially when it comes to fine quality stones. Increasing demands for tangibles that offer a hedge against inflation will continue to force prices upwards. Tie this in with a continued condition of strained relationships among countries around the world, and people will continue to look for small portable wealth for their future investments.

XXIV

Summary of Gemstone Properties

AMBER: S.G. 1.08   R.I. 1.54
Refraction: single
Color: yellow, yellow-green, reddish-honey
Transparency: transparent to translucent
Inclusions: flies, gnats, and vegetable matter
Fluorescence: orange or yellow-green . . . . LW
Other: conchoidal fractures . . . . very soft
stone . . . . resinous substance . . . . electrified
when rubbed . . . . greasy luster . . . . burns with
characteristic odor

AMETHYST: (*quartz*): S.G. 2.65   R.I. 1.54–1.55
Refraction: double
Color: light purple to deep purple
Transparency: transparent
Inclusions: usually none . . . . white cloudiness
when heat-treated for increasing color intensity
Fluorescence: none
Other: semi-hard stone . . . . conchoidal frac-

tures. . . .vitreous luster. . . .dichroism quite noticeable. . . .feels cool to the touch of the tongue

ANDALUSITE: S.G. 3.17   R.I. 1.64
Refraction: double . . . . strong
Color: brown, green, red, violet, pink, yellow-green
(some specimens change color)
Transparency: transparent to opaque
Inclusions: dark internal inclusions
Fluorescence: possibly dark green or yellow-
green . . . . SW
Other: dull to vitreous luster

APATITE: S.G. 3.18   R.I. 1.64
Refraction: double
Color: purple, blue, violet, yellow-green, colorless
Transparency: transparent to opaque
Inclusions: possibly fibrous and granular
Fluorescence: sometimes yellow-brown to orange
Other: vitreous luster . . . . conchoidal frac-
tures . . . . soft, brittle stone

AVENTURINE: (*feldspar group*): S.G. 2.5–2.8   R.I.
1.52–1.56
Refraction: double
Color: pale green
Transparency: transparent
Inclusions: glittery brown reflections
Fluorescence: none most of the time . . . . some
weak white color under LW and SW
Other: semi-soft stone . . . . easy cleavage . . . . often
called "sunstone"

AVENTURINE: (*quartz*): S.G. 2.65–2.66   R.I. 1.54–
1.55

Refraction: double
Color: greenish
Transparency: translucent
Inclusions: granular .... layers of tiny particles of hematite or mica producing a glittery effect (known as a spangled effect)
Fluorescence: none

BERYL: (*aquamarine*): S.G. 2.71–2.75   R.I. 1.57
Refraction: double
Color: light blue, blue, blue green
Transparency: transparent
Inclusions: usually free of inclusions .... sometimes small, fine, tube-like inclusions .... heat wave effect .... "fingerprint" inclusions
Fluorescence: none
Other: vitreous luster .... fragile .... doubling of back facets when viewed through crown facets .... cool to the touch .... chelsea filter shows red color .... irregular cavities ....

BERYL: (*emerald*): S.G. 2.72–2.75   R.I. 1.55
Refraction: double
Color: medium green, dark green, bluish-green
Transparency: transparent to translucent
Inclusions: wispy inclusions .... three-phase liquid, solid and gas inclusions
Fluorescence: possibly a weak orangy-red ....
SW .... none under LW
Other: vitreous luster .... conchoidal fracture ....
sinks in methyl iodide .... chelsea filter shows red color

BERYL: (*emerald-synthetic*): S.G. 2.66–2.68   R.I. 1.56–1.58

Refraction: double
Color: medium to dark green
Transparency: transparent
Inclusions: wisp-like inclusions . . . . two-phase liquid and gas inclusions
Fluorescence: dull red . . . . LW
Other: floats in 2.67 S.G. liquid . . . . chelsea filter indicates very bright red color

CHRYSOBERYL: (*alexandrite*): S.G. 3.73   R.I. 1.74–1.75

Refraction: double
Color: dull green in daylight and raspberry red in artificial light (when viewed through the table)
Transparency: transparent to translucent
Inclusions: usually none
Fluorescence: weak red under LW and SW
Other: vitreous luster . . . . conchoidal fractures . . . . strong pleochroism . . . . hard stone

CHRYSOBERYL: (*cat's eye*): S.G. 3.73   R.I. 1.74–1.75

Refraction: double
Color: yellowish-green
Transparency: translucent
Inclusions: thin vertical bands of fibrous rods in the center of a cabochon-cut stone, running vertically
Fluorescence: none to yellowish-green . . . . SW
Other: a fine quality stone exhibits a sharp and well defined line of white light

CORAL: S.G. 2.65   R.I. 1.48–1.65

Refraction: aggregate (always exhibiting light under the polariscope . . . . no change from light to dark) . . . . an aggregate is a massive crystalline mineral made up of many particles

Color: orange, red, pink, white
Transparency: semi-transparent to opaque
Fluorescence: none to a pinkish-orange . . . . LW and SW
Other: dull luster . . . . splintery fractures . . . . pink and white colored coral will effervesce in acid . . . . a soft shell

CORUNDUM: (*ruby*): S.G. 4.00   R.I. 1.76
Refraction: double . . . . strong
Color: practically all shades of red
Transparency: transparent to opaque
Inclusions: needle-like(silk) . . . . straight growth lines(striae) . . . . three sets of parallel lines crossing at sixty degrees . . . . angular inclusions . . . . black solid spots
Fluorescence: red to orangy-red . . . . LW
Other: some rubies have an oily appearance . . . .hard stone. . . .conchoidal fracture . . . . vitreous luster

CORUNDUM: (*synthetic ruby*): S.G. 4.00   R.I. 1.76
Refraction: double
Color: medium to deep shades of red
Transparency: transparent
Inclusions: Spherical gas bubbles (small) in groups . . . . curved lines
Fluorescence: very strong red to orange as seen through the table . . . . LW and SW
Other: polishing marks . . . . facets showing tiny surface fractures . . . . conchoidal fractures . . . . vitreous luster

CORUNDUM: (*sapphire*): S.G. 4.00   R.I. 1.76
Refraction: double
Color: light blue, medium blue, dark blue

Transparency: transparent
Inclusions: needle-like "silk" parallel lines in three sets crossing at 60 degrees .... dark inclusions .... fingerprints
Fluorescence: none .... moderate red .... LW .... SW
Other: hard stone .... dichroism easily visible .... vitreous luster

CORUNDUM: (*sapphire-synthetic*): S.G. 4.00   R.I. 1.76
Refraction: double
Color: medium blue, dark blue
Transparency: transparent
Inclusions: spherical gas bubbles (small) in groups .... curved lines
Fluorescence: weak to chalky-blue to yellowish-green .... SW
Other: hard stone .... vitreous luster

CUBIC ZIRCONIA: S.G. 5.91   R.I. 2.2
Refraction: single
Color: practically all colors .... the colorless cubic zirconia is the only stone that resembles the diamond at first sight
Transparency: hazy transparency
Inclusions: tiny bubbles in a fingerprint pattern .... wispy inclusions
Fluorescence: yellow to orangy-brown .... LW
Other: warm to the touch .... dull and grainy luster on girdle .... under magnification one sees rainbow reflections .... a water test indicates a drop of water will spread on stone's surface .... cubic zirconia is much heavier than diamond

DIAMOND: S.G. 3.52   R.I. 2.42

Refraction: single

Color: all colors . . . . however, most commonly colorless in its various shades

Transparency: transparent to opaque

Inclusions: cleavage cracks . . . . included diamond crystals . . . . other colorless minerals . . . . irregular inclusions . . . . black carbon spots

Fluorescence: blue is most characteristic . . . . other colors observed are green, red, and orange . . . . LW and SW

Other: easy cleavage . . . . conchoidal fractures . . . . very high luster . . . . electrified when rubbed . . . . cold to the touch . . . . "naturals" often seen . . . . sharp facet edges . . . . stands out in relief when placed in methyl iodide or bromoform . . . . hardest of minerals

FABULITE: (*strontium titanite*): S.G. 5.13   R.I. 2.40

Refraction: single

Color: colorless

Transparency: transparent

Inclusions: spherical bubbles very noticeable

Fluorescence: none available

Other: soft stone frequently substituted for diamond . . . . high brilliancy, but too much dispersion of light . . . . manmade stone . . . . conchoidal fractures. . . .vitreous luster. . . .scratches usually visible

GARNET GROUP: (*grossularite*): S.G. 3.61   R.I. 1.73   Note: All garnets are medium hard

Refraction: single

Color: green and brown

Transparency: transparent to opaque

Inclusions: small black inclusions . . . . a mass of wave-like curvings or twistings, resembling a heat-wave effect

Fluorescence: weak to moderate reddish color . . . . LW and SW

Other: vitreous luster . . . . conchoidal fractures

GARNET GROUP (*pyrope*): S.G. 3.78   R.I. 1.74

Refraction: single

Color: reddish (deep wine-red)

Transparency: transparent

Inclusions: large, round crystal grains . . . . two sets of needle-like crystals in two directions

Fluorescence: none

Other: vitreous luster . . . . conchoidal fractures

GARNET GROUP (*rhodalite*): S.G. 3.84   R.I. 1.76

Refraction: single

Color: red, violet, and pink

Transparency: transparent

Inclusions: two sets of coarse, needle-like crystals in two directions . . . . large, round crystal grains

Fluorescence: none

Other: vitreous luster . . . . conchoidal fractures

GARNET GROUP (*almandite*): S.G. 4.05   R.I. 1.80

Refraction: single

Color: red, pink

Transparency: transparent to translucent

Inclusions: two sets of coarse needles (silk) in two directions is very common here

Fluorescence: none

Other: vitreous luster . . . . conchoidal fractures

GARNET GROUP (*spessartite*): S.G. 4.15   R.I. 1.81
  Refraction: single
  Color: brown, orange, yellow, red
  Transparency: transparent
  Inclusions: dark inclusions that resemble torn
    pieces of cloth
  Fluorescence: none
  Other: vitreous luster . . . . conchoidal fractures

GARNET GROUP (*andradite*) . . . . "demantoid"
  . . . S.G. 3.84   R.I. 1.87
  Refraction: single
  Color: green
  Transparency: transparent
  Inclusions: "horse-tail" inclusions
  Fluorescence: none
  Other: vitreous luster . . . . conchoidal

GLASS: S.G. 2.3–4.5   R.I. 1.44–1.77
  Refraction: single
  Color: all colors
  Transparency: transparent to opaque
  Inclusions: prominent bubbles, elongated or spher-
    ical . . . . swirl lines
  Other: conchoidal fractures . . . . vitreous lus-
    ter . . . . brittle . . . . chips on facet edges often vis-
    ible . . . . warm to the touch . . . . a drop of water
    will spread on its surface

JADE (*jadeite*): S.G. 3.34   R.I. 1.65–1.68
  Refraction: aggregate (*see* coral)
  Color: practically all colors . . . . sometimes the col-
    ors are unevenly distributed
  Transparency: transparent to opaque
  Inclusions: more granular and less fibrous

. . . . some specimens exhibit tiny depressions on surfaces

Fluorescence: weak shades of various jade colors may exhibit a dull white or dull green . . . . LW

Other: a green color with the intensity of fine emerald is regarded as "Imperial" jade . . . . cleavage breaks more easily in certain directions than other stones because of granular inclusions (easy cleavage) . . . . tough, compact stone . . . . splintery fractures . . . . jadeite will remain suspended in methyl iodide

JADE (*nephrite*): S.G. 2.95   R.I. 1.60–1.63

Refraction: aggregate

Color: medium green, dark green (spinach green) . . . . there are other nephrite colors such as red, yellow, brown, and white which are used mostly in ornaments

Transparency: transparent to opaque

Inclusions: less granular and more fibrous

Fluorescence: none

Other: compact and tough . . . . splintery fractures . . . . may show cleavage . . . . dull luster

LABRADORITE: S.G. 2.70   R.I. 1.55–1.56

Refraction: double

Color: yellow, red, blue, green . . . . mostly gray

Transparency: transparent to opaque

Inclusions: very fine particles

Fluorescence: none . . . . may exhibit a rare weak blue . . . . LW

Other: Iridescence is very noticeable . . . . splintery fractures . . . . vitreous luster . . . . easy cleavage . . . . the blue and green colors exhibit the play of colors

LAPIS LAZULI (*lazurite*): S.G. 2.75   R.I. 1.50
Refraction: single
Color: darkish blue
Transparency: opaque . . . . it has occurred in translucent
Inclusions: particles of yellowish pyrite within the mineral that are often visible on its surface . . . . top quality stone will show little or no pyrite
Fluorescence: most often none . . . . may exhibit a weak blue or yellow color . . . . SW
Other: a soft stone . . . . dullish luster and often greasy appearance

MALACHITE: S.G. 3.95   R.I. 1.66–1.91
Refraction: aggregate
Color: bluish-green and black (both colors banded)
Transparency: translucent to opaque
Inclusions: fibrous
Fluorescence: none
Other: high luster . . . . soft stone . . . . conchoidal fractures

MOONSTONE: S.G. 2.55–2.80   R.I. 1.51–1.53
Refraction: double
Color: bluish white to bluish gray . . . . (cabochon-cut stones)
Transparency: translucent
Inclusions: bluish light effect that appears to float as stone is viewed from different directions
Fluorescence: blue . . . . LW, pale orange . . . . SW
Other: exhibits adularescence

OPAL: S.G. 2.15   R.I. 1.45
Refraction: single
Color: practically all colors

Transparency: transparent to opaque

Inclusions: characteristic rainbow flashes as stone is moved about . . . . compact masses of irregular spaces and cracks

Fluorescence: yellowish or greenish color . . . . LW and SW

Other: porous stone . . . . conchoidal fractures . . . . some stone exhibiting a dull luster . . . . fragile and brittle . . . . attacked by acids

PERIDOT (*olivine*): S.G. 3.34   R.I. 1.65–1.69

Refraction: double . . . . strong

Color: green, yellowish-green

Transparency: transparent

Inclusions: a rare occurrence

Fluorescence: none

Other: doubling of back facets . . . . conchoidal fractures . . . . vitreous luster . . . . soft stone . . . . sinks slowly in methyl iodide

RUTILE (*synthetic*): S.G. 4.25–4.27   R.I. 2.60–2.90

Refraction: double

Color: pale yellow

Transparency: transparent

Inclusions: gas bubbles

Fluorescence . . . . not known

Other: doubling of back facets . . . . high degree of light dispersion . . . . slightly harder than fabulite

SERPENTINE: S.G. 2.57   R.I. 1.56–1.57

Refraction: double

Color: many colors . . . . green used for jewelry

Transparency: translucent to opaque

Inclusions: vein-like cracks containing other mineral particles . . . . fibrous . . . . often has a cloudy appearance

Fluorescence: none
Other: soft stone .... usually cut in cabochon
.... dull luster

SODALITE: S.G. 2.24   R.I. 1.48
Refraction: single
Color: blue (usually dark)
Transparency: translucent to opaque
Inclusions: mottled texture
Fluorescence: bright orangy-red .... LW
Other: white spots on surface as compared to lapis
   with yellow spots .... has cleavage .... soft
   stone .... greasy luster .... brittle .... conchoi-
   dal fractures

SPINEL (*natural*): S.G. 3.60   R.I. 1.72
Refraction: single
Color: most colors except yellow .... blue and red
   popular
Transparency: transparent
Inclusions: eight-sided crystalline inclusions are
   very characteristic .... feathery inclusions
Fluorescence: red variety shows weak orangy-
   red .... SW and LW .... blue variety shows none
Other: conchoidal fractures .... vitreous lus-
   ter .... a hard stone

SPINEL (*synthetic*): S.G. 3.65   R.I. 1.73
Refraction: single .... will show a patchwork type
   of light and dark areas under the polariscope
   (caused by internal strain)
Color: green, violet, blue, colorless
Transparency: transparent to opaque
Inclusions: spherical gas bubbles .... internal
   cracks and strain lines .... tubular-shaped inclusions

Fluorescence: blue and green colors exhibit bright red .... colorless variety shows blue .... LW

Other: conchoidal fractures .... vitreous luster .... rapid polishing marks .... irregular facet edges .... definite cleavage

SPODUMENE: S.G. 3.18   R.I. 1.66–1.67

Refraction: double

Color: reddish-purple (kunzite) .... yellowish-green (hiddenite)

Transparency: transparent

Inclusions: no characteristic inclusions

Fluorescence: pink and orange .... phosphorescence exhibited .... LW

Other: splintery fractures .... vitreous luster .... doubling of the back facets .... semi-hard .... easy cleavage .... pleochroism evident

TANZANITE (*zoisite*): S.G. 3.35–3.50   R.I. 1.69–1.70

Refraction: double

Color: purplish-blue and violet-red

Transparency: transparent

Inclusions: usually none

Other: pleochroism exhibited .... medium soft to hard stone .... recently discovered in 1967

TOPAZ: S.G. 3.53   R.I. 1.61–1.63

Refraction: double

Color: practically all colors .... browns and oranges are popular

Transparency: transparent

Inclusions: cracks seen within stone .... can show crystalline inclusions .... two-phase liquid and gas inclusions .... irregularly shaped crystals .... most often free of inclusions

Fluorescence: yellow-orange and yellow-green
....LW

Other: a very hard stone .... easy cleavage
.... conchoidal fractures .... vitreous luster
.... pleochroism evident .... takes a good
polish .... sinks in bromoform .... doubling of
the back facets .... feels cold to the touch

TOURMALINE: S.G. 3.06   R.I. 1.62–1.64

Refraction: double

Color: all colors .... pinkish-red and green most
popular .... two colors often seen in one stone

Transparency: transparent to translucent

Inclusions: green variety shows elongated liquid
and gas inclusions in abundance .... the red variety shows the same but not as many

Fluorescence: green variety exhibits reddish-
violet .... LW .... red variety exhibits blue

Other: very dichroic .... doubling of the back
facets .... conchoidal fractures .... vitreous luster .... medium hard stone .... shows green
under the chelsea filter

TURQUOISE: S.G. 2.75 (rich blue color).... most
other shades 2.30–2.40   R.I. 1.61–1.65

Refraction: aggregate

Color: pale blue and green .... the rich sky blue is
seldom available

Transparency: opaque

Inclusions: granular .... brownish matrix veins
.... white patches visible on surface

Fluorescence: may show a weak yellow green
.... LW

Other: Conchoidal fractures .... dull luster .... soft stone .... most stones are wax-

treated to better the color . . . . a hot needle placed near the stone will cause melting of the wax when viewed under magnification . . . . porous stone. . . .heat and sunlight will fade color. . . . stone does not become electrified when rubbed

ZIRCON: S.G. 4.40   R.I. 1.81–1.90
Refraction: double
Color: practically all colors
Transparency: transparent . . . . although most have a cloudy appearance
Inclusions: curved inclusions . . . . parallel growth lines . . . . pits along facet edges very common
Fluorescence: colorless shows weak yellow (LW and SW) . . . . blue variety shows blue (LW) . . . . green exhibits weak orangy-green (SW) . . . . yellow shows weak yellow-orange (LW and SW) . . . . red exhibits yellow or red (SW)
Other: fairly hard stone . . . . strong doubling of back facets . . . . conchoidal fractures . . . . brittle . . . . heat treatment used to improve color

XXV

The Gemologist

The gemologist plays an important role in the identification of gemstones, not only for the jeweler and those working in the trade but for all who are, in one way or another, involved with diamonds and colored gemstones.

Gemology is the science which deals with the study of gemstones. The practicing gemologist is a professional graduate of the Gemological Institute of America who has passed a number of difficult examinations both in theory and practical laboratory work, involving the identification, quality grading, and evaluation of diamonds and colored stones with the aid of special scientific instruments.

Although there are other schools in the United States that offer a few basic courses in the fundamentals of gemology, they are not recognized by the jewelry industry here and abroad as being complete in their scope of subjects. The Gemological Institute of America is the only school in the country that graduates its students with a degree of "Graduate Gemologist."

When a gemstone is presented to a gemologist for appraisal, the gemologist will make no hasty decisions but will perform as many tests as necessary before any identification is made.

If there is a doubt in the gemologist's mind regarding a stone's identity, after all tests have been exhausted, he will refer the stone to another laboratory with more sophisticated testing devices, just as a general medical doctor will refer a patient to a specialist.

What other considerations are involved in appraising precious stones? There are many reasons for an appraisal and each is approached differently. The gemologist performs appraisal work for persons in the process of purchasing a gemstone; persons who are selling their jewelry; those who are insuring valuables; attorneys who are settling an estate, and insurance companies when a loss or theft occurs.

The gemologist has a responsibility to his client to see that the appraisal certificate meets certain rigid requirements in order for it to act as a valuable document. All items must be described in detail, including quality of any metal jewelry; size, weight, shape and proportion of gemstones, a diagram of the internal structure of stones, and a replacement cost evaluation that reflects the present day market. All of these factors are vital especially for insurance coverage or losses.

It is important to remind the reader to shy away from the "retail appraisal," as this is nothing more than evidence of a sale with little or no description of what was purchased. The indicated price is what was paid at the time of purchase, which may or may not have any connection with the true market value.

A knowledge of market conditions at the time of an appraisal is vital to the gemologist in arriving at a realistic monetary value. He has to be constantly in touch with numerous sources that can provide him with prices for all gemstones. The gemologist stays abreast of current developments in the field by attending gem shows and reading market trend publications and gemstone trade papers.

I find an exciting challenge every time an unknown stone is brought to my laboratory for identification and evaluation. One incident in particular comes to mind.

So let's go back a bit while I take you on a little journey into the gem lab where I was to identify this stone.

I was handed a small, round brooch of yellow gold that contained a rectangular stone in the center. Upon visual examination I found the stone to be very loosely mounted in a four-prong setting. The stone was transparent, faceted, and exhibited a medium dark blue color.

Under the gemoscope, although no special characteristic inclusions were visible, the stone's internal structure did show some fibrous and granular material. I also observed surface scratches and abrasions on the facet edges.

A refractometer reading was taken which revealed a refractive index of 1.64–1.65.

The next step was to use the polariscope, which would indicate whether the stone was singly or doubly refractive. The stone changed from light to dark and back to light again as I rotated it on the Polaroid plate, a sign that the stone was doubly refractive.

I knew there were many doubly refractive blue stones but not in the refractive index range of 1.64 to 1.65. This eliminated most of the popular gemstones like zircon, corundum, topaz, beryl, and quartz, but left tourmaline. There were lesser known stones to be considered such as apatite, diopside, and andalusite, and even the rare enclase.

At this point I could feel my adrenal glands beginning to overwork. I soon discovered when I checked the birefringence chart of these five possibilities that apatite had the lowest reading. The stone in question showed this apatite birefringence. I believed I was getting close to a positive identification.

I now turned to my dichroscope, which would indicate the strength of the stone's dichroism. As it turned out, a yellow and blue color—the two dichroic colors of apatite—appeared in the instrument. I knew I was on the right track. This information, along with the fact that the stone was soft (evidenced by its scratches and abraded facet edges) made me feel certain that the stone was apatite.

It happened that the stone fell out of its loose setting, which resulted in my being able to perform a specific gravity test. This test solidified proof of the stone's identity, since the specific gravity proved to be 3.18, which is the S.G. of apatite.

Having now identified the stone to my complete satisfaction, I next obtained its size and weight and examined its color for purity and tone. I them determined the stone's monetary value by checking the various sources from whom I receive periodic up-to-date prices according to color, quality, and size.

From this description you can see that the process of gemological appraising is not a simple matter of looking at a stone through a magnifying glass and arriving at a value and an identity for the stone.

The gemologist is a person who is deeply involved in a time-consuming profession requiring education, expensive instruments, experience, and a special knowledge of gem identification and gemstone values.

In Conclusion

For those of you who by this time have developed a strong desire to continue the study of gemology and expect to enroll in courses in the identification of gemstones, you are bound to discover a kind of fascination as you use the various scientific methods and instruments. Once addicted you will never be able to get over it; there is no cure.

Every time you see a stone that puzzles you, you will immediately want to get to the bench and start the process of gem identification.

To you readers who are not associated with the jewelry industry and do not expect to take gemological courses, but have a fascination for gemstones, this book will have opened a pandora's box of information to you. I am certain that you will have acquired a greater respect for these mysterious minerals of nature.

Especially for those engaged in collecting as a hobby, the rock hounds who are constantly seeking new places to dig for stones and the investor looking for a hedge against inflation, the contents of this book will have given you a basic knowledge in establishing the identity of unknown stones.

Glossary

ASTERISM   Optical phenonemon of a star effect which is seen in the stone through reflected light.

ALTERED STONE   A stone whose color or internal structure has been changed by some artifical method.

AMORPHOUS   When applied to gem minerals it means that the crystal structure has no shape or positive form; where the atoms are not orderly in their arrangement.

APPRAISAL   Placing a monetary value on a gemstone, based on the size, color, and quality grading.

ASSEMBLED STONE   A stone created by uniting two or more different materials to form one stone. See doublet and triplet.

AVENTURINE   A translucent greenish quartz mineral, internally granular and often mistaken for jade.

BAGUETTE   Small rectangular stone with facets termed "step up" because they resemble steps rather than the intricate facets seen on round, marquise, pear, and oval shaped stones.

BAKELITE   A plastic made by heating phenol or cresol.

BANDED AGATE   A variety of chalcedony quartz with curved colored bands.

BAROQUE PEARL   An irregularly shaped pearl.

BERYL   A mineral, light in color. When transparent and

dark green in color, it is an emerald. When blue in color, it is an aquamarine.

BRILLIANT CUT   The best method of cutting a stone, producing a round shape with the standard 58 facets.

BRITTLE   Breaking readily or crumbling when pressure is applied.

BUBBLES   A circular body of liquid containing gas.

CABOCHON   A stone with a convex oval shape and no facets.

CANDLING   A method of identification of pearls by examining them through a tiny opening in an opaque shield.

CAT'S EYE   Cabochon-cut gemstone showing a band of light running north and south, which moves when the stone is turned.

CHATOYANT   The capacity of a cabochon-cut gemstone to reflect a single band of light. See Cat's eye.

CHOKER   A necklace that usually measures 15 inches in length and fits snugly around the neck.

CITRINE   A brownish-orange variety of quartz, commonly called topaz quartz.

CLEAVAGE   The property of a gemstone to split in definite directions and leave a smooth surface where this splitting occurs.

CORUNDUM   A gem mineral known as a ruby when the color is red, and as a sapphire when the color is blue, pink, or yellow.

CROWN   The facets of a gemstone above its girdle.

CULET   A small face forming the bottom of a faceted gemstone.

DEMANTOID   The green variety of garnet, sometimes mistaken for a peridot.

EMERALD CUT   A square or rectangular step-cut shape of a gemstone.

FEATHER   An imperfection in a gemstone that resembles a feather.

FIBROUS A description of an internal imperfection that appears to resemble hair or thread.

FINGERPRINTS Cloud-like appearances of gas and liquid bubbles resembling human fingerprints.

FISHEYE A term used to denote a diamond that has a dull center due to poor faceting.

FOIL BACK A stone with silver foil backing to give it brilliancy such as that seen in a rhinestone.

FRACTURE A crack that is visible within a gemstone but not located in the cleavage plane path.

FULL CUT A gemstone that usually has a table and 32 facets above the girdle and a culet plus 24 facets below the girdle, totaling 58 facets.

GIRDLE The outer rim of a faceted or cabochon stone.

GOLDSTONE Brownish-red glass stone with tiny, bright metallic particles resembling the mineral sunstone.

HARDNESS The resistance of a mineral to abrasion.

HELIODOR The yellowish-brown variety of beryl.

JET Compact black adjusting coal with a high polish, frequently mistaken for black onyx.

INCLUSION The proper term used by gemologists when they are referring to any kind of internal imperfection, flaw, carbon spot, or any other foreign matter found within a gemstone.

INTAGLIO A carving into or beneath the surface of a gemstone as compared to a raised carving in the cameo.

LUSTER An effect produced when light is reflected from the surface of a gemstone.

LEVERIDGE GAUGE An instrument used to measure the dimensions of a gemstone in millimeters.

MABE A pearl that actually is a half pearl.

MAKE Refers to a stone's proportion and polish, the way it was made or cut.

MATRIX The rock in which a mineral is embedded, such as the well-known turquoise matrix where a piece of rock contains some turquoise.

MELEE   A very small diamond or colored stone, usually one to approximately fifteen points in weight.

MOES GAUGE   A caliper gauge that measures the height, width, and depth of a stone to determine its approximate weight, with the aid of tables.

MOHS SCALE   A scale that denotes the hardness of certain minerals.

MOMME   A measure of weight for pearls.

MOTHER OF PEARL   A hard, iridescent substance that forms on the inside layer of a pearl-bearing mollusk shell.

OLD MINE CUT   An old form of diamond cutting with the stone's girdle being rather square-looking and having a small table, and a large culet.

OLD EUROPEAN CUT   An old form of diamond cutting with a round girdle, high crown, and a large culet.

ORIENT   The iridescence on the surface of a pearl.

PASTE   Glass that is used to imitate a gemstone.

PAVILION   The facets below the girdle of a gemstone.

PLEOCHROISM   The property of a gemstone that causes it to show two or more colors when viewed in different directions through a Dichroscope.

PYRITE   Known as "fool's gold." It is tiny yellowish flecks, often seen in lapis-lazuli.

PYROPE   The brownish-red variety of garnet.

ROSE CUT   A gemstone cut with a flat, non-faceted bottom and a dome-shaped top where the facets come to a point.

ROUGH   An uncut, unpolished gemstone, fresh from the source.

SANDAWANA EMERALD   A fine color emerald stone that comes from Rhodesia in the Sandawana Valley.

SCARAB   A gemstone copied from the ancient Egyptians' fertility symbol and cut in the shape of a beetle.

SIAMESE RUBY A ruby that comes from Siam (Thailand), usually orangy-red in color, as compared to the Burmese ruby that comes from Burma and is a red to purple-red color.

SILK Tiny inclusions usually visible as shiny-white silky cloth, and needle-like in appearance. Usually seen in rubies and sapphires.

SINGLE CUT A form of gem cutting that produces only 18 facets (eight on top, eight on bottom and a table and culet).

SMOKY TOPAZ Actually smoky quartz, which is a brownish colored quartz stone with a smoky appearance.

SPESSARTITE The orange to red to brownish variety of garnet.

WIDE SPREAD TABLE Pertaining to a stone that has been cut so that the table is wide in order to give the illusion of a larger stone.

VITREOUS Glassy looking.

Reference Lists

Books

Anderson, B.W. *Gem Testing,* New York: Emerson Books, 1948.

Arem, Joel. *Gems and Jewelry,* New York: Grosset and Dunlap, 1975.

Dickinson, Joan Younger. *The Book of Diamonds,* New York: Crown Publishers, 1965.

Fisher, Peter Jack. *The Science of Gems,* New York: Charles Scribner's Sons, 1966.

Gleason, Sterling. *Ultraviolet Guide to Minerals* Princeton, N.J.: D. Van Nostrand, 1960.

Green, Timothy. *The World of Diamonds,* New York: William Morrow, 1981.

Gump, Richard. *Jade: Stone of Heaven,* Garden City, N.Y.: Doubleday and Co., 1962.

Kraus, Edward Henry and Charles Baker Slawson. *Gems and Gem Minerals,* New York: McGraw-Hill Book Co., 1947.

Kunz, George Frederick. *The Curious Lore of Precious Stones,* New York: Dover Publications, Inc., 1970.

Liddicoat Jr., Richard T. *Handbook of Gem Identification,* Los Angeles: Gemological Institute of America, 1967.

Liddicoat Jr., Richard T. and Lawrence L. Copeland.

The Jewelers' Manual, Los Angeles: Gemological Institute of America, 1964.

Parsons, Charles J. *Practical Gem Knowledge,* San Diego, Ca.: Lapidary Journal, Inc., 1969.

Rutland, E.H. *An Introduction to the World's Gemstones,* Garden City, N.Y.: Doubleday and Co., 1974.

Shipley, Robert M. *Dictionary of Gems and Gemology,* Los Angeles: Gemological Institute of America, 1951.

Sinkankas, John. *Gemstones of North America,* Princeton, N.J.: D. Van Nostrand, 1959.

Spencer, L.J. *A Key to Precious Stones,* New York: Emerson Books, 1947.

Tolkowsky, Marcel. *Diamond Design,* New York: Spon and Chamberlain, 1919.

Webster, Robert. *Gem Identification, New York: Sterling Publishing Co., 1977.*

————. *Practical Gemmology,* London: N.A.C. Press, *1941*

Weinstein, Michael. *The World of Jewel Stones,* New York: Sheridan House, 1958.

Whitlock, Herbert P. *The Story of the Gems,* Buchanan, N.Y.: Emerson Books, 1946.

Zucker, Benjamin. *How to Invest in Gems,* New York: Quadrangle/The New York Times Book Co., 1976.

Periodicals

Canadian Jeweler, 481 University Ave., Toronto, Ontario Canada M5W-1A7

Gems and Gemology, Gemological Institute of America, 1660 Stewart St., Santa Monica, Calif. 90404

Gems and Minerals, P.O. Box 687, Mentona, Calif. 92359

Jeweler/Lapidary Business, 5870 Hunters Lane, El Sobrante, Calif. 94803

Jewelers' Circular Keystone, Chilton Company, Chilton Way, Radnor, Pa. 19089

Jewelry Making Gems and Minerals, Gemac Corporation, 1797 Capri Ave., Mentone, Calif. 92359

Jewelry World, 33 Marmot St., Toronto, Ontario, Canada M4S-2T4

Lapidary Journal, P.O. Box 80937, San Diego, Calif. 92138

Modern Jeweler, 342 Madison Ave., New York, N.Y. 10173

National Jeweler, 1515 Broadway, New York, N.Y. 10036

Rocks and Gems, Behn Miller Publishers, Inc., Executive Offices, 17337 Ventura Blvd., Encino, Calif. 91316

Rocks and Minerals, Heldref Publications, 4000 Albemarle St. N.W., Washington, D.C. 20016

Rockhound, P.O. Drawer, Conroe, Tex. 77301

Manufacturers and Suppliers of Gemological Instruments and Equipment

Baskin and Sons Inc., 732 Union Avenue, Middlesex, N.J. 08846

Bausch and Lomb, Optic Center, 1400 North Goodman St., Rochester, N.Y. 14602

R.P. Cargille Laboratories, 55 Commerce Rd., Cedar Grove, N.J. 07009

Ceres Corp., 411 Waverly Oaks Park, Waltham, Mass. 02154

Consolidated Metal Products, P.O. 353 Prospect Heights, Ill. 60070

Eureka Gem Instrument Co., P.O. Box 52850 Houston, Tex. 77052

Gem Instrument Corp., 1735 Stewart St., P.O. Box 2147, Santa Monica, Calif. 90406

Gemological Instruments Ltd., Saint Dunstan's House, Cary Lane, London EC2V 8AB, England

Paul H. Gesswein and Co., 255 Hancock Ave., Bridgeport, Conn. 06605

Hanneman Lapidary Specialties, P.O. Box 2453, Castro Valley, Calif. 94546

Jewelmont Corp., 800 Boone Ave., N. Minneapolis, Minn. 55427

I. Kassoy Inc., 30 West 47th St., New York, N.Y. 10036

Okuda Jewelry Technical Institute, 49 West 47th St., New York, N.Y. 10036

Research Marketing, P.O. Box 10, Woodbury, Tenn. 37190

Rubin and Son Inc., 13 West 46th St., New York, N.Y. 10036

Sarasota Instruments, 2214 Industrial Blvd., Sarasota, Fla. 33580

Swest Inc., 10803 Composite Drive, Dallas, Tex. 75220

Ultra-Violet Products, 5100 Walnut Grove, San Gabriel, Calif. 91778

Herman W. Yecies Inc., 1275 Bloomfield Ave., Fairfield, N.J. 07006

Gemstone Suppliers

Diamonds:
Baumgold Bros., 580 5th Ave., New York, N.Y. 10036
David Brecher International, 580 5th Ave., New York, N.Y. 10036

Faculty Enterprises, 535 5th Ave., New York, N.Y. 10017
Wm. Goldberg Diamond Corp., 20 West 47th St., New York, N.Y. 10036
Kaspar and Esh Inc., 126 West 46th St., New York, N.Y. 10036
P.P. Kishore and Co., 565 5th Ave., New York, N.Y. 10017
A. Knobloch Inc., 576 5th Ave., New York, N.Y. 10036
Lazare Kaplan and Sons, 666 5th Ave., New York, N.Y. 10103
William Levine Inc., 29 East Madison Ave., Chicago, Ill. 60202
Harry Winston Inc., 718 5th Ave., New York, N.Y. 10019

Pearls:
August Gem Corp., 580 5th Ave., New York, N.Y. 10036
Imperial Pearl Syndicate, 385 5th Ave., New York, N.Y. 10016
Mastoloni and Sons Inc., 608 5th Ave., New York, N.Y. 10020
Mikimoto Co. Ltd., 608 5th Ave., New York, N.Y. 10020

Synthetics:
Baskins and Sons Inc., 732 Union Ave., Middlesex, N.J. 68846
Joseph Blank Inc., 15 West 47th St., New York, N.Y. 10036
C.G.D. Inc., P.O. Box 341861, Coral Gables, Fla. 33134
Chatham Created Gems, 210 Post St., San Francisco, Calif. 94108
Created Gemstones, P.O. Box 530, Hackettstown, N.J. 07840
Heller Hope Inc., 1180 Ave. of the Americas, New York, N.Y. 10036
International Import Co., P.O. Box 747, Stone Mountain, Ga. 30086
Kashan Inc., P.O. Box 3318, Austin, Tex. 78764

Colored Stones:

Astro Minerals Ltd., 155 East 34th St., New York, N.Y. 10016

A. Bahtiarian Inc., P.O. Box 9, 24 East Palisade Ave., Englewood, N.J. 07631

East Asia Gems, 122 S. Robertson Blvd., Los Angeles, Calif. 90048

Estrade Inc., 609 5th Ave., New York, N.Y. 10017

Geminex Corp., P.O. Box 404, San Ramon, Calif. 94583

Gems of Sri-Lanka, Impex International, 286 Hillside Ave., Pawtucket, R.I. 02860

J. Frank Golden and Associates, P.O. Box 692 Dept. M., Forest Park, Ga. 30050

Allan A. Goldman, 15 West 47th St., New York, N.Y. 10036

Idaho Opal and Gem Corp., P.O. Box 4881, Pocatello, Idaho 83201

Knupfer International, 15 West 47th St., New York, N.Y. 10036

R.L. Kuehn Productions, P.O. Box 12252, Dallas, Tex. 75225

Wm. L. Kuhn Co., 580 5th Ave., New York, N.Y. 10036

Overland Gems Inc., P.O. Box 272, Culver City, Calif. 90230

Pacific Gem Cutters, 315 West 5th Street, Los Angeles, Calif. 90013

Precious Stone Co., 580 5th Ave., New York, N.Y. 10036

Maurice Shire Inc., 609 5th Ave., New York, N.Y. 10017

Success Enterprises, P.O. Box 83, Kent, Ohio 44240

Professional Organizations

Accredited Gemologists Association, 36 N.E. 1st Street, Suite 419, Miami, Fla. 33132

American Gem and Mineral Supplier Association, c/o Glendora Lapidary, 130 North Glendora Ave., Glendora, Calif. 91740

American Gem Society, 2960 Wilshire Blvd., Los Angeles, Calif. 90010

American Society of Appraisers, Dulles International Airport, Box 17265, Washington, D.C. 20041

Appraisers Association of America, 60 East 42nd Street, New York, N.Y. 10165

Cultured Pearl Association of America, 114 5th Ave., 11th Floor, New York, N.Y. 10011

Diamond Council of America, c/o Rogers Jewelers, 124 City Center, Middletown, Ohio 45042

Diamond Dealers Club Inc., 30 West 47th Street, New York, N.Y. 10036

Gemological Institute of America, 1660 Stewart St., Santa Monica, Calif. 90404

Jewelers Vigilance Committee Inc., 919 3rd Ave., New York, N.Y. 10022

Index